Praise for

"Devi Stern has written a book that thrills me. It answers my quest and need for spiritual knowledge, but it also shows how the Kabbalah intertwines with energy medicine, and it excites and inspires. In fact, kabbalistic symbols and the energy exercises 'sync up' amazingly well to create a unique field of high vibration."

—Donna Eden, reknowned healer and author, creator of Eden Energy Medicine

"The kabbalistic underpinnings are quite solid. I found it fascinating how Devi translated them into practical meditations and exercises. This book should shine the light of Jewish mysticism out into the world and impact the world for good."

—Sarah Yehudit Schneider, author of *Kabbalistic Writings on the Nature of Masculine and Feminine*

ENERGY HEALING
WITH THE
KABBALAH

About the Author

Devi Stern, MS, EEM-AP (Chicago, IL), holds a BS from Cornell and an MS in biology from Northeastern Illinois University. She is an advanced Eden Energy Medicine practitioner and Reiki master. In addition to her healing practice, Devi teaches weekly energy wellness classes at Infinity Foundation in Highland Park, Illinois, and at the Chicago Botanic Garden. During the summers, she runs a weekly outdoor energy camp for women. She has studied and continues to study energy healing, Kabbalah, and kabbalistic healing with many teachers to whom she is very grateful. Visit her online at www.dragonflyhealer.com.

To Write to the Author

If you wish to contact the author or would like more information about this book, please write to the author in care of Llewellyn Worldwide, Ltd. and we will forward your request. The authors and publisher appreciate hearing from you and learning of your enjoyment of this book and how it has helped you. Llewellyn Worldwide, Ltd. cannot guarantee that every letter written to the author can be answered, but all will be forwarded. Please write to:

Devi Stern
℅ Llewellyn Worldwide
2143 Wooddale Drive
Woodbury, MN 55125-2989

Please enclose a self-addressed stamped envelope for reply,
or $1.00 to cover costs. If outside the USA, enclose
an international postal reply coupon.

DEVI STERN

ENERGY HEALING WITH THE KABBALAH

Integrating Ancient Jewish Mysticism
with Modern Energetic Practices

Llewellyn Publications
Woodbury, Minnesota

Energy Healing with the Kabbalah: Integrating Ancient Jewish Mysticism with Modern Energetic Practices © 2018 by Devi Stern. All rights reserved. No part of this book may be used or reproduced in any manner whatsoever, including Internet usage, without written permission from Llewellyn Publications, except in the case of brief quotations embodied in critical articles and reviews.

FIRST EDITION
First Printing, 2018

The meditative approaches in this book are not a substitute for psychotherapy or counseling, nor are they a substitute for medical treatment. They are intended to provide clients with information about their inner workings that can add another helpful dimension to treatment with a trained medical or mental health professional.

Book design by Bob Gaul
Cover design by Ellen Lawson
Editing by Laura Kurtz
For complete interior art credits, see page 303

Llewellyn Publications is a registered trademark of Llewellyn Worldwide Ltd.

Library of Congress Cataloging-in-Publication Data
Names: Stern, Devi, author.
 Title: Energy healing with the Kabbalah: integrating ancient Jewish
  mysticism with modern energetic practices / Devi Stern.
  Description: First Edition. | Woodbury: Llewellyn Worldwide, Ltd., 2018. |
  Includes bibliographical references and index.
  Identifiers: LCCN 2018010941 (print) | LCCN 2018001705 (ebook) | ISBN
  9780738757056 (ebook) | ISBN 9780738756837 (alk. paper)
  Subjects: LCSH: Healing—Religious aspects—Judaism. | Cabala. | Energy
  medicine. | Alternative medicine.
  Classification: LCC BM538.H43 (print) | LCC BM538.H43 S76 2018 (ebook) | DDC
  135/.47—dc23
  LC record available at https://lccn.loc.gov/2018010941

Llewellyn Worldwide Ltd. does not participate in, endorse, or have any authority or responsibility concerning private business transactions between our authors and the public.
 All mail addressed to the author is forwarded, but the publisher cannot, unless specifically instructed by the author, give out an address or phone number.
 Any Internet references contained in this work are current at publication time, but the publisher cannot guarantee that a specific location will continue to be maintained. Please refer to the publisher's website for links to authors' websites and other sources.

Llewellyn Publications
A Division of Llewellyn Worldwide Ltd.
2143 Wooddale Drive
Woodbury, MN 55125-2989
www.llewellyn.com

Printed in the United States of America

Contents

Acknowledgments xi

Introduction 1

Part 1: Background

1: Reconnecting to the Divine Feminine 9

2: Kabbalah: The Background and the Basics 17

3: The Kabbalistic Creation Story 27

4: The Tree of Life 33

5: *Gematria* and the Hebrew Aleph-Bet 43

6: A Different Creation Story: An Interpretation of the First Ten Letters 45

7: The Mystical Letter *Aleph* א 51

8: The Unpronounceable Name 55

9: The Infinity Sign 65

10: Love Is the Answer   71

11: Energy Medicine   83

12: Energy Medicine and Kabbalah   91

Part 2: Practices

13: Introduction to the Practices   107

14: Grounding   111

15: Breath   119

16: The Hands   127

17: Boundaries   135

18: The Belt Flow: The Rakia of Energy   147

19: Connecting Heaven and Earth   159

20: *Sh'ma* and the Kabbalistic Hook-In   167

21: A Physical Practice of *Devekut*   175

22: Infinity Eyes: Connecting to a Higher Knowing   179

23: The Light Weave   193

24: Connecting to the Cosmos with the Forty-Two-Letter Name   207

25: Energizing Blessing   225

26: Blessing Water   233

27: The Shalom/Infinity Meditation   243

28: Shabbat   251

Part 3: Healing

29: Kabbalistic Energy Healing   265

Part 4: Summary

30: The Dragonfly   281

Glossary   287

Appendix 1: The Hebrew Letters   295

Appendix 2: Gematria *and Translation of Words Cited*   297

Bibliography   299

Art Credit List   303

Index   311

Acknowledgments

A heart-filled thank you to my beloved teachers and those who contributed pieces to the puzzle that became this book:

- My first energy teacher and healer, the late Rev. Jacque Metheany, and the teachers of Crossroads Institute.

- The creators of Eden Energy Medicine/Innersource, Donna Eden and Dr. David Feinstein, for changing my life. The Innersource faculty who so enriched my training and my personal healing path, especially Dr. Sara Allen, Dr. Vicki Matthews, and Dr. Ellen Meredith.

- Dr. Shems Prinzivalli, who introduced me to the mysteries of Kabbalah and who first encouraged me to pursue the connection between energy medicine and kabbalistic healing.

- Sarah Yehudit Schneider, Rabbi Yehoshua Karsh, Rabbi Gershon Winkler, Reb Rachmiel Drizin, and Rabbi Douglas Goldhammer for their wisdom and teachings.

- Infinity Foundation, its director, Nancy Grace Marder, and my students for their support.

- Elysia Gallo, my editor at Llewellyn, for her discerning eye.
- My models: Rachel Stern, Jane Talesnik, and Sue Sherman.
- My readers for their time, corrections, and suggestions: Marty Stern, Sarah Stern, Donna Eden, Jennifer Swain, Rabbi Yehoshua Karsh, Dr. Shems Prinzvalli, Sarah Yehudit Schneider, Pnina Mazor.
- And to Judy Haber for her technical expertise and unending patience.

In memory of my dearest Abba, Rabbi Reuben M. Katz (1919–2016), who taught me, among many things, the aleph-bet.

For Marty

My life's partner and love who embodies the divine balance with every breath.

Introduction

I was born on the eighth and final night of Chanukah. My parents lit the menorah with its full array of candles, recited the customary blessings, and quickly left for Akron City Hospital where I arrived a few hours later. Why begin with this fact?

Chanukah, the holiday of lights and miracles, begins on the twenty-fifth day of the Hebrew month of Kislev. Hebrew months are lunar cycles about twenty-eight days long. Therefore, the last nights of Chanukah extend into the following month, Tevet. Because Tevet is the darkest month of the year it is associated with negative energy. I was taught that having been born on the eighth night of Chanukah, I was surrounded from birth with this consecrated light of protection, a light of miracles.

One miracle is that this book exists. Another is that I have been guided continuously, sometimes in very mysterious ways, to study both Kabbalah, the Jewish mystical tradition, and energy healing. It was certainly not I what set out to do.

In 1998 I was at a crossroads. I had been teaching dance for eighteen years on a linoleum floor and my feet hurt. Eighteen is the Hebrew symbol for *chai*, meaning life. I knew my life on linoleum was complete and I was ready to move on. I set an intention for my next calling to reveal itself.

I had trained to be a biologist but my professional path had never been direct. Right after college and grad school I had been a high school biology teacher and done medical research in endocrinology. I had left science to pursue my other love, dance. Now that, too, was ending. My dear husband, Marty, had always given me the space I needed to explore different aspects of myself. He was game for yet another ride but neither of us had a clue as to what was to come.

Strangely, it was through dance that Kabbalah entered my life. I choreographed and taught dance, primarily Israeli folk dancing and interpretive movement, to the children of the Solomon Schechter Jewish Day Schools in Chicago. When I was asked to choreograph the kabbalistic story of the creation of the world for a special presentation, I was at a loss. Despite my upbringing as a rabbi's daughter with a good Jewish education, I had been taught absolutely nothing about Kabbalah. I was clueless as to what this story was, unaware that there even *was* a kabbalistic creation story. As luck would have it, my daughter Rachel was enrolled at that time in a Kabbalah class at the University of Michigan. She explained what she had learned about the story and even helped with the staging. My eyes were opened, for I loved this strange tale of creation. After that experience, if or when the door to Kabbalah study opened somehow, I was ready to enter.

…and energy?

In 1998, as I was preparing to leave dance for the unknown, I read *Anatomy of the Spirit* by Carolyn Myss, a renowned medical intuitive. Until then, I was unaware that people could possess accurate medical intuition. Carolyn's insights thrilled me. The book contained a description of basic energy anatomy, specifically the chakras (special energy centers on the body) and their relationship to health and illness. The influence of energy had never been mentioned in all my studies of biology. I devoured everything Myss had written up to then. Her observations made so much sense to me.

When I discovered that my yoga teacher at the time, Carol Stone, was also an energy healer, I spent my birthday in 1999 having my first energy healing session. As I lay on my back, Carol simply held on to my ankles. My body shook and shivered for more than half an hour. What power had been unleashed? Was this normal? What did it mean? I had many questions and no answers. With my curiosity heightened, I knew there would be no turning back. But how to move forward was a bit murky.

To help gain some clarity I set an intention to begin a journey of self-discovery. The new millennium was coming which seemed like just the right time to begin. On January 1, 2000, I began preparing for a spiritual pilgrimage to Machu Picchu. I hoped that insights as to my future calling would be revealed to me there. For weeks I earnestly meditated, cleansed, studied, and prayed. Ten days before I was scheduled to depart for Peru, I was jolted awake in terrible pain. I had suffered a traumatic injury. Two discs had ruptured in my neck as I slept. The pilgrimage would have to take place in my own home.

At first, I worked with neurologists and other Western-trained physicians. But how this injury might have happened was a mystery. Having read *Anatomy of the Spirit* I felt there had to be more to this situation than they could see. As I lay in terrible pain, a friend called and enthusiastically recommended that I visit an energy healer who had just worked with her. That wise woman was Rev. Jacque Metheany. As soon as she laid eyes on me she exclaimed, "You belong in my school!" Jacque became my first teacher of energy healing. Her school, quite appropriately, was named "Crossroads."

And what of Kabbalah? Again, the universe had been waiting for me to meet the right teacher. Another friend called to let me know that Dr. Jodi Shems Prinzivalli, a brilliant kabbalistic healing teacher, was coming to teach in Chicago. In 2000, I also began my formal studies of Kabbalah, with an emphasis on healing.

I was on my way. They say that when the student is ready the teacher appears. I was ready and many amazing teachers followed. As I traveled along the dual path of energy healing and Kabbalah, absorbing information like a sponge, I eventually found myself in an Eden Energy Medicine workshop taught by its creator, Donna Eden. Eden Energy Medicine offered a completely different way of dealing with the energy body than I had previously encountered. It was an approach that offered specific ways for individuals to move, balance, and connect their own energies, as well as those of other people. I began to practice on myself and could feel the positive shifts immediately.

I was studying healing from two different orientations, Kabbalah and energy, and I found it impossible to keep them separate. They seemed to complement each other and together provided a more complete way of experiencing the world. Kabbalah is essentially cerebral. The main focus is on revealing and understanding the mysteries of the cosmic plan through connection to God. Energy medicine, on the other hand, involves the awareness of physical sensation: tracking and experiencing energies with the senses rather than the mind. The focus is inward to the physical and emotional, and to the natural cycles of the earth rather than upward to heaven.

It is interesting to me, in light of this book's underlying theme of balance, specifically masculine/feminine balance, that throughout its long history and until recently, Kabbalah study was restricted to men, while the vast majority of energy medicine practitioners and students are women. In retrospect I was probably drawn intensely to both fields because of the need to restore my own masculine/feminine balance.

The process of becoming a healer for others is facilitated by dealing with your own issues. Safe within the confines of a class, we students gave supervised treatments to each other and received them in return. Throughout my years of training and the years that followed, I experienced many different kinds of healing sessions facilitated both by my colleagues and my teachers. Among the issues that surfaced was the revelation of an intense inner struggle between my masculine and feminine aspects. Without my conscious consent, this struggle had impacted my life in some pretty detrimental ways.

Through both kabbalistic healing and energy medicine my masculine and feminine parts began to resolve their relationship struggles and integrate. It was as if heaven and earth, on a micro-scale of course, had come into balance in my psyche. Energy exercises offered a way to balance and connect to my physical body so I could safely rise to levels of higher consciousness and then easily return to reality. Kabbalah, with its layers of poetic symbolism, enriched and elevated my energy practices to the realm of the soul. The spiritual and physical together created a field of connection, a channel of love.

Throughout my studies of Eden Energy Medicine[1] I would learn energy wellness exercises and see, often immediately, the connection with kabbalistic symbolism and even specific prayers. After I practiced what I envisioned, and experienced the ecstatic power and the positive effects of the combination of body and soul, I knew I wanted to share what I had found. These practices continue to enrich my life.

The synthesis of energy medicine and Kabbalah is a way to heal ourselves and our relationships at every level. The practices presented in this book enable the safe exploration of higher consciousness, and help to clear blockages to love. When love can be fully given and received its light radiates out beyond us as individuals. The love spreads to create a web of connection with others. As this web of love grows larger and larger we heal ourselves, heal our relationships, and slowly but surely repair the world. But the

---

1 www.innersource.net/ Eden Energy Medicine is discussed in chapter 11.

process must begin with healing ourselves, clarifying and manifesting our soul's purpose. The practices presented in this book provide practical tools for personal growth and transformation.

Part 1, *Background,* presents a discussion and explanation of basic concepts in both Kabbalah and energy anatomy that provide the background for the practices in Part 2.

Part 2, the *Practices* help to restore and maintain balance for us as individuals and in relationships. This process can seem daunting in the turbulent times we are experiencing now. The energy componant of the practices relates mainly to the physical, emotional, and mental planes. The kabbalistic symbolism adds the spiritual plane of the soul.

Body and soul together are the co-creators of the entirety of our being. The practices are, in a sense, moving physical meditations that help connect to higher consciousness. The soul assumes its role as a partner in physical healing, and vice versa. In addition to the step-by-step photos of each practice presented in this book, videos of many of the exercises can be found at: www.energyandkabbalah.com.

Part 3, *Kabbalistic Energy Healing,* presents hands-on healing practices for self-healing or working with another person.

The last chapter of this book, "The Dragonfly," is perhaps the closest to my heart. Early in my journey, during a combined Kabbalah/energy practice, I had the vision of a dragonfly.

Little did I imagine then the mysteries this symbol would lead me to discover. As this book unfolds, the dragonfly lies waiting beneath the surface. I reveal its secrets in the final summary.

I have presented aspects of this book in classes and workshops, to a wide range of audiences, for the past fifteen years. Once, I even found myself teaching energy/Kabbalah exercises to group of women in Safed, the center of the ancient kabbalist world. It has been an amazing and challenging process to put Kabbalah and energy together in a way that someone with little or no familiarity with either subject can understand and use. Creating a balance between body and soul, feminine and masculine has been a healing journey for me and my personal process underlies every page of this book. I am both humbled and honored to be trusted to bring these teachings to you.

My hope is that the practices will facilitate individuals in gaining further clarity as to their soul's unique missions, come into greater alignment with their calling, and manifest their gifts for the good of all. For us to thrive and create societies based on cooperation, trust, and mutual empowerment, the connection and balance of body and soul is imperative.

May the physical container of love and harmony created by the practices allow you to safely receive the light of consciousness at the highest levels. May this light illuminate and heal your personal places of darkness, and clarify the choices you encounter on your soul's journey in this lifetime. May we all be empowered to transmit safety and healing into the world.

Blessings on your journey through these pages.

PART 1
Background

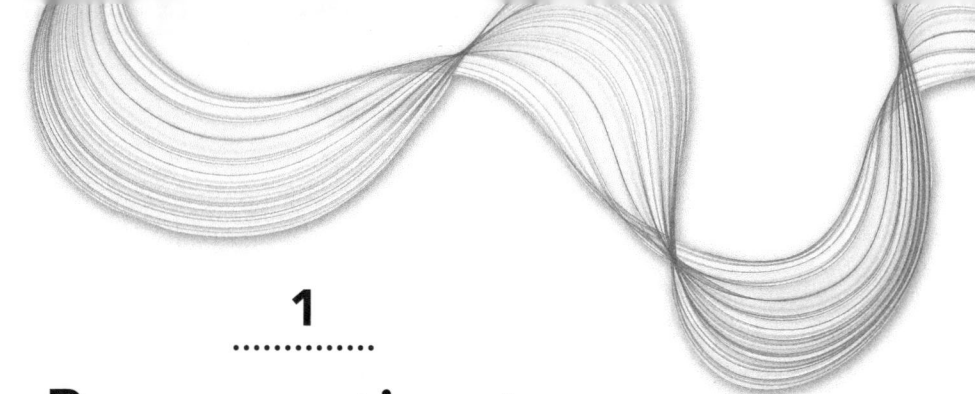

1
Reconnecting to the Divine Feminine

רָנִּי וְשִׂמְחִי, בַּת-צִיּוֹן--כִּי הִנְנִי-בָא וְשָׁכַנְתִּי בְתוֹכֵךְ, נְאֻם-יְהוָה.

Sing and celebrate joyfully, daughters of Zion, for I have arrived!
My Shechina, the Divine Feminine Presence, dwells inside you,
announces the Holy One, Blessed be He.[2]

As the long night of December 21, 2012, approached, the "end" of the Mayan calendar loomed, and many people were uneasy, interpreting that date as the end of the world. Special rituals and meditations were created for the so-called event. December 21 came and went without catastrophe, but created in its wake the mass awareness of a global shift that New Agers had long acknowledged.

    Six years later, the shift continues to progress and the struggle is palpable. The world feels unbalanced, and in this climate of rapid change, individuals are finding it difficult to maintain balance as well. We have caused much of this unbalance ourselves. Technology revamps itself constantly. The specter of global warming hovers over us. Bizarre natural phenomena such as devastating earthquakes, tsunamis, and excesses in rain and drought have become commonplace. We are rapidly depleting resources such as oil, coal, and the ocean fish that much of the world relies on for food. Even water is becoming a target of

---

2 Zecharia 2:14, special reading from the prophets for Chanukah, which I recited at my Bat Mitzvah.

conflict. Man-made threats of nuclear annihilation still exist. Terrorism and extremism dominate the news, and wars continue to rage around the globe. Slavery, sex trafficking, and other abominable abuses run rampant. Fear is exploited.

Yet amid this darkness, turmoil, and crisis, a light is shining and growing brighter. A new world order is upon us, and we are witnessing its difficult birthing process. People are becoming aware that the choices we make as individuals and societies have a far-reaching impact, and not just in the negative consequences listed above. Positive ideas and intentions also create energy fields and the power of these fields is just beginning to be studied and appreciated.[3] We are becoming more conscious of the fragility of existence, and how the choices we make now will determine our collective future, for better or for worse.

We each have a mission to fulfill: to help illuminate the darkness of our times in our own unique ways. Illumination, a higher level of consciousness, will bring us to the realization that we are all connected, that we are citizens of one world. We are at a crossroads in history. If we do connect to higher consciousness we will enable a shift to Oneness, a world of partnership, cooperation, and mutual empowerment.

The ultimate realization of Oneness consciousness is central to kabbalistic meditation, prayer, and study. Kabbalah shares the belief, with many other spiritual practices, that the restoration and rehabilitation of the value of the feminine is necessary for the shift to Oneness to be successful.

The divine feminine archetype had prevailed for thousands of years until civilizations throughout the world changed radically to a culture of male dominance. Some cultural historians, such as Dr. Leonard Shlain, mark the stages of civilization as occurring in two-thousand-year cycles.[4] By this calculation, we have reached the end of the Piscean Age which began about two thousand years ago. Symbolized by Pisces, the two-fish zodiac sign of duality, this age has been marked by masculine consciousness, hierarchy, power

....

3   A discussion of this research can be found in *The Field* by Lynn McTaggart.

4   In *The Alphabet and the Goddess* Dr. Leonard Shlain postulates that the rise of alphabetic literacy and writing shifted the principally right-brain, intuition-dominated, preliterate agricultural societies that venerated the goddess and feminine values to a left-brained, analytic, patriarchal, and mysoginistic world.

struggles, and the mistaken belief in survival of the fittest as irrefutable dogma.[5] Other historians like Riane Eisler place the transition to a male-dominant society at about three thousand years ago with the fall of the advanced civilization of Crete.[6]

This last epoch of history has been one of intense conflict, which in the end benefits no one and hurts us all by taking lives and depleting precious resources. The upheavals and uncertainties we are experiencing now are the labor pains of the birth of a new way of living. If we can rise to the challenges that face us we will usher in the age of Oneness, which some call the Aquarian Age, and kabbalists call *Olam Ha Ba*, the World to Come. In this new paradigm, the feminine is **equal partner** to the masculine. This partnership of masculine and feminine ranges from healing unbalanced parts of ourselves and our relationships, to changing what society values at its core.

Whether we are genetically male or female, we all have masculine and feminine aspects. According to the Torah, the original human was created in the image of God as a united male/female being.

In Kabbalah, masculine and feminine are relative terms. Simply put, masculine connotes bestowing or giving, and feminine, receiving. We are all feminine in relation to the generations that have come before us; we received from our parents. We are all masculine in relation to our children, giving to, nurturing, and providing for them. In relation to God, however, we are all collectively considered feminine because we are the Creation, the vessels, the receivers of God's light.

Because the Creation in Kabbalah is symbolized by the Divine Feminine, the highest manifestation of the partnership of masculine and feminine is symbolized by a divine marriage of the Infinite Creator with us, the Creation. The marriage is a symbolic union of the Divine Masculine and Divine Feminine.

The shift into Oneness consciousness is challenged by the necessity of holding opposites in harmony both within ourselves and in relationship. As opposites, masculine

---

[5] A thought-provoking discussion of Darwin's error in thinking can be found in *The Biology of Belief* by Dr. Bruce Lipton.

[6] Riane Eisler, *The Chalice and the Blade,* 56. Eisler postulates that it was repeated invasions by war-loving tribes such as the Indo-European Kurgans that drove those invaded to create weapons to defend themselves and shift their allegiance to virile warrior gods.

and feminine desires are often in conflict and can be the source of many imbalances at the personal level. In simplest terms, receiving is often much more difficult than giving. How can we feel safe to open ourselves to love at every level from love of self, to our fellow beings, and to the Divine?

We must develop the strength as individuals and societies to hold opposites, paradoxes, and conflicting purposes in a balance that respects and serves both sides.

The *Shechina*

Kabbalists refer to God's presence in creation as the *Shechina*, שכינה,[7] from the root meaning "to dwell." In Hebrew, nouns are either masculine or feminine. *Shechina*, a feminine noun, is considered the feminine expression of God. *Shechina* is also called the Indwelling Presence, the GodPresence inside each of us.

The transcendent GodPresence in the rest of the universe has many names in Judaism. These include the Creator, the Infinite Light, the Holy One, Blessed be He (*Kadosh Baruch Hu* abbreviated *K"BH*), the Upper Waters, the Name, YHVH, Master of the Universe, *Elohim*, Father, King, God.

Shechina is also a complex concept. The metaphoric, poetic language of the most studied and revered kabbalistic text, the *Zohar* (discussed in the next chapter) refers to Her in many ways. These include:

Divine presence, divine feminine, indwelling presence; the *Partzuf* (face) of *Nukva* (*NOK*), the archetype of woman, the Daughter, the *sefira* of *Malchut*, the Vessel, the Earth; Water, the lower waters, feminine waters; prayer (*tefilla*); the people Israel; *Shabbat* (the seventh day), Seven, the Hebrew letter *Zayin*/ז; the Creation, the Moon, the Mother, the Bride, Queen of the world, *Sukkat Shalom* (shelter of peace), and in certain contexts the names of God: *Adonai, Elohim,* and YHVH *Elohim*.

Like positive and negative ions and the north and south poles of a magnet, the opposites of masculine and feminine attract each other. Their attraction is the basis for the tension of all opposites, the flow of life, and underscores every chemical reaction in our bodies. The concepts of Divine Masculine/*K"BH* and Feminine/*Shechina* are spiritual reflections of this longing. When trying to decipher the abstract symbolism, poetry, and

---

7 Hebrew is read from right to left.

imagery of kabbalistic writings on the nature of masculine and feminine, it may be helpful to recall the basic underlying concept of masculine as giving and feminine as receiving.

Summary of Symbols for Divine Masculine and Feminine

MASCULINE	FEMININE
Creator	Creation
Bestower	Receiver/vessel
Kadosh Baruch Hu	*Shechina*
Heaven	Earth
Sun	Moon
Soul	Body

Although we refer to the *K"BH* as the divine masculine and to the *Shechina* as the divine feminine, no human form or any other physical form is ever attributed to either. These terms simply help us understand, to some degree, ideas that are totally beyond our scope of comprehension.[8]

In ancient cultures, the concept of divine feminine was not abstract. Throughout the ancient world, this archetype was worshipped as the goddess, often a fertility goddess related to the renewal of the earth and agricultural abundance. Statues and temples for honoring and praying to different goddesses were widespread, even in ancient Israel. When civilization shifted from the chalice to the blade thousands of years ago, the belief in and honoring of the goddess and the earth she represented was replaced by belief in a transcendent male god in heaven: a king, judge, father, and often vengeful warrior. The divine feminine and the qualities she embodied were no longer valued. Many cultures

---

[8] At some deep level, we probably all do have an understanding of this concept, maybe even a remembering of our original Oneness, for our cells reflect divine marriage in the double-standard helix of our DNA.

including Judaism outlawed goddess worship, and as a consequence, feminine attributes ceased to be honored and cherished.[9]

The ancient kabbalists were a very small group, certainly not in the mainstream, for they believed that in order to bring about the the *Olam Ha Ba*, the age of Oneness, equality of masculine and feminine was essential. The Zohar, in its symbolic and poetic language, attributes all the evils in the world to the lowered status of the feminine.[10] Kabbalists sought to restore the balance by looking to heaven through prayer and meditation. They continued to value the divine feminine as the *Shechina* and sought to elevate her by bringing down the light of the spiritual into her physical world. They believed that eventually, this process of repairing the world would culminate at the highest levels as the ultimate Oneness, the marriage of the divine beloveds, the *K"BH* and *Shechina*. Because Oneness was their ultimate goal and ours, the use of kabbalistic symbolism is ideal for the mind/body practices that follow.

It is time to resolve the long history of hierarchy, the ranking of masculine as superior and feminine as inferior. Such hierarchy is no longer sustainable. Embracing and integrating our feminine attributes, no matter our gender, is crucial for personal healing and for manifesting our unique gifts. The feminine embodies presence, strength of the heart, the nurturing of the earth and all its creatures, gratitude, creativity, depth, intuitive, inner wisdom, mutual empowerment, and peaceful cooperation. If we can learn to value these qualities in ourselves and others to the same degree we value such masculine qualities as competition, doing and achieving, activity and productivity, we will bring balance and healing to ourselves. As the energy field of our personal wholeness connects with that of others, it spreads and grows. Many believe that through this process a new world order of interconnected Oneness will eventually be born. Non-kabbalists also share this view.

The Sufi author Llewellyn Vaughn-Lee writes that it is time to give birth to our own wholeness and "awaken the soul of the world." He continues: "What is being born

---

9 An excellent discussion of this shift is found in *The Alphabet and the Goddess* by Leonard Shlain.

10 The "diminishment of the moon" and its repurcussions is discussed in *Kabbalistic Writings on the Nature of Masculine and Feminine* by Sarah Yehudit Schneider.

within the soul of the world is a quality of consciousness that comes from a union of masculine and feminine. We need to reclaim the feminine so that it can unite with the masculine in a new way, through which a new consciousness can be born."[11]

Riane Eisler writes, "The new view is of both men and women using our unique human facilities to support and enhance life… and rather than being just a *utopian dream*, a more peaceful and egalitarian world is a real possibility for our future".[12]

We are at a crossroads in history. The outcome is uncertain and our choices are critical in determining the future. The end of the Mayan calendar and the dawning of the Age of Aquarius also correspond to a major transition in kabbalistic time. The Hebrew calendar, which counts from the "birth of Adam," is now in the year 5778, approaching the end of the sixth millennium. According to the Zohar, each day of the symbolic seven days of the Genesis creation story corresponds to a thousand years. The six weekdays of the story symbolize the six thousand years we have had to prepare for the seventh millennium. Ideally, the seventh millennium will usher in the cosmic Sabbath, a time of actualized perfection, when masculine and feminine and all opposites will coexist in mutual respect, peace, and love.

Each of us can help facilitate the birthing of this new way of being by healing ourselves. We can begin by strengthening ourselves both spiritually and physically to receive, hold, and transmit more of the powerful light of higher consciousness necessary to elevate the soul of the world.[13] The Kabbalah/energy practices presented in part 2 approach body/energy and Kabbalah/soul as co-creators of this paradigm.

---

11 Llewellyn Vaughn-Lee, *Signs of God,* 97.

12 Riane Esler, *The Chalice and the Blade,* 73.

13 A fun way to strengthen the masculine/feminine balance in yourself is by enjoying your Hebrew lunar birthday in addition to your usually-celebrated solar-year birthday. Because the Hebrew calendar is based on the moon, Hebrew birthdays vary from year to year in relation to solar birthdays. Find your Hebrew birthday at chabad.org. This lunar birthday may occur before or after your solar birthday. If the birthdays are six days apart, for example, celebrate the entire span as your personal union of sun and moon, masculine and feminine. On the date exactly halfway between the two birthdays, you will be in perfect balance.

2
Kabbalah: The Background and the Basics

Kabbalah as Receiving

Kabbalah is the body of ancient teachings of the Jewish mystical tradition. Kabbalists, like other mystics, search for the meaning of life, the purpose of our existence. The major focus of study is the relationship between the Infinite Unfathomable Creator and the finite created realms, in other words, between God and us.

Kabbalistic study is esoteric, employing meditation and prayer to reach higher states of consciousness and connect with the Divine Oneness of the universe. In Kabbalah, consciousness is referred to as light. *Ruach Hakodesh*, literally "holy spirit," is the term used to denote the influx of higher consciousness, enlightenment, and divine inspiration. The intention of kabbalistic practice is to repair the world by bringing in and spreading this special light of *Ruach Hakodesh*.

The Hebrew word *kabbalah* is usually translated as "that which is received." In addition to the goal of receiving enlightenment, this definition reflects the fact that Kabbalah was an oral tradition, transmitted from masters to carefully chosen students. Its legendary beginnings lie about four thousand years ago with the biblical patriarch Abraham, the first recognized monotheist. Some even credit Abraham with creating the teachings found in the first written kabbalistic text, *Sefer Yetzira*, the *Book of Formation*. What was received by Abraham, and others that followed, was transmitted unrecorded, over and over again down through the generations.

Torah study, the basis of Kabbalah, is often symbolized by the word *pardes*/פרדס, the Hebrew word for "orchard."

The four letters in the word PARDES:

    P (פ peh)

        R (ר resh)

            D (ד dalet) and

                S (ס samech)

stand for the four levels of Torah study:

פ P= *pashut*: the simple literal meaning of the words

ר R= *remez*: what is hinted at just below the surface

ד D= *drash*: interpretation through stories and lessons

ס S= *sod*: the secrets, hidden from but a very few

Kabbalists at the highest levels engaged with the mysteries of *sod*, the secrets. A Kabbalah master could, however, only impart a fraction of the depth of the material to his students. The students would need to deepen and fill in the teachings through their own bliss-filled influx of higher consciousness, the light of *Ruach Hakodesh*.

Spending long periods of time in higher states of consciousness can be challenging so stability was an important consideration in selecting students. Ideally, students were Jewish scholars, stable, married men aged forty or older. Rarely, a younger protégé—or even more rarely, a woman—might be included. Studying Kabbalah was an all-consuming commitment, the study of a lifetime, making marriage very important. Wives provided the grounding of a home and family, the opportunity for stable sexuality, and emulation of the divine marriage. Wives also worked to allow their husbands the luxury of full-time study.

Thankfully, the tradition of restricting kabbalistic study to men no longer applies. After the loss of the leading European kabbalists in WWII, the old boundaries of gender, age, and even religion could not be maintained or enforced. For the first time, anyone could access this treasure that was once kept secret. Although it helps immensely to have a learned teacher, masters are no longer required for a student to receive. Ancient texts, often with detailed commentaries, are now widely available in English and sources such as the internet provide a plethora of teachings for every level of ability.

Today, after many years of study, I, a woman, have been blessed to experience firsthand how layered, rich, thrilling, and often totally confusing kabbalistic teachings can be. Texts often contain esoteric references, multiple interpretations (some of which may conflict), symbolism, and words that seem to make no sense at all except to those with knowledge at the deepest levels. Mastering the most profound truths requires immense discipline and guidance, as it has since the beginning. Our modern lifestyles do not allow the gift of engaging in full-time study except to a very lucky devoted few.

Yet, there are also kabbalistic concepts that are practical, easily grasped, and have implications for Jews and non-Jews alike. These ideas are universal and are the basis of this book. They have the power to help create the world of peace and connection we all envision for the future. Each of us can receive kabbalistic teachings and ideas, based on our own level and capacity. We stand on the metaphoric shoulders of the kabbalistic giants of yesterday.

History

Because Kabbalah was a secret and well-guarded oral tradition, the origins of our earliest written manuscripts, the keys to ancient knowledge, are shrouded in mystery. For example, the authorship of the oldest known text, *Sefer Yetzira*, the *Book of Formation*, is attributed by some to the Patriarch Abraham and others to Rabbi Akiva (considered the greatest mystic of his time), but no one really knows.[14] Several different versions of the book exist because they were based on oral teachings that were passed down in different locations over the centuries. Even the Zohar, or Book of Radiance, the most studied and well-known kabbalistic text, has unclear origins. According to Jewish legend, Rabbi Shimon bar Yochai wrote the Zohar in the second century while hiding in a cave for thirteen years. (He was escaping the persecution of Jewish scholars suffered throughout the Roman occupation of ancient Israel.) Others claim the Zohar was written by Moses de Leon in thirteenth-century Spain. Some claim that de Leon channeled the words of Bar Yochai. Despite the mystery of its origins, the Zohar provides a rich

---

14 Rabbi Aryeh Kaplan, trans., *Sefer Yetzira*, xvii. Rabbi Akiva lived in the first century CE.

and complex source of connection to the Torah and to the masters who once devoted their lives to Kabbalah study.

Spain was the home of many of the greatest kabbalists outside of ancient Israel. Spanish Kabbalah flourished for many centuries under Muslim rule until, in the infamous Inquisition of 1492, the Jews and Muslims were both expelled, ending a golden age of scholarly coexistence. As a result of this uprooting, a number of well-trained and highly disciplined kabbalists settled in Israel, in the safety and isolation of the walled mountain city of Tzfat (Safed). There they joined an already established community of mystics.

The leader of a select group of about a dozen men was Rabbi Isaac Luria (1534–1572), called the Ari (lion), the creator of the lineage most studied today. The Ari was a brilliant interpreter of Zohar. Even though the printing press was already in widespread use, the Ari published nothing. His insights and visions were so overflowing that he refused to record his extraordinary ideas for posterity. Thankfully, his student, Chaim Vital, took excellent notes and we are fortunate to have Vital's texts with which to study the Ari's teachings today.

The esoteric language of the Zohar is like poetry. It speaks in code, metaphors, and symbols. It is layered with highly guarded ideas, obscure references, and secret language meanings. Comprehension at any level is a scholarly undertaking and the Ari and his followers devoted themselves to unravelling its mysteries. With the Zohar as their guide, they practiced what is called *Ma'ase Merkava*, the Work of the Chariot. Based on the prophet Ezekiel's vision of the Throne of Glory, this work involved elevating oneself through prayer and meditation to ecstatic states to connect with and bring down *Ruach Hakodesh*, the light of elevated consciousness.

To this end, except on the Sabbath, the group followed a highly self-disciplined, ascetic life style. During the six weekdays of study, they kept their physical needs tightly reined to prevent matters of the body from interfering with the intensity of their focus on the spiritual realms. Even now, many Orthodox Jewish men wear a special garment called a gartel[15] to symbolically separate the urges and desires of the lower body from those of the mind and spirit.

....

15   *Gartel*, a simple black or white garment worn as a symbolic belt, is Yiddish for "belt." The word comes from the same source as the German *Gürtel,* and the word "girdle" also comes from this root.

Any physical sensations could be considered problematic. Even the meditative head movements and breathing practices taught by Rabbi Abraham Abulafia in the thirteenth century were rejected as too radical by most rigorous Kabbalah students.

The Ari instructed his followers that any connection whatsoever to the desires of the body and the physical world would sabotage their attaining an influx of *Ruach Hakodesh*, the light of higher consciousness.[16] He taught that one should "separate the soul from the body to such a degree that that he no longer feels any relationship to his physical self." Because their goal was to reach higher states of consciousness and from these elevated realms bring the light of truth into the world, they believed that the level of prayer, meditation, and study necessary to achieve these states must not be disturbed by physical needs. Eating and sleeping were kept to a minimum, and, ideally, sexual desire and activity limited to the Sabbath.

An interesting aspect of the Ari is that he was a healer as well as a scholar, gifted in diagnosing through both face reading and pulse testing.[17] However, his interpretations, understandably, were grounded in Torah and Kabbalah. He was a doctor of the soul.[18]

The study of the soul, God, and creation led kabbalistic rabbis and masters long ago to explore what we'd today consider New Age topics. They detailed such ideas as astral travel, reincarnation, prophesy, the nature of the dream state, the reliability of information discerned from dreams, the powers of angels and the forces of evil.[19] Maybe they would not have been too surprised to see the integration of kabbalistic ideas and energy medicine practices presented here!

---

16   Chaim Vital, *Sha'arei Kedusha, The Gates of Holiness.*

17   Pulse testing is also a basic form of diagnosis in Traditional Chinese Medicine.

18   Lawrence Fine, *Physician of the Soul, Healer of the Cosmos: Isaac Luria and His Kabbalistic Fellowship,* is an excellent book on the life of the Ari and his followers.

19   Many of these ideas are discussed in *Derech Hashem, The Way of God,* by Rabbi Moshe Chaim Luzzato, known as the RaMCHaL, 1707–1746.

Kabbalah and Relationship

Hebrew verbs usually have three-letter roots. The root letters of the word Kabbalah are KBL קבל,[20] meaning "receive," but KBL, in the form meaning "receive," never appears in the entire Torah. Instead, the three times this root does appear in the Torah, KBL refers to a detailed description of the *makbilot*, two special sets of fifty loops that connected two tapestry panels inside the portable tabernacle called the *Mishkan*. The Israelites carried the *Mishkan* with them throughout their forty-year sojourn in the wilderness after leaving Egypt. The *Mishkan*, from the same root as *Shechina*, was considered to be God's dwelling place thoughout the desert journey. The tapestry panels encircled the Holy Ark containing the Ten Commandments. The Ark eventually was placed in the Holy of Holies in the Temple in Jerusalem.

The *makbilot*, tapestry loops, were connected to each other by golden clasps. This sole meaning of the root KBL in the Torah brings us to the second meaning of the word Kabbalah, "connection or relationship." Kabbalah is, at its core, all about relationship and Kabbalah emphasizes one relationship in particular: the Creator with the Creation.

According to the Zohar, the Creator, the Unnamable Infinite ONE, had everything except an *other* with whom to be in relationship. All of creation is the manifestation of that will for an "other." Everything began with the ONE with the intention that eventually, filled with memories and experiences, all would return to ONE again. Reunification with the ONE refers to the "world to come," the time of perfected relationship, Messianic times. Now, in our time, Oneness can be manifested as wholeness in ourselves, a deep knowing that we exist in total connection and harmony with each other and with all of creation, and that our actions are in alignment with this knowledge.

Although religions tend to separate people by dwelling in differences, mystics understand that at the highest levels of consciousness these differences disappear. Ideally, religious beliefs provide ladders, different means to rise to the same place of connection. Kabbalistic ideas of Oneness are embraced across religious and cultural lines. The shift in world consciousness happening now is a phenomenon that affects everyone. If

---

20   Rabbi Yitzchak Ginsburgh of the Gal Einai Institute provides this reference: (5764#29), www.galeinai.org.

we are to survive and thrive, we must evolve into societies based on cooperation and trust, encouraging and empowering each others' highest purpose.

Despite the fact that we can conceptualize this ideal of connectedness, we struggle with practicing Oneness in our day-to-day lives: as individuals in relationship with our inner selves; in our relationships with others; and in our relationship with the concept of God.

For instance, as individuals, we all have hidden places of darkness and shame, shadow parts which tend to rule our lives. Light is the kabbalistic symbol of higher consciousness. Healing our shadow parts by bringing them into "the light" brings us wholeness, balance, and vitality. When we clearly see these disowned aspects of ourselves they lose the power to drive our unconscious thoughts and behaviors.

Our personal level of wholeness affects our relationships with others. We are complex, flawed individuals attempting to have loving intimate relationships with other complex, flawed individuals. Often we are drawn to people who trigger our own issues. Many relationships we have are not of our conscious choosing and yet we must find a way to accommodate and even learn from them. Difficult relationships are often the key to personal growth.

Finally, there is faith, the ultimate relationship, our relationship with the Creator. All of these relationships influence each other, from God to us, from us to God, and everything in between.

The Torah, the basis of Kabbalah, is a guide to relationships at all levels, from the personal to the cosmic:

1. First is our relationship to ourselves. For example, in Genesis, Jacob wrestled with an "angel," interpreted as an aspect of his own shadow self, and transformed as a result. Our own wholeness is the basis of healthy relationships with others.

2. The interpersonal relationships presented in the Torah are often dysfunctional so that we can learn from them and apply their lessons as a guide for handling difficulties we encounter in our own lives.

3. Our relationship to the Creator, the Source of Infinite Light, is the key to connecting with higher levels of consciousness. We each have the power to bring down the divine light for the sake of our own healing and to help illuminate and repair our dark and fragmented world.

When Moses shattered the first set of the Ten Commandments, the tablet containing the first five dealing with our relationship to God was separated from the second tablet, those dealing with our relationships to each other. When Moses received the second set of unbroken tablets, the ten were reunited. The lesson here is that relationship to God should be reflected in our interactions at every level. Because the *Shechina*, God's Presence, lies at the core of our being, every relationship has an aspect of the divine. Kabbalists, such as the Ari and his followers, understood this. They knew that a prerequisite to accessing the light was to live a life according to the rigorous Jewish code of charity, integrity, good deeds, honesty, piety, and personal purity in relationships both with others and within oneself.[21]

Many of the more esoteric kabbalistic texts contain coded instructions as to how to reach higher levels of consciousness resulting in meditative experiences of union with the ONE. Practices included *devekut* meaning "cleaving to God" through constant connection, and *yichudim* meaning "unifications" usually by meditating on intertwined divine names. The resulting enlightenment, the influx of *Ruach Hakodesh*, could then be channeled into the progressively denser "vessels" of human thought, emotions, and actions, and from there into the rest of material reality for the sake of repair.

It should be noted that this process consisted entirely of mental constructs. As previously mentioned, the physical body, home to the divine feminine, was not only excluded but considered an obstacle to achieving such union. The kabbalists loved and honored the divine feminine but did not connect this concept to their own physical bodies.

A loving relationship with self, others, and with God begins with healing ourselves at all levels. At the core of this wholeness is the task of bringing balance to the physical body as the vessel of the soul. Adam, the primordial human of Genesis, was created in the image of God as both masculine and feminine. This ideal being is the model for the world to come: a union of Creator/masculine with Creation/feminine, of soul and body. Daniel Matt's statement that God is "the energy that animates the universe ... father and mother equally" underlies the world we are trying to bring into being: equal, connected, and balanced; as above so below; as below so above. From the harmony and love created in ourselves comes repair of the world.[22]

---

21   Chaim Vital, *Sha'arei Kedusha, Gates of Holiness.*
22   Dr. Daniel Matt, translator of the Zohar, as quoted in the *United Synagogue Review*, Spring 2006.

From the cosmic to the cellular, kabbalistic symbolism enmeshed with physical energy practices facilitates a reuniting of the divine masculine and feminine archetypes. In Kabbalah, the spark of an idea, considered masculine, can only become manifest through the vessel of the physical body, considered feminine. Manifestation of these ideas into reality is essential now.

The *Shechina* is the embodiment of the Creation. She is the light of the divine presence in all of us. It is time for Her light, OUR light, the consciousness of creation, to reach its full potential. When we are in alignment with our soul's purpose, manifest our unique gifts and encourage others to do the same, the separations that divide us will be transformed into channels of unbound love and connection. Creator and Creation will again be ONE. This process is the sacred mission of Kabbalah. It is called *tikun olam*, the repair of the world and begins with our own *tikun*, personal healing. The next chapter reveals the mystical origins of *tikun olam*.

3

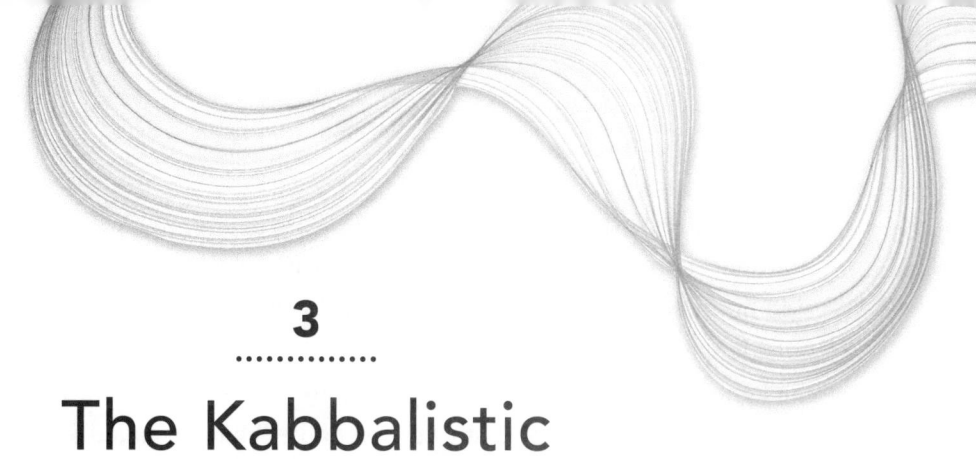

The Kabbalistic Creation Story

Shivirat Ha Kaylim/The Shattering of the Vessels

In the beginning, God's infinite light filled the entire universe. There was no room for anything else. There was only God and therefore no possibility of relationship. According to the Zohar, the driving force behind creation was God's desire for an autonomous "other" with whom to create the possibility of relationship. The Zohar describes a long and rather intricate process that sets the stage for the creation story as told in Genesis. The following is a brief synopsis of the Genesis prequel.

Because the infinite light was overwhelming, allowing no room for anything else, God drew back the light from a small space, creating a void. This withdrawing of the light was called the *tzimtzum*. Into the "empty" space, a narrow ray of light was projected. This light would eventually organize into the vessels or *sefirot* of the Tree of Life (chapter 4), the template of the created world as we know it.

However, before the Tree evolved into its current form there were several failed attempts to organize the light into vessels. In summary there was:

Plan A: The Bound World

Ten emanations of God's light, primitive *sefirot*, were all contained in a single vessel. They had no individual way to express themselves. This world failed.

Then came…

Plan B: The World of Points

The lights were each placed in separate vessels. These vessels now had individual expression but no connection to each other. They were unaware that any other light existed outside themselves. There was no possibility of relationship. The vessels could receive the light, but without any way to give to another they became so full of light that they shattered. This is the kabbalistic version of the Big Bang called *Shivirat Ha Kaylim*/shattering of the vessels.

And finally:

Plan C: The Tree of Life

After the shattering dispersed fragments of the vessels from Plan B throughout the universe, the Tree of Life was created. The *sefirot* in the form of the Tree had both individual expression and interaction. This time around, relationship was paramount. The rectified *sefirot* could both give and receive the light of the divine life-force. Giving and receiving is the model for our lives. We are individuals fulfilling our purpose in the context of relationship. The Tree is discussed more fully in the next chapter.

Tikun Olam

The idea that a perfect and infallible God would need several tries to create the world is a philosophical conundrum.

The Ari taught that the shattered vessels were an important part of the process of creation because they represent the origin of free will. Rabbi Eliahu Klein, in *Kabbalah of Creation*, explains the Ari's teaching: "If it became known to humanity that the Creator failed initially with cataclysmic mistakes, and nevertheless recreated and re-established existence as it is, then all human beings can do the same with their lives… Divine failure is God's way of creating the possibility within human consciousness of repairing what has been destroyed."[23] This process of repair is called *tikun olam*, literally repair of the world, and is symbolically based on redeeming the shattered sparks.

When the vessels shattered, some of the light returned to the higher realms where it had originated, but some fell lower and lower, until it reached the the lowest plane of

---

23   Rabbi Eliahu Klein, *The Kabbalah of Creation*, 70.

reality, the physical world. There, the shards of light that had made up the vessels coarsened. They became *klipot* or shells/husks (singular *klipa*), dense knots of unactualized potential, surrounding, obscuring and trapping the sparks. *Klipot* contain fragments of the original light from the shattered vessels. Our job is to unconceal, reveal, and elevate the sparks, for they are fragments of the divine lights of our souls.[24] The process takes work, like refining oil or freeing diamonds from rock.

Tikun olam is the main intention of kabbalistic meditation and study. In our day-to-day lives *tikun* occurs through the life lessons we learn and the consciousness we integrate as a result of our growth. No matter what religion we practice if any, we can "free the sparks" by living with integrity, being kind, doing good deeds, offering charity, blessings, and prayers, and learning from our mistakes. The work we do to heal our individual wounds and shadow places may be the richest source of our growth for Kabbalah teaches that there are concealed sparks even in the core of our darkest shames and most severe trials. Recall that the shattered first set of the Ten Commandments were kept in the *Mishkan* and honored along with the tablets that were whole. Our broken or unconscious parts contain the opportunity for us to grow and should be honored as such.

Shattering is often a part of life, reflected in expressions such as "falling apart," "coming unglued," or "losing it." We shatter because as in *Shivirat Ha Kaylim*, the give and take, push and pull of our homeostatic equilibrium has become unbalanced. Shattering, even in the form of a minor annoyance, is an opportunity to examine what triggered us. With that new self-awareness, that now revealed spark of consciousness, we have the opportunity, as the Ari suggested, to put ourselves back together in a new and improved way. Interestingly, the Japanese have a beautiful way of expressing a similar concept. *Kintsukuroi* is the art of repairing broken pottery with a special gold lacquer to emphasize the cracks. Broken vessels that have been reassembled are more prized than the original, whole piece.

---

24 Technically, the word *tikun* means to create a vessel that enables the revelation of some increment of previously transcendent light—Sarah Yehudit Schneider, Still Small Voice Correspondence School: Zohar class, 5/15/16.

Free will offers us the choice to change, or not change, in every moment. Doing the personal work necessary to clarify our soul's purpose allows us to manifest our gifts, revealing and shining out our unique light to the world. In kabbalistic terms, as we reveal the truths of our being the rectified sparks rise, returning to their original divine source. They bring down new light, new consciousness, and the world is repaired through us one spark at a time. Rabbi Simon Jacobson states: "These sparks must be elevated in holiness for the world to achieve perfection as per the divine plan."[25]

The divine plan is revealed when in Genesis, *Elohim,* the God-force of creation, pauses throughout the six-day process with the words:

"And God saw that it was good." וַיַּרְא אֱלֹהִים כִּי טוֹב

Restoring God's original plan of the goodness of creation is one of the main goals of *tikun olam*. The illusion of being separate from the light of the divine is the kabbalistic definition of evil. The opacity of our skin and bodies is regarded as a *klipa* for it gives the illusion that we are separate. Only in our world, the physical world of the *Shechina*, can good come close enough to evil, and light come close enough to darkness, to perform *tikun*. In higher realms, like attracts like, so such transformation is not possible. Opposites repel except in the physical world. According to the Zohar, the highest form of *tikun* is the balancing of opposites, the ability to hold paradox, and it can only be done by us because we live in the physical world.

According to the Zohar, God created Creation to actualize the potential of relationship with an autonomous other, symbolized as the *Shechina*. The work of kabbalists is to bring light to world through *tikun olam* so that eventually Creator and Creation will be One as in the very beginning. When all the sparks have been raised, Creation will be "enlightened" and we will delight in the *Olam Ha Ba*, the world to come.

Tikun olam begins with our individual journeys of personal growth and underlies the practices in Part 2. The practices strengthen us to receive, hold, and reveal more of our inner light, our true divine essence, the *Shechina*.

---

25 Rabbi Simon Jacobson, www.meaningfullife.com.

Duality and the Nature of Light

Creation began with the statement: Let there be light/*Y'hee aur*/יְהִי אוֹר. Light is the fabric of everything that was subsequently created, including us. In Kabbalah, everything is made up of light and vessels for the light, which are said to be light in a denser form. The analogy of physical light can be used as a way of describing metaphysical divine emanations. The light of divine emanations is the link to higher consciousness and its delights. Both physical and metaphysical light illuminate what is concealed. Both are transmitted immediately and stay in constant connection with their source. White light divides through a prism into seven colors much as the Tree is divided into the seven lower *sefirot*. Although this appears to be a multiplicity, in both cases all seven derive from the One.

Scientists have discovered that light exists simultaneously as particles called photons, and as waves. Because we are made of light, we also then, exist as particles and waves. This concept can be very helpful when trying to resolve the idea of duality verses Oneness. Like light, we are both physical and spiritual. Our photon-ness is matter, our physical being, our individuality. Being physical, photons can be thought of as a metaphor for the *Shechina*. The wave aspect can be thought of as cosmic consciousness, the divine flow, metaphorically the *K"BH*. Thus the union of the *Shechina* and the *K"BH* becomes a metaphor for wholeness and "enlightenment."

We seek to be in sync with the cosmic flow. It is the flow of Oneness, the highest frequency or vibration we can attain. Having a high vibration means we feel positive, at peace with ourselves and others.[26] The challenge is to connect with the highest vibration of Oneness and yet fulfill our individual destinies. A solution can be found in the term *tikun olam*, repair of the world. The word *olam* in *tikun olam* has another meaning besides "world." *Olam* also means hidden, so *tikun olam* can also be translated as "repair of what is hidden." Our inner work is to illuminate and activate the potential of our concealed divine sparks so we become more and more in sync with the divine flow of higher consciousness. As we free the sparks, we raise our vibration. Individually and collectively we are able to hold more light.

---

26   Check out: "The Benefits of Being in a Higher Vibration" by Pamela Dussault, http://m.huffpost.com/us/entry/positive-energy_b_1715767.html.

In order to reach the highest level, we must become whole in ourselves by doing the spiritual work of illuminating our darkest shadow parts. According to the Zohar, every soul, including the darkest forces of society, must be included in this process. Eventually, we will become light again, as it was in the beginning.

4

The Tree of Life

The **Tree of Life**, or *Etz haChayim* (עץ החיים) in Hebrew, is the kabbalistic blueprint, the holographic guide to how God's light is revealed in creation. This blueprint applies to individuals, relationships, societies: everything and everyone. The Tree also represents the anatomy of the human soul, masculine/feminine relationships, and the spiritual path to enlightenment.

The Tree is introduced in the very first line of Sefer Yetzira, the oldest kabbalistic text. There it states "With thirty-two wondrous paths … God created the world." The word for paths used is *netivot*. *Netivot* are personal paths, for everyone has an individual mission to accomplish in their lifetime.

The thirty-two paths are interpreted in Sefer Yetzira as the ten *sefirot*, the vessels of light that make up the Tree, plus the twenty-two Hebrew letters that connect the *sefirot*. A *sefira* (pl. *sefirot*) is a channel of divine energy or life-force. The ten *sefirot* reflect different qualities of God's light. Although nothing can be said about God as the Infinite One, the *sefirot* as divine emanations can be both described and contemplated. Each *sefira* transmits a particular insight or capacity of awareness. These include such attributes as justice, compassion, mercy, and majesty.

In the Tree, the *sefirot* are arranged in three columns. The center might be considered the trunk while the sides are polar opposites. Because the Tree is the blueprint for creation, every possible set of opposites exists in it.

The qualities of the *sefirot* on the right, such as compassion, are expansive in nature and are considered more masculine. In relation to the right, the left side is considered more feminine. The qualities of the *sefirot* on the left are contracted in nature, such as judgment and the creation of boundaries. The central column is the column of balance between the opposites, and when right and left are balanced, the central column acts as the conduit for bringing in new light.

LEFT	CENTRAL	RIGHT
Bina בנה understanding	Keter כתר crown/connection to higher consciousness	Chochma חכמה wisdom
Gvurah גבורה boundaries, judgment, might	Da'at דעת knowing	Chesed חסד compassion loving kindness
Hod הוד gratitude, surrender	Tiferet תפארת beauty, balance	Netzach נצח victory, control, endurance
	Yesod יסוד foundation	
	Malchut מלכות kingdom, realm of the Divine Feminine	

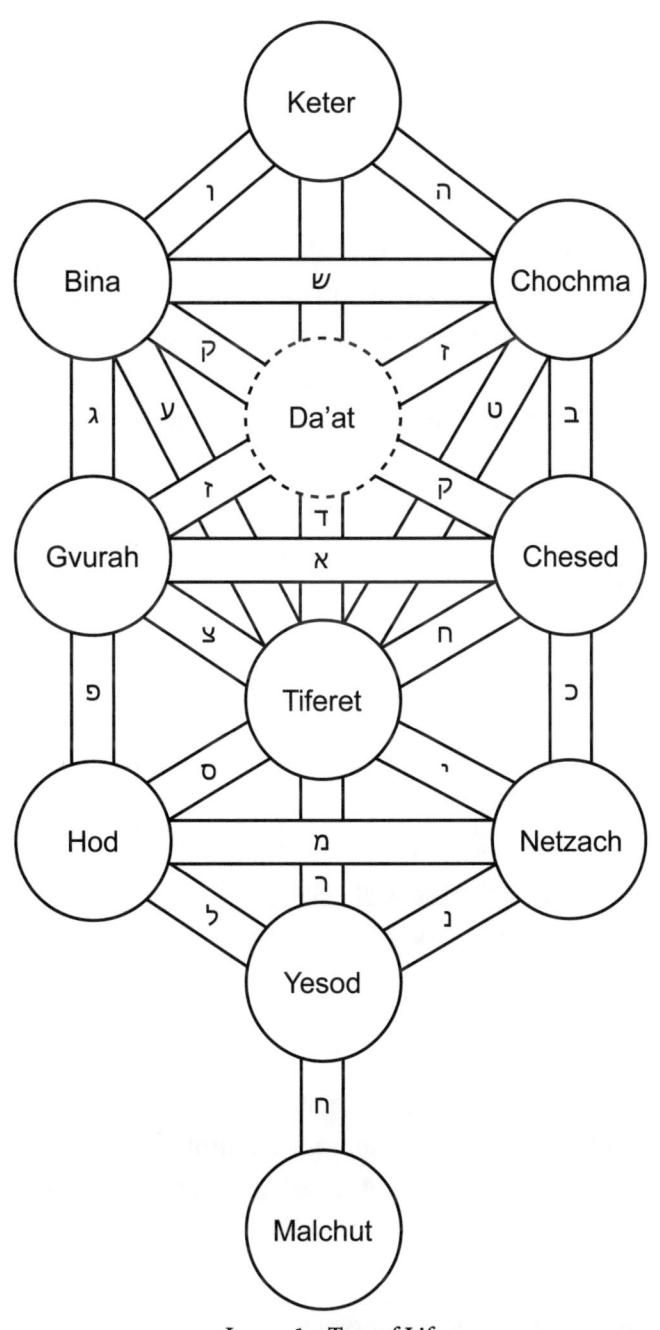

Image 1—Tree of Life

In this diagram of the Tree of Life, the circles represent the *sefirot*. The twenty-two channels between them each contain a specific letter of the Hebrew alphabet. The letters create pathways connecting the *sefirot*.[27] The pathways bring stability to the Tree and create relationships through these connections.

The *Sefirot* of *Keter*, *Da'at*, and *Malchut*

Keter/crown, the highest *sefira*, is actually the root of the Tree. The Tree is upside down compared to a tree in the physical world because the Tree is made of divine light, not wood. *Keter* is the root because it is the *sefira* closest to the influx of the divine light that feeds it and it is where light enters the Tree. In energy practices, "root" refers to grounding, being supported and nourished by the earth. In Kabbalah, the root is the connection to the Source of Infinite Light so the root is heaven.

Keter is our link to cosmic consciousness, our higher selves, our souls. It is the connection to the spark of inspiration for everything we choose to manifest and create in our lives. *Keter*, being so elevated, is not usually accessible with the conscious mind.

Sefer Yetzira states that there are ten and only ten *sefirot*. Sometimes, because the realm of *Keter* is inaccessible, *Da'at*/knowing is included as the tenth *sefira*. *Da'at* lies directly below *Keter* on the Tree and represents those aspects of *Keter* that have been brought to consciousness. It serves as a unifying link between *Keter* and the other *sefirot*. It connects the conscious mind to the unconscious, hidden aspects of the self. *Da'at* is also the channel between the heart and mind.

The light of the divine life-force enters through *Keter*/crown and filters its way down the Tree, enlivening the *sefirot*. By the time the light reaches the lowest *sefira*, the physical world of *Malchut*/kingdom, it has been depleted. Like the moon, *Malchut* has no light of her own. *Malchut* serves as a vessel for the light that comes from above and seeks to be filled by it. When the light of higher consciousness is actively pulled down into our physical world, the world of creation, the sefirotic home of the divine feminine, the *Shechina*, the potential of divine light from above can become manifest.

---

27 There are slightly different versions of the twenty-two letter pathways. This is the arrangement taught by the Ari. The Tree is also nonlinear and holographic.

"Rising up the Tree" from the portal of *Malchut* in order to access higher and higher levels of consciousness is referred to as *Ma'aseh Merkava*, the way of the chariot. *Ma'aseh Merkava*, refers to the prophet Ezekiel's ascent and vision of the Throne of God. Ma'aseh Merkava practices were regularly performed by the Ari and his students. Their rigorous lifestyle was meant to strengthen their "vessels," in order to "rise up the Tree," bring down, hold, and transmit more light.

"Vessel" refers to *Malchut*. A strong *Malchut* is essential for stability in the Tree. In kabbalistic healing as I was taught by Dr. Prinzivalli, the strengthening of *Malchut* as the vessel is always the first priority. *Malchut* creates the container for the light, for healing and repair at every level. Without a strong *Malchut* the intensity of the light that enters can be overwhelming, even unsafe.

Because the Tree is the blueprint of creation, having a strong *Malchut* has ramifications both for us as individuals and in relationships. As individuals, we all have areas of shadow that can be healed by bringing them into the light of consciousness. The vessel of *Malchut* creates grounding and safety in which to heal these parts.

Malchut is also the space for safely resolving conflicts arising from the tension of opposites, such as in our intimate relationships. The purpose of sanctified marriage is to create an expanded vessel capable of holding both partners, strong and flexible enough to resolve conflicts without being shattered.

The Tree is also a way of looking at the nature of conflict resolution within societies and between countries. The Tree is a hologram, and at the macro level we all exist in one container, the *Malchut* of the Creation. If that container, the Universal Divine Feminine becomes strong enough, we can resolve conflict, empowering and raising each other for the good of all. The task begins with each of our individual Trees.

The Tree in the Physical World

Although the Tree is a mental construct, archetypal and symbolic, it can be helpful to imagine it on a body. However, because the Tree is made of light, the body is not in the physical realm, per se. Instead, the body is that of a primordial being made of light/*aur* (אור), called *Adam Kadmon* in Kabbalah. The *sefirot* have associations with our physical bodies based on the metaphysical anatomy of *Adam Kadmon*. These associations are very helpful when applying kabbalistic symbolism to physical exercises. But primarily the Tree provides a map of the qualities and values we need to work with in order to return to the original Oneness. This Oneness is exemplified by *Adam Kadmon*, who existed before the Garden of Eden, and was made up of both man and woman.

According to *Midrash*, the stories that help to interpret the Bible, Adam and Eve were light-beings. When they were expelled from the Garden of Eden, they left the spiritual plane and became human. Their bodies of light, *aur* (אור), were replaced by an enclosure of physical skin, spelled differently but also pronounced *aur* (עור). Part of the *Havdala* service on Saturday night that marks the end of the Sabbath, and the weekly departure of the *Shechina*, includes examining the thin skin around our fingers. As the ritual candlelight reflects through them we are reminded that we once were light and seek to be united with the light once more.

The *Partzufim*

The essence of Kabbalah is relationships. (We'll soon see that this is the case with energy medicine as well.) The *sefirot* of the Tree are organized into a family to help explain the relationships between them. This family is composed of *Partzufim* (faces, singular *Partzuf*). The *Partzufim* are described in anthropomorphic terms to help us better understand complex ideas. They are symbols, metaphors, and no images are associated with them. The *Partzufim* can also be considered sub-personalities within each of us. In addition, *Partzufim* are related to different "universes" or planes of existence.

ARCHETYPE	PARTZUF	CORRESPONDING SEFIROT
The Ancient One Great-grandfather/Grandfather	Arik Anpin Atik Yomin	Keter
Father	Abba	Chochma
Mother	Ema	Bina
Son/Man	Ze'er Anpin (Z"A)	Chesed/Gvurah/Tiferet/Netzach/Hod/Yesod
Daughter/Woman	Nukva or NOK	Malchut

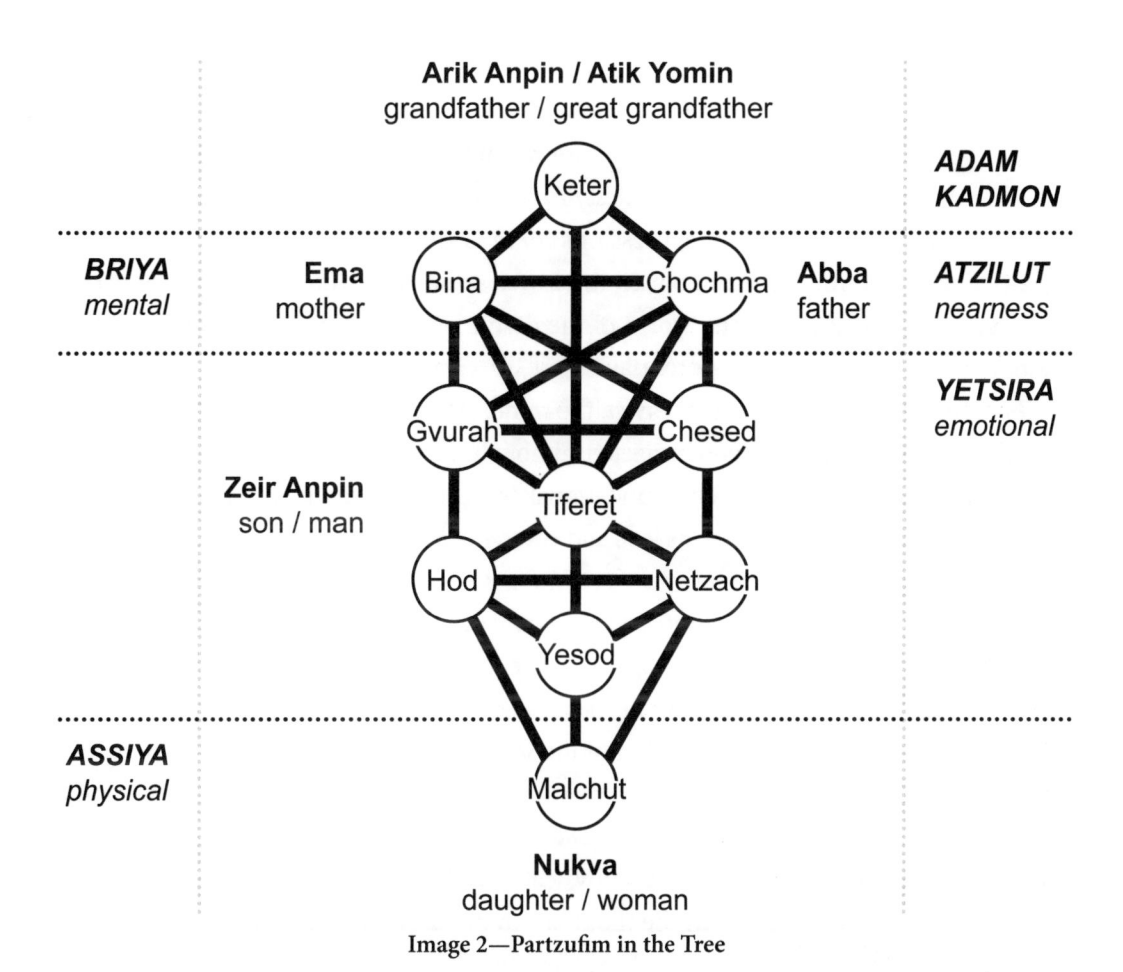

Arik Anpin / Atik Yomin
grandfather / great grandfather

ADAM KADMON

BRIYA *mental* **Ema** mother **Abba** father **ATZILUT** *nearness*

YETSIRA *emotional*

Zeir Anpin son / man

ASSIYA *physical*

Nukva daughter / woman

Image 2—Partzufim in the Tree

The *Partzufim* in the Tree

Description of the *Partzufim/Faces*

We begin at the root, *Keter*/crown, which is the top of the Tree. *Keter* has two personas: *Arik Anpin*, the Long Face, the *Partzuf* of grandfather, and *Atik Yomin*, the Ancient of Days, the *Partzuf* of great-grandfather. *Keter* is the closest connection to the light, to Source, our link to cosmic consciousness, our higher selves, soul. This is the world of *Adam Kadmon*, the primordial being who preceded the manifestation of the lower four varities. We, as humans, cannot fathom this plane of existence. Moving down the Tree, *Abba*, the Father, is composed of the *sefira* of *Chochma*/wisdom. In the metaphysical anatomy

The Tree of Life 39

of *Adam Kadmon*, *Abba* represents the right brain. Abba represents the universe of *Atzilut*, the spiritual plane, from the Hebrew root meaning "closeness."

Abba/Father receives a spark of inspiration from *Keter* and transfers the light to the left brain, his partner, *Ema*/Mother, the *sefira* of *Bina*/understanding. In *Ema* the spark expands to include all possible expressions. *Ema* is the Mother of manifestation, and "births" the now refined idea down to the lower *sefirot* including our physical world. Without the physical world, the world of the divine presence, all inspiration would remain in *Ema* as unmanifested potential.

Ema represents the universe of **Briya**, the mind. *Abba* and *Ema* as Father and Mother are beloveds, never apart, always connected, although the nature of that connection is variable. *Abba* and *Ema* also represent foundational aspects of the divine masculine/feminine archetypes, sometimes referred to as love and reverence.[28]

Ze'er Anpin (Z"A) is the archetype of son/man. Z"A is sometimes called the Six because it is composed of the next six *sefirot* as you go down the Tree. In the center of the Six and sometimes representing them is *Tiferet*/beauty, the heart. The Six also correspond to the divine masculine archetype, the *Kadosh Baruch Hu (K"BH),* and emotional universe: **Yetzira**.

Nukva (NOK) is the personification of the *sefira* of *Malchut*. NOK is the archetype of daughter/woman and also refers to the *Shechina*. NOK and Z"A, representing man and woman, have a very special relationship, and she is sometimes called the seventh *sefira* of Z"A. NOK corresponds to earth, the physical universe—*Assiya*. This is our world, the world of matter, the only world where thought can manifest into action.[29]

Lying at the lowest point in the Tree, the physical universe of *NOK* is the farthest from the influx of divine light. As a result, *NOK* has no light of her own. She is symbolized as a vessel that longs to be filled by the light, the influx of guidance from above. When this happens and the "light" associated with the masculine/Z"A enters the "darkness" associated with the feminine/NOK, potential can become reality.

This process can be looked at as a mini-reflection of the very beginning of the creation story. To recap, the universe was once totally filled with God's light until the *tzimtzum* made a space devoid of light. In that space, the divine will could manifest the

---

28   Rabbi Aryeh Kaplan, *Meditation and Kabbalah*, 238.

29   Interestingly, the word *matter* derives from the word *mater*, Latin for "mother."

Creation, an autonomous other. Since we were created in the "image of God" we have a symbolic space within us, *NOK*, where OUR will can become manifest. Autonomous means we have have free will. We have the choice in every moment to change and grow in accordance with our soul's purpose. Change and growth are only possible because of the space *NOK* provides. She is the cauldron of transformation. She represents the *Shechina*, the divine presence in each of us. One way to honor the *Shechina* is to manifest the light of our souls in the physical world, to flourish and express our individuality.

NOK receives as much light as she is strong enough to hold. The journey of our lifetimes is to strengthen ourselves to hold more and more light, for the more light we can hold, the greater the expression of our soul's actualization of its unique potential.

In the Ari's circle, uniting the divine masculine and feminine archetypes represented as *Z"A*/*K"BH* and *NOK*/*Shechina* through meditation or prayer was a way to achieve states of higher consciousness—that is, bring in the light. Indeed, the divine union of the *K"BH* and *Shechina* is the kabbalistic intention of every Hebrew blessing. Uniting *Shechina*/earth and *K"BH*/heaven in order to connect to higher consciousness also underlies the practices in part 2.

The Tree of the Future

The Tree as presented reflects the hierarchical nature of the present world, called the World of *tikun*/repair. The higher the *sefira* lies in the Tree, the closer it is to the Infinite Light. Our kabbalistic goal is to rise higher in the Tree in order to access the light of higher consciousness, and bring it down for repair of the world. When all the sparks have been raised, the Tree will no longer be a columnar hierarchy, but a circle.

In the circle Tree of the World to Come, the *Olam Ha Ba*, each soul, each lightbody will live in spiritual bliss, having attained their full potential. Each will have equal access to the Infinite Light at the center.[30]

---

30 Sarah Yehudit Schneider, *Kabbalistic Writings on the Nature of Masculine and Feminine*, chapter 7.

5

Gematria and the Hebrew Aleph-Bet

The twenty-two letters of the Hebrew alphabet (aleph-bet) are considered sacred because they are the original language of the Torah, also called the Old Testament, and of Jewish prayer. Kabbalistic texts use this alphabet whether they are written in Hebrew or its ancient sister language, Aramaic.[31] This is the same Hebrew alphabet used today.

Like other alphabets, the letters of the aleph-bet have specific sounds and shapes. In addition to the shape and vibrational energy of its sound, every letter in Hebrew has a story and a numerical value based on its order such as: A=1, B=2, C=3. A full listing of the Hebrew letters and their corresponding numerical values are given in Appendix I. The letters are described in the Zohar and in Sefer Yetzira as the building blocks, the DNA if you will, of creation. God spoke creation into being. Speech is made of words and words are made of letters. In Kabbalah, Hebrew words are said to contain the energy and power of the letters that compose them.

The numerical values of the letters are also significant. The term *gematria* refers to the numerical value of both individual letters and the value of the words, phrases, and sentences they form. **The numerical value of words and groups of words is the sum of the values of the letters composing them.** We have already mentioned that the essence of Torah and Kabbalah is the study of relationship. One way kabbalists establish relationship is through *gematria*. *Gematria*, in its simplest form, means that **words or even**

---

31   The Zohar is written in Aramaic.

sentences with the same numerical value have a deep and special relationship with each other. Words with equal numerical values are often considered to be equivalent. *Gematria* is the basis of many teachings and meditative practices.

For example, in Sefer Yetzira, the Book of Formation, the oldest known kabbalistic text, the importance of numbers as a way to establish relationship is explored. The simplified first line of the book states: "With thirty-two wondrous paths … God created the world." Thirty-two is interpreted as the sum of the twenty-two letters of the Hebrew alphabet plus the ten *sefirot*.

What further insights can we glean from words and ideas that share gematria thirty-two? Thirty-two is the value of the letters of the Hebrew word for "heart," *lev/* לב. So "thirty-two paths" might be interpreted that the source of the creation of the universe was and continues to be the heart. In fact, the God-force of the Creation, called *Elohim*, appears exactly thirty-two times in the story. In addition, thirty-two is the *gematria* of the word *Yachid*, the concept in Kabbalah of the singular force that preceded creation. *Yachid* is a totally unfathomable concept, the cause behind all causes, and yet its *gematria* helps us to understand that *Yachid* is at the heart of every point of time and space. Universally, the heart is regarded as the center of life-force and the seat of love, whether looking at energy chakras, the Tree of Life, or any other system. Simply put, whenever thirty-two shows up, look for a connection to the heart and vice versa. Because the heart is where the body and soul communicate it serves as the focal point in several of the practices in part 2.

Today, computer programs have enabled *gematria* calculations and interpretations far beyond what the ancients could have imagined. We will, however, be using very simple applications of *gematria*. The relationships of words through numbers hold wonderful secrets! There is a chart with all the words whose *gematria* is presented in this book in appendix 2.

6

A Different Creation Story: An Interpretation of the First Ten Letters

Despite its apparent simplicity, the Hebrew alphabet is regarded by kabbalists as containing the deepest secrets of creation. Sefer Yetzira introduces the twenty-two Hebrew letters as the actual building blocks of creation, directly connected to the Divine Source of Infinite Light. According to the Zohar, each of the primordial twenty-two letters had a specific energy and role in creation. In other words when, in Genesis 1:3, God said "Let there be light," the actual letters that make up the word for light/אור/*aur*: *aleph*/א *vav*/ו and *resh*/ר, formed a unique vibration that physically produced light. In addition, the first ten letters and their *gematria* reveal a symbolic creation story of their own.[32]

א *Aleph* (A)—1 is the first letter. It is so important that we will return to discuss it several times. *Aleph*/א is the first letter of *Elohim*/א-להים, the God-force behind the creation story recounted in Genesis. Although *aleph* is first in the alphabet it is not the first letter in the creation story as you might expect. Because *aleph*/א is the first letter of *Elohim*, the *Aleph*, the One, was already present, so it does not have the honor of being the first letter in the Torah. That honor goes to:

---

32 This interpretation is based on a presentation made by Rabbi Itzchak Marmorstein at an Ophanim kabbalah yoga workshop I attended many years ago. www.jewishyoganetwork.org.

ב *Bet* (B)—2 means house (*bayit*). *Bet* is the first letter of the first word in the Torah, "*B-reishit*"/בְּרֵאשִׁית, usually translated as "in the beginning." One interpretation of the reason that *bet* is the first letter of the creation story is that two symbolizes relationship and, as we have discussed, the essence of Torah is relationship: to self, to others, and to God. Another interpretation is based on the physical shape of the *bet*. At the beginning of the creation story everything opens to the future (remember that Hebrew is read from right to left). If you try to go back you hit a wall.

ג *Gimel* (G)—3 See the "leg"? *Gimel*, now stable like a tripod, prepares to leave the house (*bet*/ב/*bayit*) and walk out into the world.

ד *Dalet* (D)—4 means door. It is the door through which the *gimel* walks into the world. *Dalet*, as 4, is sometimes used to signify the four-letter Name of God, which can be represented by the letters YHVH in English. This name is sometimes referred to as the tetragrammaton, meaning four-letter name.

ה *Hei* (H)—5 The *dalet* grows a foot which breaks away in order to take action in the world. *Hei* is also the sound of exhaled breath…hhh.

ו *Vav* (V)—6 after the *hei*/foot steps out into the world, it stretches into a *vav* and looks like a spine standing tall. The actual meaning of *vav* is a "hook," something that connects. *Vav* is not only a letter but the word "and," the word of connection, of relationship. *Vav*, as the word "and," is the most commonly occurring word in the Torah.

Vav, as six, represents **masculine** energy. This idea comes from the story of creation itself. The six days of creation were the days of action. Getting the job done is the nature of masculine/yang energy. Recall that *Ze'er Anpin* (Z"A), the son/man archetype in the Tree, is also called the Six because it is comprised of six *sefirot*.

As kabbalistic symbols reveal themselves in the pages to come, remember that *vav* has two separate associations, as "and," the connector, and as the Six, the expression of the masculine. It will be clear which one is being referred to.

VAV and ZAYIN/the Groom and Bride
6 *Vav*/ו and 7 *Zayin*/ז represent the relationship
between masculine and feminine.

ז *Zayin* (Z)—7 looks like a *vav* wearing a wedding hat. Seven represents the **feminine**. The seventh day is called *Shabbat*/Sabbath from the same root in Hebrew as *sheva*/seven. Shabbat is the day of rest and renewal which followed the six days of active creation. God blessed and sanctified the Sabbath as a sacred oasis in time, a time for being, receiving, and integrating. The six days of activity are balanced by the seventh, the day of receptivity.

The Sabbath is often represented as a bride returning to her beloved or a queen reuniting with her king. *Nukva/NOK*, the daughter/woman archetype in the Tree also associates with seven, for she is called the seventh *sefira* of *Z"A*.

Symbolism of 6 *Vav*/ו and 7 *Zayin*/ז

The Jewish star, the six-pointed *Magen David*/Shield of David, is a symbol of the relationship of six and seven. The six points of the star stand for the Six, on the Tree, the six *sefirot* of the son/man archetype, *Z"A*. The seventh *sefira*, *Malchut*, *NOK* the daughter/woman, lies in the center. The points are the six days of creation, of the work week, surrounding *Shabbat*, the Sabbath.

Image 3—Star of David with Shabbat

The star is also symbol of the balance of masculine/yang and feminine/yin.

The upward-pointing triangle, symbolizing masculine energy/yang, is the rising energy of fire. The downward-pointing triangle represents water, feminine energy/yin, which always moves down. When fire and water meet as they do in the star, they create the Kiss of Heaven, referred to in the Zohar as "Holy Steam."

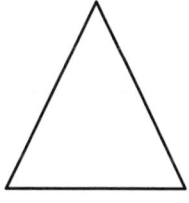

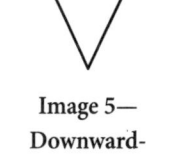

Image 4—Upward-Pointing Triangle

Image 5—Downward-Pointing Triangle

A Different Creation Story: An Interpretation of the First Ten Letters 47

Numerical Relationships of 6 Vav/ו and 7 Zayin/ז

1. Multiply the numbers

Vav times Zayin

6 x 7 = 42

A forty-two-letter name of God is mystically derived from the creation story that opens the the book of Genesis. Like other very sacred names, the forty-two-letter name cannot be pronounced. However, this name, which signifies duality coming into unity, can be used powerfully in healing. One such practice is detailed in chapter 24.

2. Add the numbers:

Vav plus Zayin

6 + 7 = 13

Thirteen is the gematria of the Hebrew word for love, *ahava*/אהבה.

When *vav*/6 and *zayin*/7 move forward in their relationship, join in love and take the next step, they reach 8, the letter *chet*.

The Wedding

Image 6— Chet with Bridge

ח *Chet* (CH)[33]—8 According to the Ari, when the *vav*/ו and *zayin*/ז stand together, they create the *chet*/ח shape which is sometimes written with a little bridge connecting them.

Together the *vav* and *zayin* create and symbolize the marriage canopy central to a traditional Jewish wedding ceremony. This canopy, the *chuppah*/חופה, begins with the letter *chet*. The word for life, *chayyim*/חיים, also begins with the letter *chet*. The *chet* chuppah is made of the groom/*vav*/ו on the right and the bride/*zayin*/ז on the left. Above them rises a tall fragile roof that unites them into one letter, the letter of life, the new life that begins with the wedding ceremony. The *chet* as *chuppa* is the symbolic container for this sacred "re"union of masculine and feminine, groom and bride.

---

33   Hebrew pronunciation which is indicated in parentheses after each letter, has equivalent sounds in English except for the *ch* sound as in the letter *chet*, The *ch* sound is guttural and sounds like a very gentle clearing of the throat. The *sefira* of *Malchut*, and the words *baruch* (blessed), and *echad* (one) are all pronounced with this sound, which can take some practice.

Under the chuppa in a traditional ceremony, the bride circles the groom seven times. This is a reenactment of the seven days of the creation story and according to the Ari, bonds the bride and groom on a cosmic level, ensuring a successful marriage.[34] To seal the union, seven blessings are also recited. One of these blessings is for the creation of an "Adam." "Adam" refers to the primordial Adam, *Adam Kadmon*. *Adam Kadmon* was a light-being, male and female both, who could contain these opposites in harmony and stability.

Chet is the number eight. In our number system, "8" looks like an upright infinity symbol. Although Hebrew presents a different shape for eight, the *chet* can also represent an infinity symbol in the sense that as the *chuppah* it unites opposites in balance.

ט *Tet* (T)—9 is the gestation. *Tet* is a shaped like a container; it is the only letter that is "upside down." With a bit of imagination, it looks like a womb, and nine "months" after the *vav*/6 and *zayin*/7 marry under the chuppa of *chet*/8, the little projection on the right of the top of the ט springs forth as the letter *yud*.

י *Yud* (Y)—10 The tiny letter yud is the product of the union of opposites, *vav*/masculine and *zayin*/feminine, and so contains all possibilities within it. The Zohar regards *yud* as the cosmic stem cell, the architect who fashioned the building blocks of creation—that is, all the other letters.[35] In this regard, *yud* (especially the upper tip) is called the divine spark. The literal meaning of the word *yud* is "hand," which is spelled the same as the letter *yud* but pronounced slightly differently: *yad*. So *yud*/יד = hand/*yad*/יד. *Yud* is also the first letter of the most holy Name of God, YHVH/יהוה. Divine spark, hand, component of holy Name(s): we will delve deeper into these ideas and other secrets of *yud's* significance in future chapters.

The end of this alternate creation story brings us full circle, for *yud* is also the number 10. The numbers 1 + 0 add to 1, where the story began and where we now continue.

---

34   Rabbi Eliahu Klein, *The Kabbalah of Creation*, 50.
35   It is interesting to note that name of the Greek letter *iota*, derived from the Hebrew yud, is also a way of indicating the smallest thing … as in the expression "not one iota."

7

The Mystical Letter *Aleph*
א

Infinite 8
א

א is the universal mathematical symbol for **infinity**.[36] The 8 in this drawing has thirteen segments, a significant number. David Friedman, an artist and kabbalist living in Safed, in creating the Infinite 8 above, says, "Eight represents beyond time and space—the realm of the Infinite and the Eternal—the realm of miracles and the supernatural."

Aleph is the first letter of the Hebrew alphabet and therefore has the numerical value of one. Many Names for God begin with *aleph*:

Image 7—Infinite 8

---

36   That *aleph* is a symbol of infinity was revealed to me in the solution of the *New York Times* crossword puzzle (#0923) 9/23/06. I immediately verified this information and still have that puzzle!

El/א-ל/the Almighty[37]
Elohim/א-להים/the aspect of God who spoke creation into being
Adonai/א-דני/My Lord or Master
Ehiye Asher Ehiye/אֶהְיָה אֲשֶׁר אֶהְיָה/I Will Be What I Will Be:
   the Name revealed to Moses at the burning bush
Aur Ein Sof/אור אין סוף/the Infinite Light

The Ten Commandments begin with the letter *aleph* as do many significant words.

One	אחד	/*echad*
Infinity	אין סוף	/*ein sof*
Love	אהבה	/*ahava*
Light	אור	/*aur*
Air	אויר	/*avir*
Earth	ארץ	/*eretz*
Fire	אש	/*aish*
Man	איש	/*eesh*
Woman	אשה	/*eesha*
Mother	אמה	/*ema*
Father	אבא	/*abba*
Adam	אדם	/the first man, humanity

As the number one, the *aleph* is a symbol of oneness, of unity. However, the *aleph* is also a symbol for the balance of oneness with multiplicity, a place where opposites can meet and coexist. Many of the *aleph*'s secrets will be revealed in the chapters to come. Let's begin with the most obvious, the nature of its shape.

א

---

37   Out of respect and custom, dashes have been inserted into the Holy Names when written in Hebrew.

The *aleph*, though whole as it stands, is symbolically composed of other letters. The parts above and below the diagonal line are identical. The diagonal line both separates and connects the two identical parts.

The parts above and the part below the line can be thought of as *yud*s י.

Separating and connecting the *yud*s is the letter *vav*/ו oriented diagonally instead of straight up and down.

Recall that each letter has a number value. *Aleph* as a whole is 1, but add up the value of the three component letters to discover an additional *gematria*:

	י	upper *Yud* = 10
א	ו	*Vav* = 6
	י	lower *Yud* = 10

      add to 26

Aleph = 1
 and *Aleph* = 26
So according to this construct
    26 = 1

This strange equation leads us to the next chapter, "The Unpronounceable Name."

8

The Unpronounceable Name

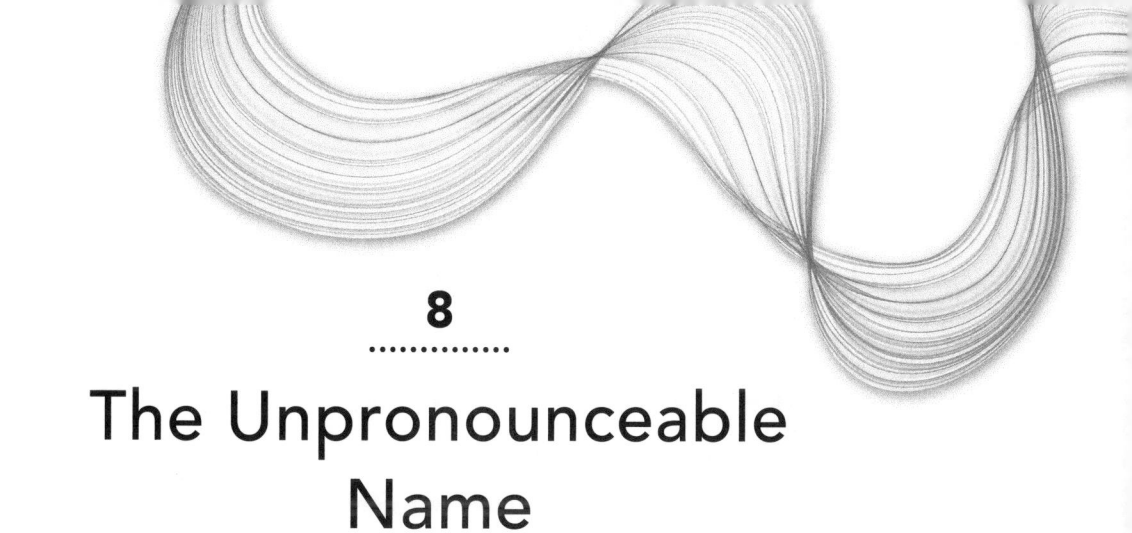

Judaism, and therefore Kabbalah, rests on the belief in a singular unity called God, the Divine Source of Infinite Light, beyond description or comprehension. Even physicists, who postulate the presence of a force underlying and unifying everything in the universe, call this unity the God particle.

In Hebrew, pronunciation depends on vowels, which are lines or dots surrounding the letters in various positions. For example, the letter *tet*/ט, which has the sound "T," could be pronounced TEE, TAY, TOO, TAH, TEH, etc. In both modern Hebrew and the Torah the vowels are not written but can be inferred. There is one major exception. The most sacred name of God, י-הוה, sometimes represented in English as YHVH, cannot be pronounced, even in the Torah or in prayer, because it has no vowels that we know.

Only the *Kohen ha Gadol,* the High Priest of the ancient temple in Jerusalem, had the honor to pronounce the Name. Once a year, during a special service on Yom Kippur, the holiest day of the Jewish calendar, he would enter a chamber called the Holy of Holies. The Ark of the Covenant, containing the tablets of the Ten Commandments, was kept in this most sacred area. In the Holy of Holies the *Kohen* would pronounce the Name YHVH/י-הוה as it manifested in that moment. The power of the Name would bless the people for the coming year. It is said that if the High Priest, despite his intense and painstaking preparations, somehow lost his focus and mispronounced the Name, he would die on the spot. He entered the Holy of Holies with a rope tied around his waist as a precaution so that in case that remote possibility actually occurred, the other priests could pull him out and send in a replacement.

Because no one today can pronounce YHVH/י-הוה, it is sometimes referred to in English as Yahweh or Jehovah.

YHVH/י-הוה is usually referred to by kabbalists as:
- *HaShem,* meaning "the Name,"
- The tetragrammaton, meaning the four-letter name,
- A permutation of YHVH pronounced *Havayah,*
- A variation of YHVH spelled YKVK,
- *Dalet,* meaning four.

Although there are many names for God in Hebrew, YHVH/י-הוה is the Name of Names. It represents the Unity, the force of Oneness at the core of cores that connects everything in the universe. Although we really cannot describe this infinite power in any way there are many secrets coded in the Name. They give a glimpse into the unfathomable nature of this concept of God that will help to enrich the practices in part 2.

God Exists Beyond Time and Space

YHVH/י-הוה is a permutation of and encompasses the Hebrew words for *past, present,* and *future*:

If you take the word
>
> **WAS**
>
> היה
>
> HAYAH

superimpose on it the word for the present, what
>
> **IS**
>
> הוה
>
> HOVEH

and superimpose them on it the word for the future, what
> **WILL BE**
> יהיה
> *YIHIYEH*

the word that results is:
> י-הוה
> *YHVH*

YHVH is the junction of everything past, present, and future. YHVH encompasses all time and space but is beyond time and space, symbolizing the process of both being and becoming.

Vertical Representation

The name י-הוה looks quite different when written vertically.

yud י
hei ה
vav ו
hei ה

Writing the name vertically helps relate the letters to the Tree of Life. The resemblance to the shape of a person in no way implies that God has a physical body but it helps us wrap our minds around ideas that we as humans cannot possibly fathom.

The Letters Represent Four Planes of Existence

The letters of YHVH/י-הוה represent the four superimposed worlds depicted in the Tree of Life. The tip of the *yud*/י, extends into *Keter,* the primordial realm of Adam Kadmon that gave rise to the Four Worlds.

yud	י	spiritual/*Atzilut*
hei	ה	mental/*Briya*
vav	ו	emotional/*Yetzira*
hei	ה	physical/*Assiya*

Just as the four letters of the Name are ONE, the four worlds are mystically connected to each other creating the whole of existence. According to the Ari, as explained by Rabbi Chaim Vital in *Gates of Holiness*, humans are the only beings in creation who exist in all four worlds simultaneously. In Genesis (1:26) is written:

And God said: "Let us make man in our image, after our likeness."
וַיֹּ אמֶר אֱלֹ הִים נַעֲשֶׂה אָדָם בְּצַלְמֵנוּ כִּדְמוּתֵנוּ

"In God's likeness" refers both to the male and female essence of the primordial human being and also to the idea that humans uniquely contain all four worlds. Humans alone were created near the light of the ten *sefirot* of the Tree to be able to access and cleave to the light and draw it down into the lower worlds. The worlds need the actions of humans to draw heaven to earth.

The Letters Represent the Partzufim

The letters of YHVH/הוה-י represent the faces, or personas that are often used to explain relationships between the *sefirot* within the Tree. You may recall that these "faces" are called *Partzufim*.

They are:
Crown of the *yud*/י (great) grandfather/*Arik Anpin* and *Atik Yomin*

Keter, the *sefira* that crowns the top of the Tree, corresponds to the apex of the *yud*/י in YHVH. This tip is also called a crown, the crown of the *yud*. The crown of the *yud*, as the closest point to divine light, receives the spark of inspiration for everything we choose to manifest and create in our lives.

Yud/י Father (*Abba*, composed of *Chochma*)

 Abba receives the spark of inspiration from *Keter* in the form of the body of the *yud*/י in YHVH. In *Abba*, all thoughts and actions exist only in potential. In order for the potential to become manifest, the spark is carried to the left brain, *Ema*, the *sefira* of *Bina*.

Hei/ה Mother (*Ema*, composed of *Bina*)

 Ema and *Abba* are always together.

The *Yud*/י and *Hei*/ה, *Abba* and *Ema* together form a Name of God, written YAH/י-ה

Vav/ו the son/man (*Ze'er Anpin* or *Z"A*, the next six sefirot)

 Z"A represents the *Kadosh Baruch Hu (K"BH)*

Hei/ה the daughter/woman (*Nukva*, composed of *Malchut*)

 represents the *Shechina*/partner of the *K"BH*

Summary

LETTER	PARTZUF/SEFIRA	UNIVERSE
apex of י	Arik Anpin/Atik Yomin	Adam Kadmon (primordial "man")
י	Abba/Chochma	Atzilut (spiritual)
ה	Ema/Binah	Briya (mental)
ו	Ze'er Anpin (Z"A): Chesed/Gvura/Tiferet Netzach/Hod/Yesod	Yetzira (emotional)
ה	Nukva (NOK): Malchut	Assiya (physical)

The Letters Symbolize the Balance of Heaven and Earth

YHVH/הוה-י represents the balance between

Heaven: YH/יה

the divine masculine, also called *K"BH Kadosh Baruch Hu,* the transcendent God, the Creator and the *potential* of creation

and

Earth: VH/וה

the divine feminine or **Shechina,** the *manifestation* of creation, the Indwelling God-presence in us and every other aspect of the creation.[38] *Lecha dodi* (meaning "come, my beloved") is a mystical prayer sung on Friday evenings to welcome the return of the Sabbath/Shechina as the bride of the K"BH (see chapter 28: The Sabbath). The refrain, reflecting the seventh day, has seven words. The seven words are divided into two parts. The first part has fifteen letters. Fifteen is the gematria of יה/YH. The second part has eleven letters. Eleven is the gematria of וה/VH. Together they add to twenty-six, the gematria of YHVH.

It is interesting to note that the letter *vav*/ו, representing manifestation, even looks like an extension of the potential of *yud*/י.

The Letters Symbolize the Different Levels of the Soul

Each letter of the tetragrammaton represents a different level in the anatomy of the soul.[39] For the purpose of this book, the levels will be referred to collectively as the *Neshama* נשמה.

A Problem Solved

The inability to pronounce the Name aloud poses a problem, as YHVH/ הוה-י appears constantly in both the Torah and in Jewish prayer. The solution is that, whenever the Name YHVH/הוה-י is written, it is pronounced as a different word entirely, *Adonai,*

....

38 A beautiful example of the union of YH and VH is hidden in the refrain of *Lecha Dodi.*

39 Information on the anatomy of the soul can be found at http://www.chabad.org/kabbalah/article_cdo/aid/380651/jewish/Levels-of-Soul-Consciousness.htm.

meaning "my Lord" or "Master." Speech is a physical phenomenon. Because speaking א-דני the name Adonai is a physical phenomenon, saying Adonai/א-דני instead of YHVH/הוה-י is considered part of the physical world, the realm of the divine feminine, the Shechina. In this context, the unpronounceable name YHVH/י-הוה symbolizes the transcendent God/the Kadosh Baruch Hu (K"BH), while Adonai/א-דני symbolizes the God within the physical universe, the Shechina, the divine presence. Every time Adonai/ א-דני is pronounced when YHVH appears creates a union of divine masculine and י-הוה/feminine. In Sephardic prayer books the two Names, YHVH/י-הוה and *Adonai*/ א-דני, are often written as one word.[40] The final H/ה of YHVH/י-הוה, which symbolizes the physical world (*assiya*) expands and shelters the letters of *Adonai*.

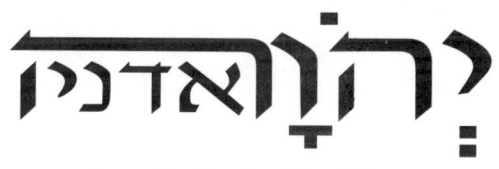

יְהֹוָואדני

Image 8—The Combined Name

The Names YHVH/י-הוה and *Adonai*/א-דני, representing divine masculine/י-הוה and feminine/א-דני, combine in another beautiful name for this union, י-הוה אדנ-י.

Both the first letter of YHVH/י-הוה and the last letter of *Adonai*/א-דני are *yuds*/י. Together they create the Name

YY/י-י

often found in traditional prayers and blessings.

YY is also pronounced *Adonai*.

---

40 The Sephardic branch of Judaism is descended from the Jews of Spain who were expelled in the Inquisition of 1492. The other main branch of Judaism, the Ashkenazik, originated in Eastern Europe.

Returning to the Aleph

With this new information let's reexamine the letter *aleph*/א, ONE, and see how it reflects the beautiful symbolism of the name YY/י-י. Recall that the deconstructed *aleph*/א can be thought of as:

                י *yud*
         ו *vav*   א
 י *yud*

According to the Zohar, the *yud*/י above the *vav*/ו (diagonal line) symbolizes YHVH/י-הוה, Heaven/*K"BH*/Oneness.

The *yud*/י below the *vav* represents *Adonai*/א-דני, Earth/*Shechina*/the multiplicity of Creation.

Vav/ו is the word **"and,"** so
The *Aleph* (ONE) can now be interpreted as follows:

Yud/י, *K"BH*, the divine masculine/Heaven
            and
Yud/י, *Shechina*, the divine feminine/Earth
are   ONE.

Aleph holds masculine and feminine, heaven and earth, the relationship of Oneness and all possibility of diversity in balance.

Aleph is like a yin/yang symbol. Yin is dark, feminine. Yang is light, masculine. The ancient Tao symbol for this union of opposites also shows that both equal halves are essential to create the whole.

Image 9—Yin/Yang Symbol

The *Gematria* of YHVH/יהוה-י

Adding together the values of the letters:

10	Yud	י
5	Hei	ה
6	Vav	ו
5	Hei	ה
26		

We know, from the symbolic deconstruction of *Aleph*/1 that:
א = 26 = 1

In *Aleph*, 26 = 1
א = 26 = 1
gematria of YHVH = 26
26 = 1
YHVH is ONE

These relationships have exquisite ramifications, soon to be revealed.

9

The Infinity Sign

**Image 10—
Infinity Sign**

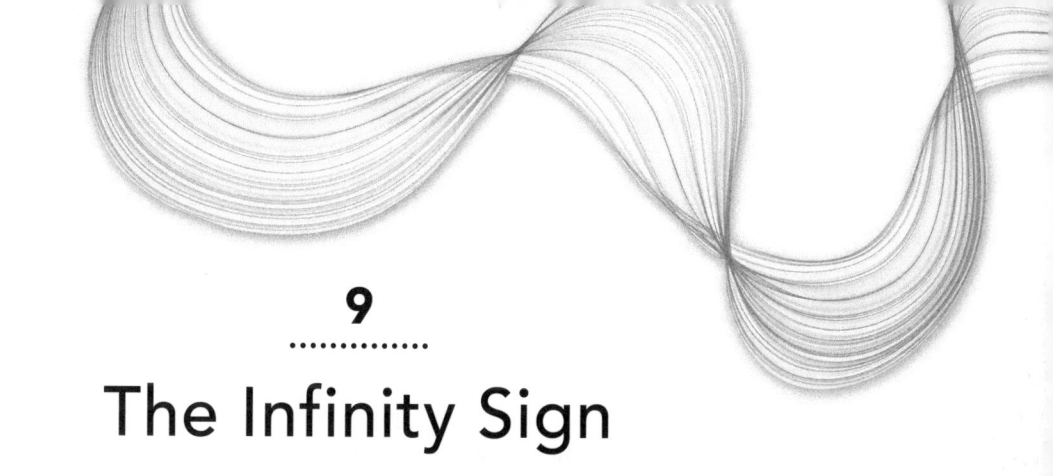

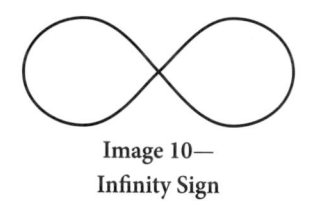

The infinity sign is a universal representation of endlessness and eternity. It is also a symbol of relationship, the connection of all that exists, specifically through the tension of opposites. It is a reflection of the atomic dance of positive and negative forces, the tension of push and pull that keeps the entire universe in balance. When representing the opposites of masculine and feminine, the constant movement within the unity of the symbol allows for simultaneous bonding and individuation. This connection is represented as yang/masculine and yin/feminine in Taoist philosophy and Chinese medicine, and appears in Kabbalah as well.

In Kabbalah

Sefer Yetzira, the oldest kabbalistic text, describes the Tree of Life, blueprint of the cosmos, as: "the end is in the beginning," (1:7) "their limit has no end," and "running and returning" (1:6). These phrases also describe the infinity sign.[41]

The theme of "running and returning" also occurs in Genesis, where one of the pivotal scenes of transformation is Jacob's dream of angels ascending and descending a ladder which connects heaven and earth. A similar description is found in Ezekiel's vision of the heavenly throne/chariot, called the *Merkava*. The *Merkava* vision, which the Ari and his followers studied so diligently, details the mechanism of bringing higher consciousness, the light of heaven, down to earth. The Zohar details the actions of the

---

[41] I have found infinity signs on reproductions of ancient kabbalistic amulets.

Merkava itself and the heavenly creatures who support it. The creatures ascend to the *Merkava* in order to bring down the light of higher consciousness. This is called "running." They then descend to the physical plane in order to integrate and distribute the new light. This process is called "returning." My Zohar teacher, Sarah Yehudit Schneider, describes this pulsation of "running and returning" as the heartbeat, the pulse, of spiritual life.[42]

The infinity symbol has three parts: the two sides and the center. The center of the symbol both connects and separates the polarities on either side. The center is an active boundary and because the opposites meet there it is also the space where healing and resolution occur. The center also corresponds to the final boundary Ezekiel encountered before he rose to the highest level of his vision and saw the *Merkava*, the throne of glory. The final boundary in the vision is called the *chashmal*/חשמל.[43] The word *chashmal* itself is a meeting of opposites, *chash*/חש meaning silence and *mal*/מל meaning speaking. In Sefer Yetzira, *chashmal* is said to represent the boundary between the physical and the spiritual. In a way, the practices in this book reflect the concept of *chashmal*, the reconnection of body and soul.

The infinity symbol can also represent balance within the Tree itself. The *sefirot* of the left/feminine and right/masculine columns may have opposing purposes. The two sides of the Tree find balance in the central column, which acts as the power center of an infinity sign. There in the center, opposites can meet in harmony and resolve their differences. According to the Zohar, when the *sefirot* of the central column are activated by the balance of left and right, the central column becomes a channel for the new light of higher consciousness to enter the world.

---

42 Sarah Yehudit Schneider, Still Small Voice Correspondence School: Zohar Class, 8/16/15.

43 *Chashmal* has no real translation in Ezekial's vision. It is referred to as electrum and in modern Hebrew became the word used for "electricity."

Image 11—Influx of Light

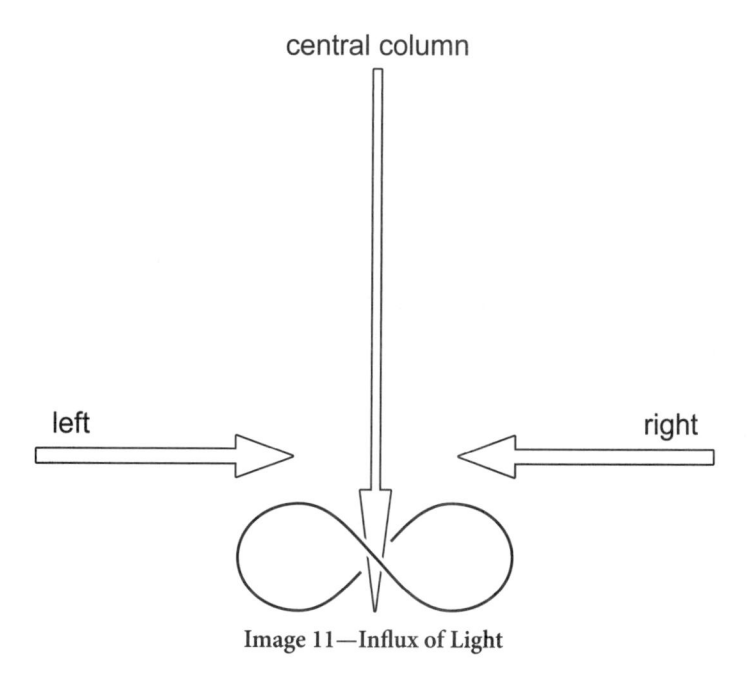

The influx of new light, higher consciousness, is also symbolized in the Zohar by the letter *aleph*, which holds within it both the spark of an idea and all possible manifestations. The *aleph* is in a constant state of vibration because of the attraction of the two polar opposites symbolized by the *yuds*, nonduality and multiplicity. They run and return like the two ends of the infinity sign. The *vav* ("and") between them, like the central column of the tree, is the place of meeting and transformation.

In Energy Medicine

Energies connect and communicate to a large extent in infinity shapes. Donna Eden, founder of Eden Energy Medicine, observes healthy energy moving in infinity/figure eight patterns both within individuals and between people in positive relationships. We have infinity patterns in the energy aura that surrounds us, in every organ, tissue, and cell, and down to the double helix of DNA. The infinity sign is the pulse of the physical world. When I first learned this, a defining relationship between energy and Kabbalah became evident.

Healing of the body and even clearing the energy of a physical space can be fostered by creating infinity patterns with the hands. Simply tracing these patterns over an area that is bruised, broken, or just painful promotes healing. Smudging a room with sage or lavender smoke in infinity patterns helps to clear it of unwanted energies. Kabbalistic symbolism, as we shall soon see, can be added to elevate this process.

In addition, Eden Energy Medicine teaches that infinity patterns are actually radiant circuits, energies of light, and are described in Chinese medicine as direct connections to the soul.[44] The radiant circuits are hyperlinks that can travel anywhere in the body. They are the golden energies of joy, responsible for healing "miracles." Is it merely a coincidence that the renowned scholar and healer Reb Nachman of Breslov (1772–1810), who took a spiritual approach to the origins of physical illness, proclaimed "joy is the greatest healer"? I believe he saw the lights of the radiant circuits.

A Final Note About Light and Infinity

In Hebrew, God is often referred to as the *Ein Sof*/אין סוף meaning the Infinite (literally "without end") or *Aur Ein Sof*/אור אין סוף Infinite Light. Both of these names begin with the letter א/*aleph*, which, coincidentally, is the mathematical symbol for infinity.

In addition,

Ein sof/Infinity (אין סוף)

and

Aur/Light (אור)

have the same *gematria*, 207, which makes them equivalent in a deep way.[45] We can think of the infinity sign then as a symbol of divine light, both energetically and kabbalistically.

....
44   Donna Eden in Radiant Circuits Class: April 27–May 1, 2016.
45   *Gematria* is usually based on the numeric values of the letters as per their order in the aleph-bet. This is the case here, even though final forms of two of the letters occur.

When using the infinity sign for healing or as a symbol of many of the ideas presented here, remember the underlying secret of the relationship between light and infinity.

Infinity = Light = Infinity

10

Love Is the Answer

"Who we are is Divine Love, and that is Infinite."
—Wayne Dyer

It is time to bring together many of the concepts we have explored so far: the Hebrew letters, *gematria*, the unpronounceable Name, the Tree, the *Partzufim*, the infinity symbol, the letter *aleph*, the balance of opposites, and the union of the *Shechina* and the *K"BH*. Where they all merge is love.

Love has the power to heal the world. In *Power vs. Force*, a classic treatise on consciousness, Dr. David Hawkins scientifically calibrated recognized levels of consciousness from the lowest, shame: level 20, to the highest, enlightenment: 700 to 1,000.[46] According to Hawkins, the tipping point to higher consciousness is 200; below 200, the primary impetus is survival. He wrote that we could easily solve all the problems our world now faces if mankind were to raise its collective consciousness much above 200, the level of integrity and courage. Luckily, higher levels of consciousness disproportionally balance out lower levels. The higher the level of consciousness a person possesses, the more negativity they cancel out. In fact, Hawkins wrote that only 15 percent of the world's population actually calibrates above 200 but this small minority has the weight to counterbalance the remaining 85 percent. One person can truly make a difference.

---

[46] David R. Hawkins, MD, PhD, *Power Vs Force*, 55–74. The levels were calibrated using applied kinesiology. The methods of determining the data are thoroughly discussed in the book.

According to Hawkins, truly spiritual states appear at a calibrated level of about 500, love. We generally think of love as an intense emotional state. It can include physical attraction, desire, and attachment, and can fluctuate depending on circumstances. The love referred to here is a higher love. It is an emulation of the goodness of divine love. It is an unvarying, healing, all-inclusive state of being that brings true happiness.

We can begin to understand this higher level of love by kabbalistically examining the nature of our being. Although most people are genetically clearly male or female, we all have masculine and feminine aspects to our psyches. They can represent the tension of all opposites within us. Their conflicts can prevent us from finding the wholeness and inner peace necessary to fully manifest the gifts of our souls. The Tree of Life provides a template for examining the tension of opposites.

You may recall from earlier chapters that, in the Tree, the expansive *sefirot* of the right side are considered masculine. In relation to the right, *sefirot* of the left side are considered constricting and feminine. Creating balance between *sefirot* that lie opposite each other in the left and right columns activates the *sefirot* of the central column. For example, in the right column, the *sefira* of *Chesed* overflows with lovingkindness and compassion. The partner of *Chesed* in the left column is *Gvura*. *Gvura* is the *sefira* of judgment and boundary-making. I mention these two *sefirot* because bringing *Chesed* and *Gvurah* into balance has been especially challenging for me. My *Gvurah* is stronger than *Chesed* and shows up as judgment and boundaries that restrict the flow of compassion. When these two right/left attributes are in balance, and compassion has appropriate boundaries, the *sefira* of *Tiferet*, beauty, which lies between them at the heart, is activated. When I am conscious that I am judging and consciously open to compassion, I can actually feel my heart open. For others, *Chesed* is stronger and their overcompassionate natures result in an imbalance of giving to others. Their *Gvura* boundaries need strengthening. Finding the balance between the relationship of right and left, masculine and feminine, is a repair, a *tikun*, that can transform our lives.

When the *sefirot* of the central column such as *Tiferet* are activated by the balance of left and right, the central column becomes the channel of enlightenment, and brings down *aur chadash*, the new light of higher consciousness. As Hawkins showed, the doorway to spiritual states, the state of higher consciousness, is love. Bringing in this new light for the healing of the world is the main intention of kabbalistic study, meditation, and prayer. That is why, according to the Zohar, the healing of relationships is the highest level of *tikun*, repair.

The Tree is a template for examining relationships at every level:
in the self, with others, and with God.

The Self

A model of love in the Tree is the relationship between the *partzufim* of Z"A/man and NOK/woman.

Recall that:

Ze'er Anpin/Z"A, the archetype of son/man, is also called the Six, because it is composed of six *sefirot*. Six is also associated with the letter *vav*/ו because the *gematria* of *vav*/ו is six. Z"A, *vav*/ו, and six all represent the masculine.

Nukva/NOK is the archetype of daughter/woman. She is symbolized by the letter *zayin*/ז, *gematria* seven, and represents the feminine.

Placing six and seven, as *vav*/masculine and *zayin*/feminine, in an infinity sign helps us to visualize these complex ideas in a simple way. Six and seven can represent *all the opposite aspects* within our selves. First we must become aware of our sixes and sevens. Then, when sixes and sevens harmonize and consciously balance, they add to thirteen.

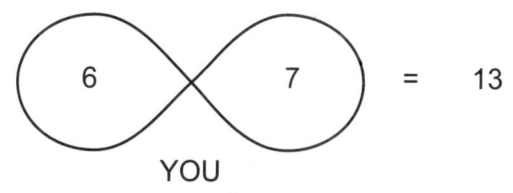

Image 12—Infinity Sign 6 + 7 = 13

6 + 7 = opposite parts of you in balance
6 + 7 = 13
13 is the *gematria* of love/*ahava*/אהבה
Therefore, creating balance creates love.

Repair of the self, balancing our sixes and sevens and restoring love is a journey that can take many paths. Good deeds, prayer, meditation, therapy in its many forms, and kabbalah/energy exercises are all ways to facilitate our growth by bringing in the light that illuminates and repairs our dark places. Every reconnection of six and seven creates a field of thirteen, of love.

Thirteen is also the *gematria* of the word *Echad*/ONE/אחד
so every connection of six and seven encourages the creation of oneness, of wholeness.

<u>13= Love= ONE=1.</u>

In addition to being the *gematria* of "love" and "one," the number thirteen has an additional dimension in Kabbalah. Thirteen channels connect the higher lights of the superconscious with the conscious levels of soul. Called the thirteen *midot*, Attributes of Mercy, they are channels of love, compassion, mercy, kindness, and empathy.[47] They are described in the Zohar as the "thirteen-petaled rose"—the greatest secret of life, the key to repairing whatever is broken. The thirteen *midot* are also considered a very perfected, elevated, exalted integration of masculine and feminine through the sefirot of *chesed* and *gvurah,* which find balance in *Tiferet,* the heart.

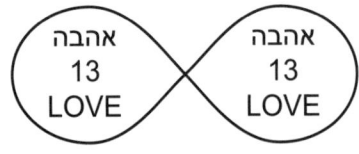

Image 13—Infinity Sign of Love

Relationship with Others
When your balanced 6 + 7 = 13 parts
connect with

---

47 Thirteen Divine Attributes of Mercy are found in the book of Exodus (32:10) after the incident of the Golden Calf, when God threatened to destroy the people of Israel rather than forgive them. God taught Moses the Divine Attributes of Mercy for the people to use whenever they needed to beg for divine compassion. Reciting them is an important part of the atonement process of the Yom Kippur service.

another's balanced 6 + 7 = 13 parts
LOVE connects with LOVE
Together they are 26.
26 is the *gematria* of the Name YHVH/י-הוה.
YHVH ~ 1
26 = 1

26 ~ YHVH ~ ONE

Every balanced, loving relationship creates 26, an expression of YHVH.

Balanced relationships are a source of Oneness.

You	Another				
Echad	*Echad*				
13	+	13	=	26	= 1
1	+	1	−	YHVH	~ 1
1	+	1		=	1

Every connection of 13 and 13 equals 26 = 1.
**YHVH is the manifestation of LOVE
that connects us all in the fabric of existence,
and
It all adds up to ONE.**

The Cosmic Connection

As we continue to do the work of personal growth and repair, more and more internal conflicts, sixes and sevens come into the balanced state of thirteen, love and oneness. Although conflicts may arise, the increased level of wholeness created within forms a framework for compromise and resolution of new issues. On the path to manifesting the unique gifts of our souls, remember that conflicts can be regarded as *klipot* surrounding divine sparks. Resolving the conflict reveals the sparks, which contain the necessary lessons of the journey. Each time a six and seven resolves into thirteen, we become more conscious, meaning we become more able to bring in, contain, and contribute more of the light of our unique gifts to the world.

When conflicts arise in relationships, personal wholeness encourages compromise and resolution, for there is less baggage to be triggered or defended. As we honor our own mistakes as sources of growth, we can also find the space within ourselves to honor the other's process, their unique path, and what the relationship is meant to teach us. The space for the other to be self-expressed is a reflection of the divine pulling back, the *tzimtzum* that made the creation possible.

On a higher level, the *6/Z"A* stands for the *K"BH* and the *7/NOK* represents the *Shechina*. As below so above. When our sixes and sevens unite into thirteen, *Shechina*, the God within us comes into union with the *K"BH*, the transcendent God. Every connection creates more love. Person by person, relationship by relationship, the cosmic spiritual "internet" expands. We are individuals and yet we are ONE.

One of the greatest minds of our generation, Jean Houston, refers to uniting the love within ourselves to the love of the cosmos:

> *I believe that accessing the depth of love within ourselves and feeling it united with the flowing love of the cosmos will open our lives to new dimensions… That union of love with love will free us to be who we really are—living, breathing human expressions of the eternal power and care of the universe.*[48]

"Love within ourselves… united with the… love of the cosmos" can be visualized using the Flower of Life. The Flower is an ancient symbol of sacred geometry representing a basic geometric blueprint of existence. The Flower helps to illustrate the interconnectedness of all life.

The Flower of Life

Imagine yourself as a self-expressed and balanced individual, a petal in this infinite web of life.

---

48   Email communication, 5/5/17.

Image 14—The Flower of Life

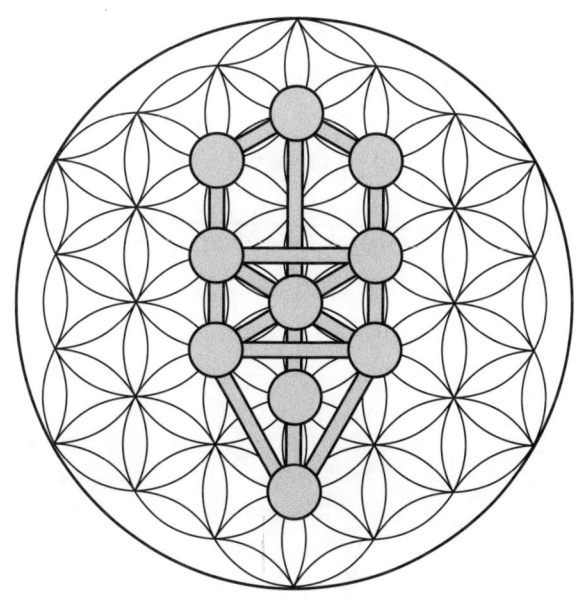

Image 15—The Tree of Life Superimposed on the Flower of Life

Love Is the Answer

You = a petal = half of an infinity sign

Each person/petal = 6 + 7 = 13 = LOVE/אהבה

Every connection in the Flower is a connection of 13 + 13.

Every connection of 13 + 13 adds to 26,

26 is the *gematria* of YHVH/י-הוה

YHVH/י-הוה is ONE

Every connection of 13 and 13 equals 26 = 1.

YHVH/י-הוה is the connection of love and love. Love is the greatest power in creation, whether it is inside us, in our relationship to others, or as a reflection of our connection to the Creator.

Is this a metaphysical "God particle" astrophysicists seek? Whenever LOVE joins LOVE, the result is a manifestation of YHVH/י-הוה that is equal to ONE. Our personal work is carried through our relationships and connects us to the power of God's infinite love. In the end, when every soul has been repaired, we will all be connected through YHVH, through love, and we will all be ONE with each other and with the Creator.

Aleph/א Redux

Revisiting the *aleph*/one provides a beautiful way to conclude this chapter on love. Recall that the *gematria* of the deconstructed *aleph*=26.

י *Yud* = 10
ו *Vav* = 6   א
י *Yud* = 10

According to the Zohar, the *yud*/י above the *vav*/ו (diagonal line) symbolizes Heaven/K"BH and the *yud*/י below the *vav* represents Earth/*Shechina*.

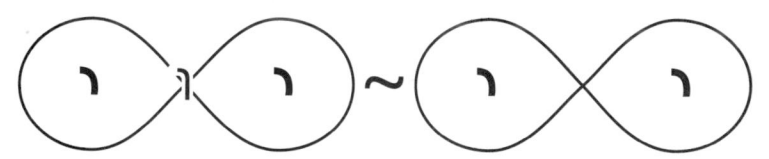

Recall also that *yud/yud*/י-י is a divine Name that incorporates the divine masculine and feminine. This Name is symbolized in the letter *aleph*. Instead of using *vav*/6 and *zayin*/7 to represent masculine and feminine, the upper and lower י s of the *aleph*, as divine masculine and feminine, can be placed in an infinity symbol. *Vav*, the connector between them in the *aleph*, can either be written in the center or understood as the connection between them.

Image 16—Double Infinity Symbols with Yuds

When the componant letters of the *aleph* are symbolized by an infinity sign, they also represent, the union of heaven and earth/K"BH and *Shechina*.

In the practices in part 2:

The infinity sign of love

can often be interchanged with

the infinity sign of the א.

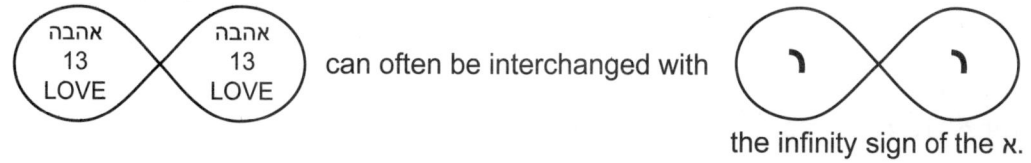

Image 17—The Infinity Sign of Love with the Infinity Sign of א

They each have a *gematria* of 1.

They each also have a *gematria* of 26.

They each are a source of 13 + 13, love and love. They appear frequently in the practices because "love is the metaphysical glue that holds all of existence together." [49]

---

[49] Rabbi David Cooper, *Ecstatic Kabbalah*, 52.

Love Is the Answer 79

Fun with *Gematria*

Raz/רז is the Hebrew word for mystery, and though as mystery, it will always remain essentially unknowable, let's use *gematria* and see what lies at its core. You may recall that *aur*/light/אור and *Ein Sof*/infinity/אין סוף both share the same *gematria*, 207. *Raz* also has a *gematria* of 207, so light, infinity, and mystery are deeply connected.

Write the words *aur* and *raz* one over the other, like the relationship of numbers in a fraction.

light/*aur*	ר/ו/א	אור
mystery/*raz*	ז/ר	רז

The letter *resh*/ר is found in both words. As if reducing a fraction to find its lowest common denominator, cross out the *Resh*/ר on both top and bottom.

In *aur*/אור this leaves *vav*/ו + *aleph*/א   א ו
In *raz*/רז this leaves *zayin*/ז   ז

Remember that:
vav/6/ו represents the (Divine) masculine

and
zayin/7/ז represents the (Divine) feminine.

Aleph connects *vav*/6 and *zayin*/7. *Aleph*, the equivalent *gematria* of YHVH, is the bridge to 6 + 7 = 13, to love. *Aleph*, the ONE, can be regarded as the force at the center of the mystery of light. It is an infinity sign that holds (divine) masculine and feminine, opposites, within itself and is the place where two can unite without losing their individuality.

א
Love/infinity/YHVH/mystery/inspiration/divine marriage/
oneness and multiplicity in balance:

Aleph and its beautiful symbolism is a foundation of part 2.

11
Energy Medicine

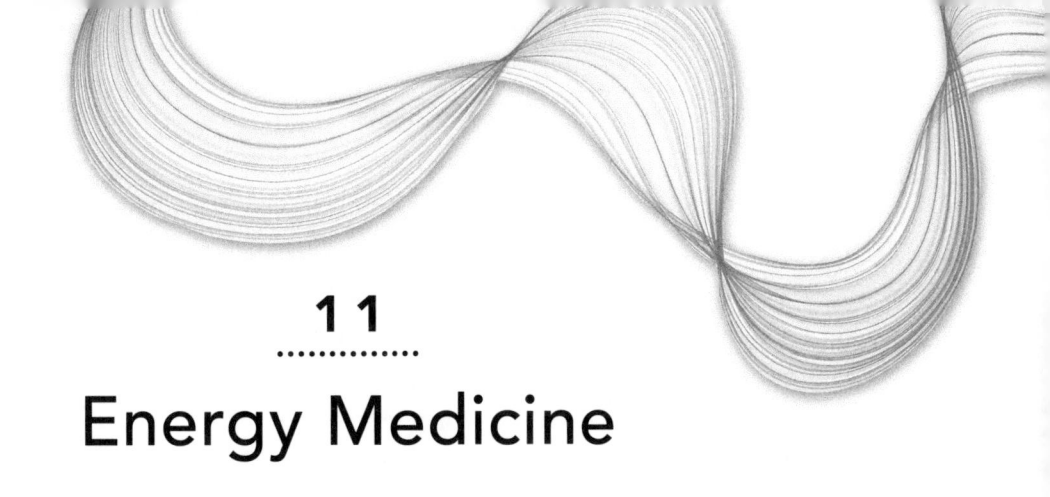

Energy medicine is an acknowledgment that we are made of energy and that our health and vitality depend on the balance and flow of these energies. One hundred years ago, Albert Einstein proclaimed that energy is all there is. He showed that the physical matter we could readily sense and energy that most of us could not, were really forms of the same thing. Our thoughts, emotions, and our dense physical bodies are all made of energy. The energies of our bodies are dynamic and communicate with each other, weaving through the physical, emotional, and mental planes with an anatomy that has been charted for thousands of years.

According to Nobel laureate in medicine Albert Szent-Gyorgyi, "In every culture and every medical tradition before ours, healing was accomplished by moving energy."[50] The word "medicine" in "energy medicine" refers to the restoration of balance, flow, and vitality in the energy body, as well as the upkeep necessary to encourage the body to use its innate wisdom and heal itself.

Energy medicine, like Kabbalah, dates back thousands of years. Also like Kabbalah, it is enjoying a modern renaissance, becoming more and more popular as an alternative and complement to Western medicine. Western medicine focuses on alleviating disease symptoms in an already unbalanced system and pharmaceuticals, with their ever-present side effects, are often the treatment of choice. In contrast, energy medicine is a holistic approach, focused on maintaining wellness and resilience. Energy medicine

---

[50] http://www.azquotes.com/quote/997585.

takes advantage of the body's innate healing ability, and when disease occurs, encourages this ability by restoring disrupted energy balance and flow.

I had studied energy healing in several programs before I met Donna Eden. I was attracted to Eden Energy Medicine because as a scientist by training, it provided me with a more logical way of dealing with a subject that is nonlinear and intuitive. I appreciated that there were textbooks for reference. Like Kabbalah, teachers can impart the basics but it is up to the student to deepen the teachings through practice and experience. Although skeptical by nature, I was immediately convinced of its value.

Donna Eden was born with the ability to see energy clearly. Some people can see auras. Donna can see every detail of energy anatomy including meridians, chakras, and their colors. Although it's a bit unnerving to know that your deepest secrets may be revealed when she looks at you, it feels very safe because of her enormously open heart. Many people who see energy do not know how to interpret what they see. Donna worked with thousands of clients and studied extensively to be able to use her gift to teach others. Touch for Health gave her the tools of applied kinesiology, sometimes referred to as muscle testing or energy testing, that allows energy to be assessed even without seeing it.[51]

Eden Energy Medicine (EEM)[52] empowers individuals to balance and care for their own energy bodies. *Energy Medicine,* a textbook of wellness practices by Eden and her husband, Dr. David Feinstein, was first published in 1997. Since then, the field of energy medicine has grown enormously. There are trained EEM practitioners and students all over the world. YouTube brims with Eden Energy exercise videos. Eden Energy medicine includes the great traditions of Chinese medicine and the yogic chakras as well as other healing practices. It is very inclusive. Practitioners continue to add to the effectiveness of exercises and treatments based on their own experiences. We teach each other and everyone benefits.

The mission of Eden Energy Medicine is to empower the individual to balance and care for their own energy body thus raising the vibration of the planet one person at a time. There are many forms of energy work available today: Reiki, zero-balancing, and

---

51   www.touch4health.com.
52   www.innersource.net.

polarity therapy to name a few. Most rely on trained practitioners in contrast to self-care and empowerment. For lasting changes, self-care is essential.

Students, clients, and practitioners alike work with their own energies regularly. Eden exercises help to activate the body's innate healing power through a series of simple exercises called the daily routine. The daily routine helps to keep energies humming, enabling maximum vitality no matter what stresses an individual is coping with. The exercises also create a foundation for deeper work. Simple activities such as stretching and moving the body help by creating space for energy to flow. Hands move energy powerfully and can restore balance by connecting specific areas or points. The body then can do what it innately knows how to do, heal and stay healthy.

An EEM practitioner learns to assess imbalances and blockages in a client's energy body. After working to correct these, the practitioner helps determine which additional exercises will be the most beneficial for lasting change. It is then up to the client to work with the energies themselves between sessions. With regular practice the body becomes healthier and more resilient.

Most of the practices in part 2 have Eden or Eden-inspired exercises as their foundation.

Energy Anatomy

Eden Energy Medicine recognizes nine different systems that make up our energy anatomy. These include chakras, meridians, an electric system, an underlying grid of support, an aura that surrounds the body like a cocoon of light, and a special group of energies called the radiant circuits. These systems are all in continual movement and constant communication and each affects the others. All are addressed by EEM, but for our purposes we will focus on four of them: [53]

---

53   There is an additional energy pattern Donna Eden observes which she calls the diamond inlay. Connecting to both heaven and earth, it is strangely similar to the geometric shape of the Tree of Life. This may be the topic of future inquiry.

1. The chakras
2. The meridians
3. The aura
4. The radiant circuits

The Chakras

Because the practice of yoga has become widespread, many people are familiar with its concept of chakras. From the Sanskrit word for "wheel," chakras are energy patterns, centers of spinning energy that occur all over the body. The major chakras are seven vortexes of energy that run up the center of the body from the base of the torso to the crown of the head. There are chakras over the root/womb (sacrum)/solar plexus/heart/throat/third eye (between the eyebrows) and crown of the head. They influence bodily functions and emotions. Like an energy memory database, chakras contain imprints, records of every significant thought or experience you have ever had.

The Meridians

The meridians are fourteen interconnected channels of energy that flow like a river through the body. They are the basis of Oriental medicine and acupuncture. The meridians connect all of the body's organs and systems providing instant communication and feedback with both the internal and external environment. Except for the central channel and governing channel which run respectively up the front and up the back, the meridians are bilateral.

The Aura

The aura is a field of light energy that surrounds living beings. Like a cell membrane, its primary function is as a filter, protecting the body from toxic or disruptive energies, and bringing in beneficial energies.

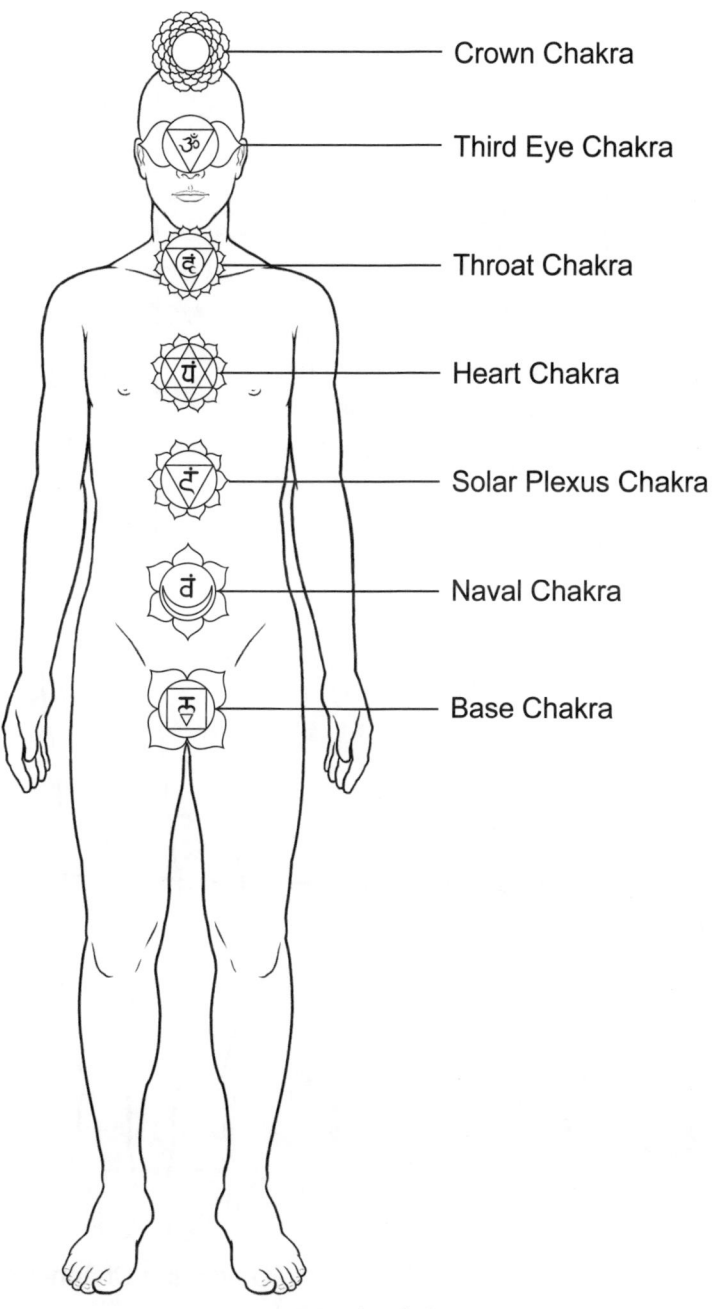

Image 18—The Chakras

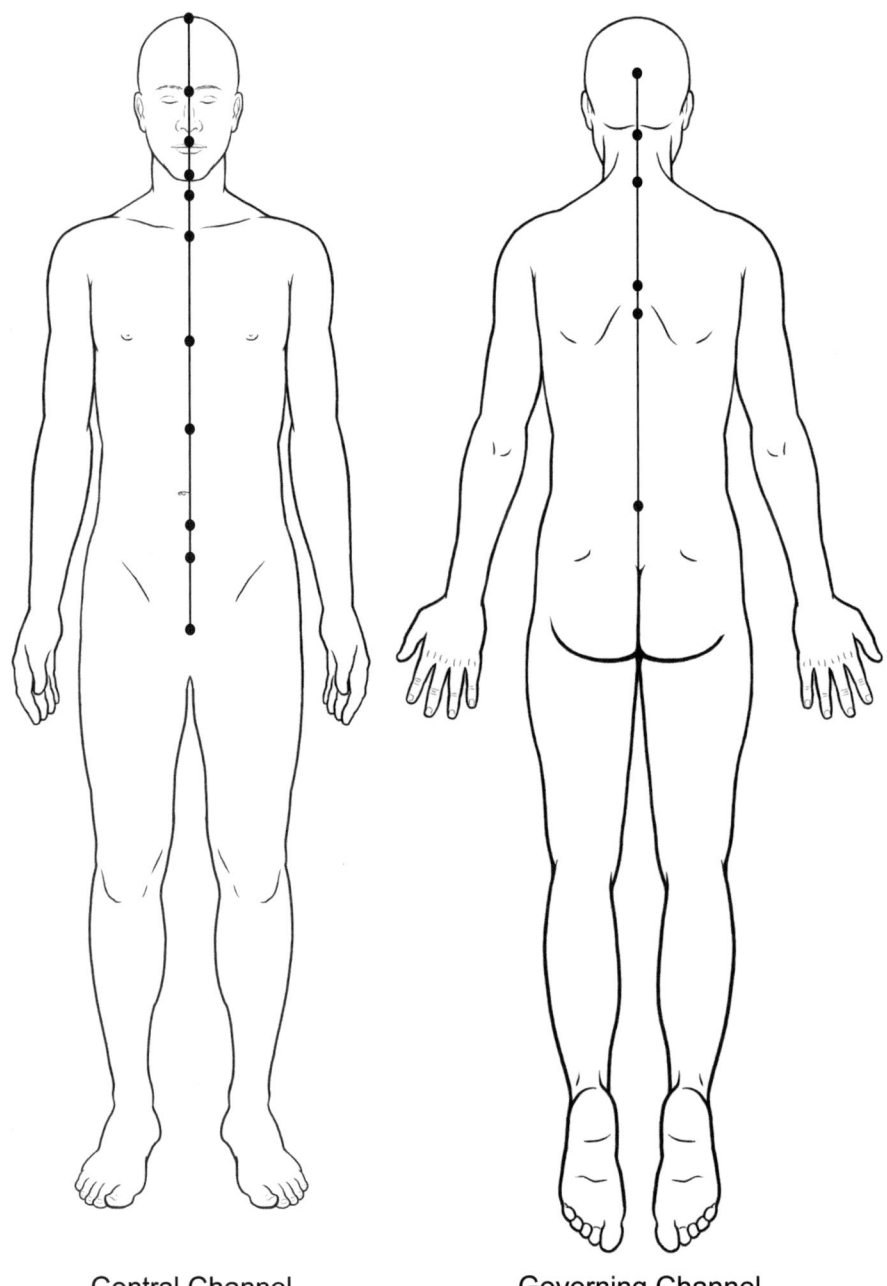

Central Channel   Governing Channel

Image 19—The Two Channels

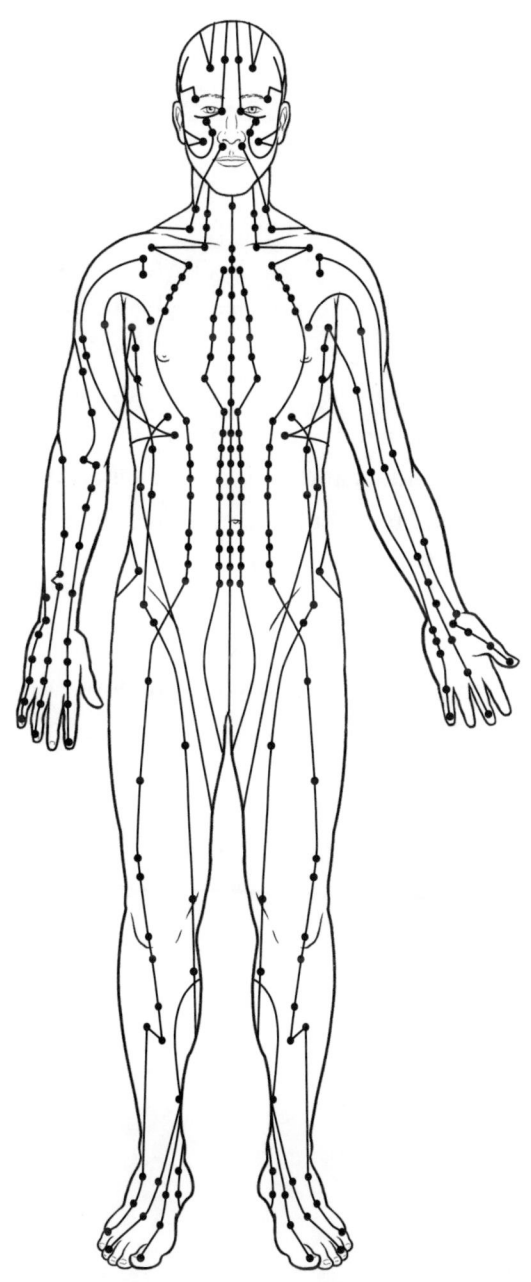

Image 20—The Meridians

The Radiant Circuits

The radiant circuits are the energies of joy and miracles that literally "light you up." They can travel anywhere they are needed in the body. Some say these subtle energies of light connect directly to the soul. Because they are light, they can be thought of as our direct connection to the divine, the realm of Infinite Light.

Radiant circuits are activated when you laugh with abandon, are in the "zone," experience the majesty of nature, or are captivated by beautiful music. You are in a state of awe or bliss and may experience goosebumps or chills. You may feel yourself as part of an expanded reality, even a state of Oneness with the universe where time stands still. In addition, radiant circuit energy is contagious. When someone's lights are turned on they activate the lights in others and everyone benefits. We are naturally attracted to these higher vibrations like iron filings being drawn by a magnet. Because radiant circuit exercises are a natural bridge between the physical and the spiritual they are the foundation of several practices in part 2.

We will look at these four aspects of energy anatomy in more detail in the next chapter, specifically how they relate to Kabbalah.

12
Energy Medicine and Kabbalah

The ancient scholars and healers whose teachings are the foundation of Kabbalah and energy medicine observed life from very different perspectives. Today, we can appreciate their perceptions as part of an expanded worldview.

To review, Kabbalah is based on an attempt to understand the nature of God and our relationship as the Creation to the Creator. The mission of Kabbalah is seeking connection to the Creator, the Source of Infinite Light, symbolized as heaven, to bring down the light of higher consciousness. Kabbalists like the Ari, who sensed energy, interpreted his sensations in the context of the anatomy of the soul and connection to God.

By contrast, energy medicine comes from the world of creation, of nature, of the earth. Over the centuries many cultures have described the anatomy of the energy body and have practiced energy healing. For example, medicine men of several Native American peoples, Peruvian shamans, and other indigenous healers created practices and rituals that were attuned to the energies of the earth. Indian yogis and Celtic healers worked with the energy of the chakras based on their own traditions, rituals, and beliefs. The diversity of interpretations of the same phenomena provides a richness and depth to our own understanding of healing.

Chinese medicine, a foundation of Eden Energy Medicine, is based on thousands of years of observing natural cycles and their relationship to physical wellness and disease.

The elements that make up these cycles—water, wood, fire, earth, and metal—are physical substances, grounded in earth metaphors.

There have always been those who could perceive energy with their senses. The interpretation of these perceptions over time became a way of looking at the world. Although one looked to heaven and the other to Earth, Kabbalah and energy medicine intersect and complement each other in fascinating ways.

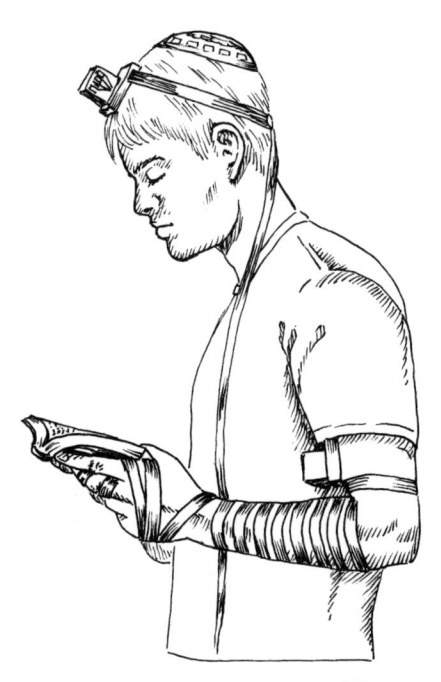

Image 21—Man Wearing Tefillin

Take, for example, the ancient morning pre-prayer ritual of putting on tefillin by adult Jewish men. Although it has no known connection to Chinese medicine or philosophy, this ritual uses acupressure points to connect to God. Putting on or "laying" tefillin involves wrapping leather straps around the arm, hand, and head in a carefully prescribed manner. Attached to the straps are leather prayer boxes which are placed on the head and nondominant biceps. The careful positioning of the straps and the placement of the boxes is ritually applied acupressure to elevate the spirit and clear the mind for prayer. Many of the points stimulated by the straps correspond to Chinese acupuncture's Window of

Heaven points that connect heart and mind. Here is an example of an actual kabbalistic relationship to the physical body, but its purpose is to ascend higher.[54] The body is yoked to heaven, but not to earth.

I recently became aware of another intriguing intersection of Chinese medicine and Jewish ritual. When a section of the Torah is read in the synagogue, the passage is displayed by lifting the open scroll. The congregation rises singing praises to the Torah and it is customary in some communities to point the pinkie finger at the scroll. Pointing at the Torah with the pinkie was an unfamiliar custom to me and I was very curious as to its origins. An internet search revealed that there are many opinions as to the source of this custom and no definitive answer. Yet this custom provides a glimpse into the possibility of ancient connections. The path of heart energy, the heart meridian, ends at the tip of the pinkie finger. Pointing with the pinkie finger carries heart energy directly to the Torah.

Despite the difference in their approaches, Kabbalah and energy medicine are both based on the nature of and healing of relationships. A person in harmony within themselves, with others, and with their environment flows with a positive life-force energy that affects all their interactions. Health and vitality require balance and flow between all the levels of existence: physical, emotional, and mental. Kabbalah adds the level of the spiritual, the relationship to God. Imbalances or blockages at any level can create disease patterns in the others, so it is important to look at the whole picture, energy and Kabbalah both.[55]

Chakras and the Tree of Life

Although the Tree is a construct imagined on a primordial man made of light, it can be useful to imagine the Tree on an actual physical body. The late kabbalist Leonora Leet, in the *Secret Doctrine of Kabbalah*, likened the *sefirot* to the chakras. It's a compelling comparison that helps illustrate how the kabbalists and the yogis of India interpreted the same

---

54 Steven Schram, "Tefillin: An Ancient Acupuncture Point Prescription for Mental Clarity," *Journal of Chinese Medicine* no. 70, October 2002.
55 Ibid.

human energy patterns through the filters of their own beliefs, culture, and era. These interpretations are all valid and serve to enhance the nuances of our understanding.

For instance, the yogic tradition and Kabbalah share the idea that we are sanctuaries of divine light and the stronger our "vessel" is, the more light we can hold and transmit. The traditional Sanskrit greeting, *namaste*, means "the divine light in me recognizes and honors the divine light in you."

To review, the chakras are concentrated energy centers. The word *chakra* comes from a Sanskrit root meaning "wheel" or "disc." The chakras are vortexes, spinning at specific points on the subtle energy body. There are many chakras but seven major ones run up the center of the body. For example, the third chakra is in the center of the solar plexus. Our well-being is directly related to the health of our chakras. Chakras can be worked with directly on the body. Energy testing allows for assessment and correction of imbalances and other issues that have direct impact on the mind, emotions, and physical body.

Although in the diagrams below the *sefirot* may look like chakras, remember that the Tree is a mental construct, composed of archetypes, symbols, and qualities. It is a non-linear hologram, existing simultaneously in the physical, emotional, mental, and spiritual realms. Imbalances in the *sefirot* can also be assessed and rebalanced but the techniques for healing such imbalances are not physical. As I was taught by Dr. Shems Prinzivalli, kabbalistic healing can take place totally in the mind of the healer.

Roots in Heaven/Roots in Earth

The chakras are often referred to by number. The numbering begins with connection to the earth. The root chakra is considered the first, the crown is the seventh and highest. In the Tree, this is reversed. The crown, *Keter*, is also the highest point, but is considered the ROOT because it is the closest to the *Or Ein Sof*, the Source of Infinite Light. It is said that the Tree is upside down because the roots of the tree are in heaven. *Keter* could therefore be considered the first *sefira* but numbers are rarely if ever used when referring to *sefirot*.

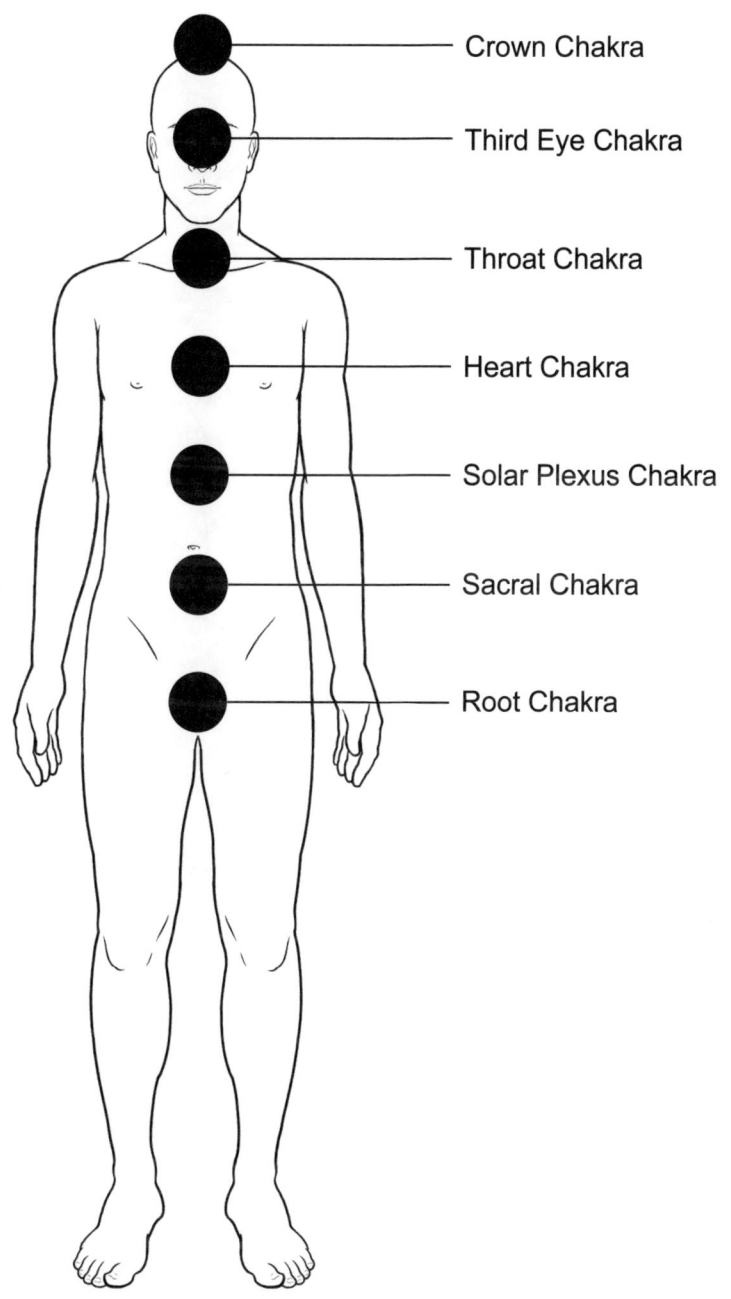

- Crown Chakra
- Third Eye Chakra
- Throat Chakra
- Heart Chakra
- Solar Plexus Chakra
- Sacral Chakra
- Root Chakra

Image 22—The Chakras Revisited

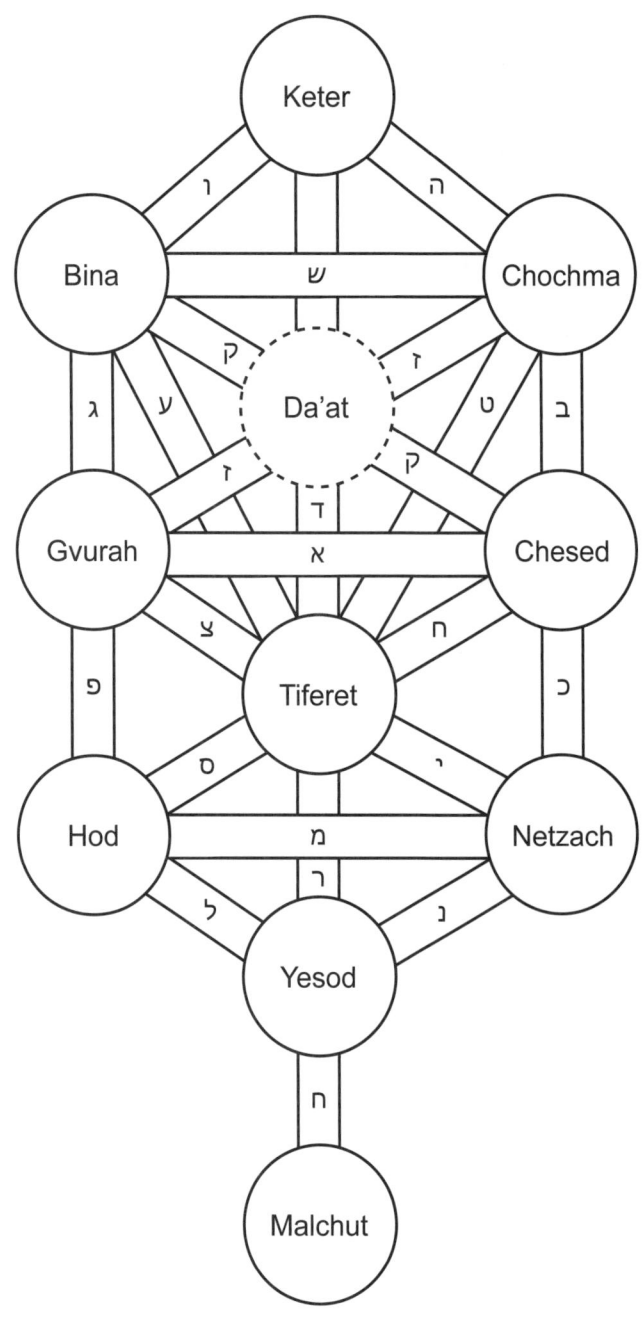

Image 23—Tree of Life

The seven major chakras run from the earth to the crown up the central channel on the front and through the body. The Tree also has a central column and the *sefirot* on the central column share many similarities with the corresponding chakras, specifically the first, second, fourth, sixth, and seventh.

Central Column Sefirot Compared with Chakras

1. The first chakra, the **root chakra**, can be compared to *Malchut*.

The root chakra is the physical connection to the earth. It holds patterns of survival, safety, security, tribal/family history, and expectations.

Malchut is a complex concept. In addition to the qualities represented by the root chakra, *Malchut* is the expression of the the divine feminine/*Shechina*, and the physical world.

Recall that the Tree is made of light, but *Malchut*, like the moon, has no light of her own. Because *Malchut* is the farthest *sefira* from *Keter* and the connection to the Infinite Light, all the light has been distributed to the other *sefirot* before it can reach her directly. Instead, she has a unique role. She receives and holds the light that filters down from the *sefirot* above it creating stability in the entire Tree. The stronger, more resilient, and stable *Malchut* is, the more light the Tree can hold. Interestingly, I have experienced this when studying kabbalistic texts. The words on the page can have so much spiritual energy that reading or hearing them sometimes causes our study group to feel dizzy and unstable. We stop and focus on *Malchut*, consciously returning to the solidity of our physical bodies before we continue with the text.

Kabbalistic healing is also enabled by the strength of *Malchut*. In energy healing, grounding is essential and is largely a function of the root chakra. In kabbalistic healing, it is the *sefira* of *Malchut* that creates the stable and safe vessel necessary for healing.

2. The womb (sacral) or **second chakra** can be compared to *Yesod*.

The second chakra shares with *Yesod* the qualities of bonding, sexuality, creativity, joy, and wonder. Because Kabbalah is male-oriented, *Yesod* is referred to extensively as the male phallus. This is in contrast to the names "womb" or "sacral chakra" used for the second chakra.

   3. The **fourth chakra** lies over the the heart and so is referred to as the heart chakra.

The heart chakra lies at the center of the seven main chakras: three chakras lie above and three below. The heart chakra holds the energy of love for self and others, caring and compassion, as does **Tiferet**, which means beauty. *Tiferet* also lies at the center, the center of *Ze'er Anpin* (Z"A), the six *sefirot* that make up the son/man/archetype.

   4. The **sixth chakra** is located at the third eye, between the eyebrows.

It corresponds to *Da'at*, a "quasi" *sefira*, which literally means "knowing." The third eye chakra is, like *Da'at*, the source of intuition, inner knowing, and cosmic vision.

Da'at creates the balance between *Chochma*/wisdom and *Bina*/understanding, the right and left brain. In the metaphysical anatomy of *Adam Kadmon,* this aspect of *Da'at,* like the sixth chakra, lies at the third eye. It is connected to the corpus callosum, the anatomical bridge separating the cerebral hemispheres. Another aspect of *Da'at* connects the mind and heart. *Da'at* is a balance point for the tension of opposites and a gateway where divine inspiration, *Ruach Hakodesh*, is said to enter the body.

   Because of its unfathomable nature, *Keter* is sometimes not included with the lower *sefirot*. The Sefer Yetzira says there are exactly ten *sefirot*, so when *Keter* is hidden and not included in the ten, *Da'at* is counted as the revealed aspect of *Keter*.

   5. The crown chakra at the top of the head corresponds to **Keter,** also called the crown. *Keter*, like the crown chakra, is the connection to spirit and universal Oneness.

Many healers and scholars also recognize eighth and ninth chakras that lie above the head and connect to higher consciousness.

The Right and Left Columns

The seven main chakras run up the central line of the body. This corresponds to the central column of *sefirot*, the "trunk" of the Tree. In addition, the Tree also has columns on the right and left side whose *sefirot* are polar opposites. The central column is the column of balance between them.

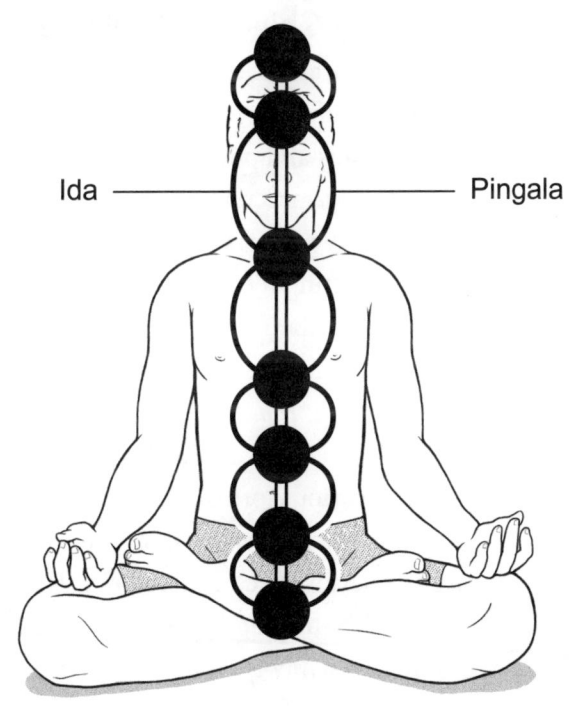

Image 24—Seated Man showing Chakra/Nadi Connections

Is there a corresponding balance in the chakras?

Although it is beyond the scope of this book, it can be noted that the yogic/Hindu tradition recognizes channels of energy called *nadis*. Two of these channels intertwine and snake up the central channel on the left and right side of the body intersecting at the chakras.

According to the Hindu tantras, there are seventy-two thousand or more nadis through which stimuli flow like an electric current from one point to another. The nadi system was in place in the East long before the chakras, meridians, or the Tree. It is interesting to speculate that perhaps observation of the nadis long ago evolved into the chakras, meridians, and even the Tree.

The Tree and Chinese Medicine

Chinese medicine is based on the natural cycles of the earth. Energy is visualized in interconnected channels called meridians that flow through the body like a river. The meridians correspond to different organs and physical systems, the seasons of the year, and properties of yin/feminine and yang/masculine.

In a more abstract way, the twenty-two letters of the Hebrew alphabet form stabilizing channels on the Tree of Life, connecting the *sefirot* like meridians.

In Chinese medicine, as in the Tree, the right side of the body is considered more yang/masculine and the left side yin/feminine. However, gender is a relative term in Kabbalah. Although two of the ten *sefirot*, *Bina*/the *Partzuf* of *Ema* (Mother) and *Malchut*/the *Partzuf* of *NOK* (daughter/woman), are considered more feminine, the Tree is a hologram so genders are present in various forms and relationships with each other in each *sefira* and *partzuf*. In Chinese medicine gender is specific. Of the fourteen meridians, seven are considered yang and seven are considered yin. The fourteen form seven yang/yin pairs, related to each other like husbands and wives.

Heaven and earth are also universal symbols of masculine and feminine. In Kabbalah they are represented in the Tree by the *partzufim* of *Z"A* as the *K"BH* and *NOK* as *Shechina*. These are abstract concepts with many rich layers of meaning to reveal. In the Chinese meridian system the ideas of heaven and earth are based a natural rhythm, specifically the direction of the meridians' flow. The majority of yang energies (heaven), such as stomach, gall bladder, and bladder, begin in the head and flow down the body. In contrast, most yin energies (earth) such as kidney, liver and spleen, begin at the feet and flow up the body.

This concept of male energies coming from above to below, and feminine energies rising from below to above is also found in the letter *aleph*. The upper *yud* represents the masculine flow of consciousness from above to below and the lower *yud* the feminine that attracts the masculine from below to above.

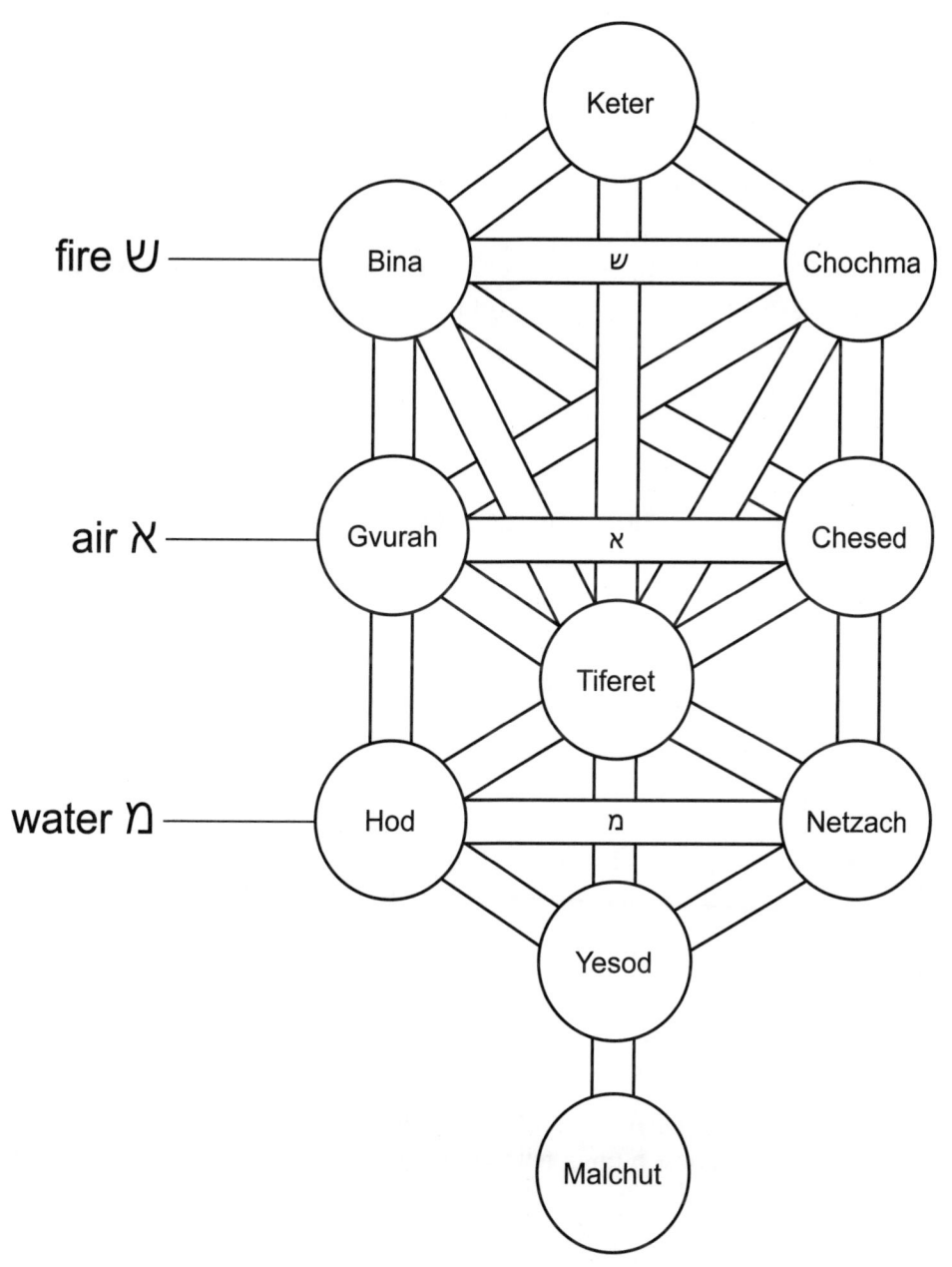

Image 25—Elements and the Tree of Life

Energy Medicine and Kabbalah

Elements and the Tree of Life

The Chinese meridians correspond to five basic elements: water, wood, fire, earth, and metal.

Elements are also found in the Tree. The three letters that lie in the horizontal connections between the right and left columns are called mother letters and represent elements of fire, air, and water. Between *Binah*/understanding and *Chochma*/wisdom is ש/*Shin*, fire. Between *Chesed*/compassion and *Gvurah*/judgment is א/*aleph*, air. Between *Netzach*/endurance and *Hod*/gratitude is מ/*mem*, water.

Earth element is a foundational element in Chinese medicine. Earth in the Tree is understood to be a synthesis of fire, air, and water. There is no letter for Mother Earth.

Kabbalah and the Radiant Circuits

The anatomy, state, and elevation of the soul is studied extensively in Kabbalah. There are five different layers of soul that associate to parts of the Tree, to the family of *partzufim*, the different worlds, and the Name YHVH. They range from the lowest animal soul, the *Nefesh*, to the highest soul that is part of the Oneness, *Yicheda*. For our purposes, we will call them collectively *Neshama*/soul. The soul is the life-force and is considered pure as is stated in Judaism through the daily affirmation: "YHVH, the soul you have given me is pure."

I was surprised to find a discussion of the soul in energy medicine, but not surprised to discover that the soul is associated with the energies of light called the radiant circuits. The radiant circuits are the energies of joy and healing miracles.[56]

As previously described, the radiant circuits do not travel in meridian pathways but can go anywhere they are needed. When activated by feelings of wonderment, awe, or bliss, the body instantly lights up all over. In these moments you may also feel yourself as part of an expanded reality, even a state of oneness with the universe. Physical sensations, such as chills or goose bumps, tell us our lights are on, even if we cannot see them.

---

56 They have many names such as strange flows, extraordinary vessels, or wondrous wires. Referring to them as radiant circuits helps connect them directly to ideas in the Zohar, the Book of Radiance.

The lights spread from person to person and we often experience this phenomenon in ourselves when we witness activated radiant circuits in someone else. When people see a bride walking down the aisle, or a new mother holding her baby, we recognize them as "radiant," "glowing," and "lit up" and their lights activate ours.

The Infinite Light is a way of referring to God the Creator and it is divine light that activates the Tree of Life. We can even imagine the radiant circuits as divine sparks for the radiant circuits are often described as the energetic link between heaven and earth. In fact, Donna Eden has observed that radiant energy enters a baby at birth from heaven and earth simultaneously. These two energy flows connect in the heart and become the heart chakra.

Keeping our "lights on" helps to create balance and healing on all levels. Several practices in Part 2 weave kabbalistic symbolism into Eden radiant circuit exercises. These include tracing infinity patterns, and the chapters on Boundaries, the Rakia Flow, and the *Sh'ma* Hook-In.

It is time to spread the light.

PART 2

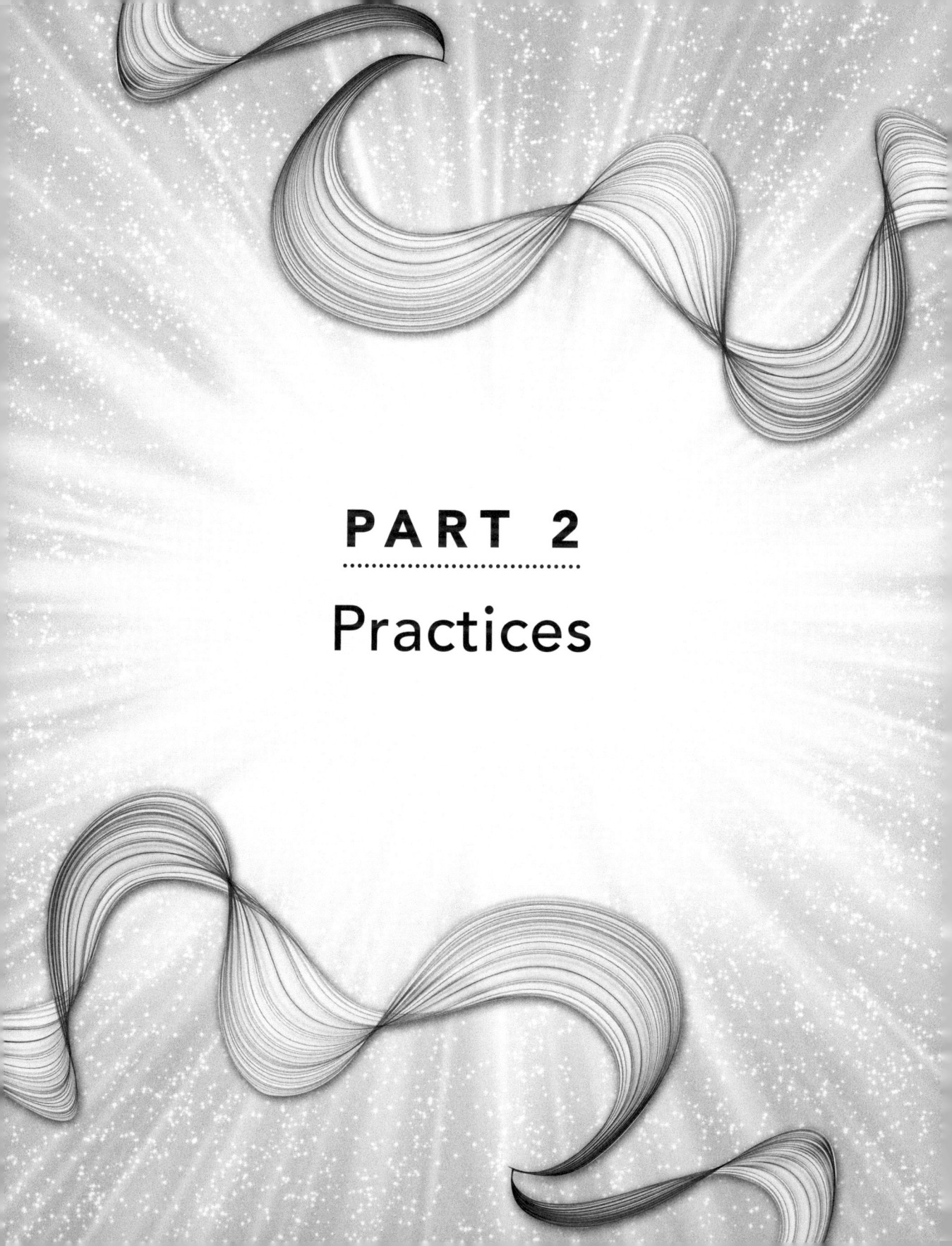

Practices

13

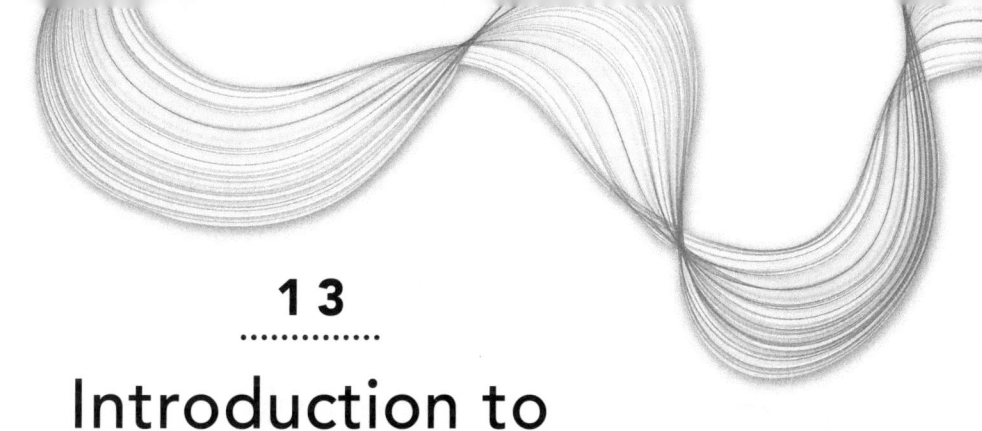

Introduction to the Practices

Body-Centered Mystical Practices for Balance, Healing, Transformation, and the Enhancement of Prayer

We are each here to fulfill the missions our souls created for us to accomplish in our lifetimes. Our souls link us to the cosmos and to the Creator. But it is only through the physical world, the world of the divine feminine, that we can satisfy our soul contracts. The soul connects to the divine plan and the body puts the plan into action. In order to manifest what we were born to do, it is essential that we be solidly connected to our physical bodies even as we connect to higher guidance.

Our paths are not always simple, direct, or even clear. When the body and soul are balanced and communicating in an easy flow, it becomes easier to discern our choices and clarify the path we are meant to take to fulfill our unique destinies. When we are truly aligned on this path we resonate with vibrations of flow and harmony that repair both ourselves and the world.

The four universes of Kabbalah and the energy world are essentially the same: physical, emotional, mental, and spiritual. While energy medicine works primarily with the physical body, emotions, and the mind, and Kabbalah with spirit, the worlds are all intertwined. An imbalance or a healing on one plane can affect the others.

The Ari believed that healing on the spiritual plane would translate to healing in the other universes as well. Many do believe that only healing at the level of spirit is true healing. But while we are alive, the physical body is the home of the soul. The body is the instrument through which the soul fulfills its mission in our lifetime. Ignoring the needs of the physical to accommodate the spiritual leaves out half the picture. Without the physical realm to act on them, the ideas and inspirations that fuel our reason for being just remain ideas.

Kabbalistic symbols elevate the mind as the body works to integrate this energy, which is the light of higher consciousness. The practices bring in, balance, and align the light of the soul and its unique mission with the energy of the physical body. The practices connect us, as individuals, to the fabric of cosmic Oneness. The practices can help access guidance and the clarity to fulfill our personal missions. They also can be used for healing.[57]

We are often out of physical/spiritual alignment. Many of us find it hard to be souls confined by the limits of our physical bodies and may, as a result, live primarily in our thoughts. On the other hand, some of us feel detached and isolated from the spiritual realm which is always there to guide us.

For example, if prayer has become a rote recitation rather than a transcendent experience try adding the practices recommended for the enhancement of specific prayers. Whether you are praying formally or in personal meditation, the practices strengthen the balance between body and soul. The words may bring visceral sensations and new insights for the practices encourage the connection to love, light, and higher consciousness.

The practices can also be used simply to put life in perspective. Perhaps stress is overwhelming. Perhaps you are feeling down or a little off. Maybe you feel strangely disconnected from your body after sitting at a computer for hours. If you sense you are out of balance in any way, the practices presented have the added benefit of helping to restore equanimity. There is an old Jewish custom of carrying two slips of paper, one in the right pocket and one in the left. On one paper is written: *"The entire world was created just*

---

57 The Hebrew "Misheberach" prayer, recited for those who are ailing, calls for healing of both body and soul. The popular Debbie Friedman version can be found at www.youtube.com/watch?v=HX5TWsfykSs.

for me." [58] On the other paper is written *"I am but dust and ashes."* [59] The goal is to be between the extremes in a centered place of balance and wholeness. Wholeness in Hebrew is *shalem*—the same root, שלם—as the word for peace, *shalom*. By connecting the realms of the physical and the spirit the practices help to facilitate personal wholeness and the creation of inner peace.

The practices can be performed as individual exercises or grouped together in various combinations. I have experimented with different sequences and invite you to do so as well. If possible, smile. Smiling turns on the energies of light, the radiant circuits, which are thought to be soul lights. The radiant circuits are also activated by feelings of love and gratitude, or by being in a special place in nature or in your mind. Ideally, practice in a slow, relaxed way in a room with minimal distractions, or outside in nature.

Set an intention, and perhaps ask a question you would like clarified. Feel free to modify and make the practices your own. Add the suggested prayers, those of your choosing, or none. Although they may have visualizations in common, each exercise is complete in itself.

Group practice enhances the experience by creating a larger field of high vibration. Whether practicing alone or with others, the spiritual radiance created spreads like the ripples of a pebble tossed gently in a pond. When we raise our own vibration by coming into alignment with the light of our souls, we create a morphogenic field that helps others to do the same. The oneness we create in our own being through the alignment of body and soul is the template for the universal Oneness we seek.

It may be helpful to skim through the practices and pick an exercise that resonates with you. Work with that practice and its nuances before you continue to another. Or try them all in the order presented. The videos at energyandkabbalah.com are a guide to the physical movements. Feel free to experiment. Keep a journal if you like to keep track of which exercises are most beneficial in achieving your goals.

Suggestion:

Although the relevant concepts are repeated within the description of each practice, it may be helpful to review several themes presented in part 1.

---

58 Talmud-Sanhedrin 38a.
59 Genesis 18:27.

These include:
1. The infinity sign of love
2. Symbolism of the letter *aleph*/א
3. Visualizing the letters of the most Holy Name YHVH/יהו-י
4. Symbolism of the letter *yud*/י

Become as familiar as possible with the symbols and the concepts of love and oneness they represent. Allow these ideas to center in the heart and ride with the breath (chapter 15). The mind then becomes a partner in the practices rather than the focus, and you will be able to experience the range of sensations more fully. Remember to smile!

14
Grounding

An ancient legend tells the story of four illustrious rabbis who embarked on a mystical journey through the levels of the *pardes*/פרדס/orchard. You may recall that the letters in *pardes* symbolize the levels of Torah study, the basis of Kabbalah. The rabbis were attempting to reach the highest levels of consciousness, the kabbalistic world of *sod*, secrets.

According to the legend, only one of the four who entered the *pardes*, Rabbi Akiva, entered in peace and left in peace. Of the other three rabbis, one died, one became insane, and one completely abandoned his faith. What protected Rabbi Akiva? One interpretation is that Rabbi Akiva survived because he stayed grounded, connected to the earth. Because he was in contact with his body and the physical world he was able to handle the magnitude of the experience, while the others could not. He had created a balance of spiritual and physical within himself resulting in a strong vessel that withstood the challenge of holding the intense light of higher consciousness. Because Rabbi Akiva stayed in his body, he emerged from the highest mystical realms of the *pardes* even stronger and wiser.

Working with kabbalistic ideas and symbolism can create altered states of consciousness. Grounding to the earth is an essential preliminary to energy, meditative, or kabbalistic practices to ensure that you are firmly in your body. It is very easy to get carried away in esoteric study, and leaving the body for a length of time can be quite detrimental. It can be difficult to return to reality and in some cases to discern reality from imagination.

Even the pressures of ordinary life can cause us to "escape" out of the present moment and detach from the rigors of being a soul confined to a body. In working with clients, the first thing I check is the stability of grounding. For a myriad of reasons, from the shifting of the earth's magnetic poles to having been caught in traffic, many people are not grounded moment to moment.

Conscious grounding helps to create a stable container for balancing and reconnecting energies on the physical, emotional, and mental planes. Grounding also helps to stabilize the *sefira* of *Malchut*, creating a vessel that is strong and secure enough to hold the light of intense spiritual vibration. The mind may then travel and return safely to the physical body, as Rabbi Akiva exemplified in the *pardes*.

Atoms and molecules are electromagnetic force fields. Our cells are made of atoms and molecules so we are electromagnetic beings. Electricity and magnetism connect us to those same forces in the earth. We are held by the force of gravity, and like a lightning rod or any other electric device, we must be connected to the ground in a way that allows energy to enter and leave the system.

When we are earth-grounded, we feel secure in our bodies, supported, solid, connected. People who are not grounded may feel depleted if fresh earth energy is not entering to "juice" them. They may also pile up so much excess energy they "explode" with emotion. When people say they are "burned out" or "fried," in a way they really are.

Grounding can occur at different levels. For example, we experience physical connection to the earth through a harmony with the force of gravity. Emotional grounding allows our emotions to move freely and enables us to easily discharge unwanted thoughts. When both the physical and emotional bodies are grounded, we can bring our minds and hearts into harmony with others and with our higher selves.

Grounding is largely a function of the root chakra and the kidney meridian. The root chakra, similar to the *sefira* of *Malchut* in the Tree, stores information dealing with survival, safety, and of being held securely in time by the ancestors. It is the connection to Mother Earth that feeds the higher chakras. It replenishes and heals us.

In the poetic language of Kabbalah, *Malchut* is also the realm of the *Shechina* and the world of *Assiya*, physical matter. *Malchut* creates the vessel that stabilizes the entire Tree. Having no light of her own, *Malchut* instead attracts, receives, and holds the influx of divine light from above. The stronger the vessel *Malchut* creates, the more light the Tree can hold. A stable *Malchut* is necessary for lasting healing and repair while a weakness in *Malchut* brings instability to the entire Tree.

Physically clearing the energy of the root chakra and/or entraining to the vibration of a healthy *Malchut* are excellent ways to ground, but require some training. We will focus on simpler and more immediate ways to reconnect to earth energy, first through an energy practice alone and then through a combination of energy and kabbalistic symbols.

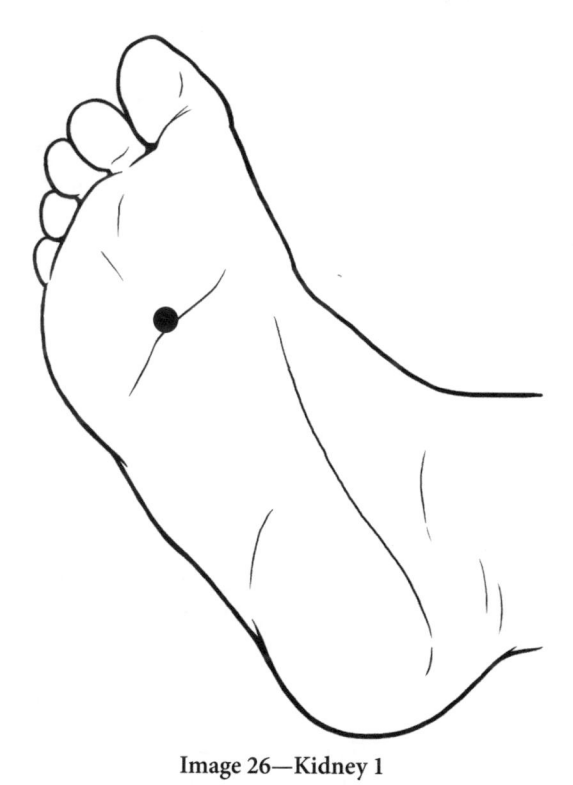

Image 26—Kidney 1

The Energy of Grounding

We ground to the energy of the earth through the lower parts of the body. Besides the root chakra, a primary doorway to this energy is Kidney 1 (K1), the acupressure point called the Wellspring of Life. K1 is the first point on the kidney meridian. It lies on the ball of the foot. Kidney energy runs up the front of the body, continually delivering life force energy also called chi, and in Kabbalah, *Ruach*.

There are many easy ways to practice conscious grounding no matter where you find yourself at.

Indoors:

- Gently stamp on the floor and consciously feel your connection to the earth through the bottoms of the feet.
- Massage or stretch K1 with the fingers or rub the ball of the foot with the back of a stainless steel spoon.
- Sit in a chair with your feet flat on the floor and rest your hands on your thighs. This is called pharaoh posture because it is the position of seated pharaohs found in ancient Egyptian carvings.
- Stand on sea salt crystals while you shower.[60]

Outdoors:

- If you have access to a large tree, stand (preferably barefoot) with your tailbone and back against the trunk. You are connecting to all the surrounding area where the tree's roots extend. Close the eyes and feel the expansion of your own roots.
- Walk barefoot on wet grass or on a beach.
- Lie on the ground with bent knees. Feel the connection to earth through your tailbone and feet. Breathe deeply.

Kabbalistic Grounding

The following grounding technique is based on Earth Docking, created by my colleague Ellen Meredith, a gifted and intuitive energy healer.[61]

---

60 For a complete energy routine for the shower, visit www.dragonflyhealer.com.

61 An excellent discussion of grounding can be found at Ellen Meredith's website: www.listening-in.com/grounding_intro.php.

Sit with your feet flat on the floor. If possible, remove your shoes and activate the K1 point by rubbing it with your fingers or the back of a stainless steel spoon.

Place your hands and arms gently on your thighs, or use them to follow the energy as it rises up the body.

Project the image of the four-letter Name onto your body.

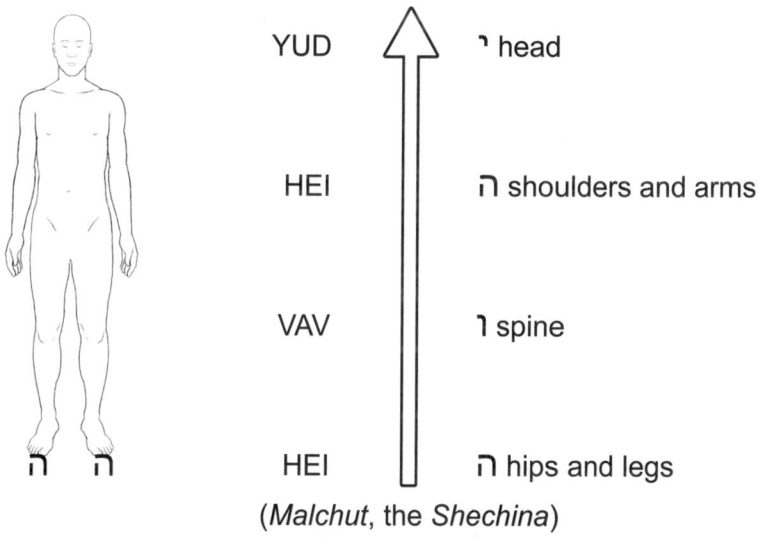

YUD — י head

HEI — ה shoulders and arms

VAV — ו spine

HEI — ה hips and legs
(*Malchut*, the *Shechina*)

Image 27—Kabbalistic Grounding

Imagine doors on the bottoms of your feet connected to Kidney 1. Open the doors. Imagine you are extending the sides of the letter *hei*, like roots down from your feet, deep into the earth. Stop about eight feet down. Here the energy is very stable. Imagine you are plugging your *hei* roots into energy outlets, as if you were plugging in an electric appliance like a toaster. Feel the energy rise up each leg through the *hei* and up the body through the *vav*, upper *hei*, and *yud*. Let the energy release through the crown like a fountain.

YUD

HEI ה

VAV ו

HEI ה

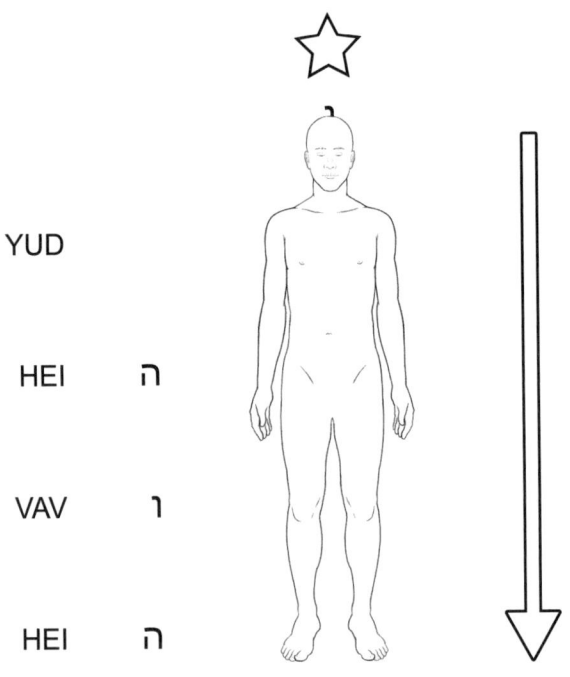

Image 28—Connecting to Heaven

Connecting to Heaven

The focus here is on earth grounding to balance the cerebral and spiritual nature of Kabbalah. But both heaven and earth energies must be in balance to create the stable dance of yin/yang, of life. In general, yin/feminine/earth energy enters through the lower part of the body; yang/masculine/heaven energy enters through the top of the head.

As in Kabbalah, the masculine energy connects to the light of heaven. If an influx of spiritual energy is needed, it is possible to do earth grounding in reverse. If we imagine the Tree of Life on a physical body, the top of the head is the *sefira* of *Keter,* meaning crown, corresponding to the crown chakra. *Keter* also corresponds to the top tip of the Y/י in the Name YHVH. Also called a crown, the crown of the *yud* is our closest connection to the Infinite Light of Source.

Imagine the tip of the *yud* connecting to your special soul star lying about eighteen inches above the head. (Some call this the eighth chakra.) The soul star is your connection to *shefa*, the cosmic flow. Imagine this life-force energy entering through the crown, traveling down through the Name into your roots, and repeat the pattern with your breath and imagination as long as desired.

15
Breath

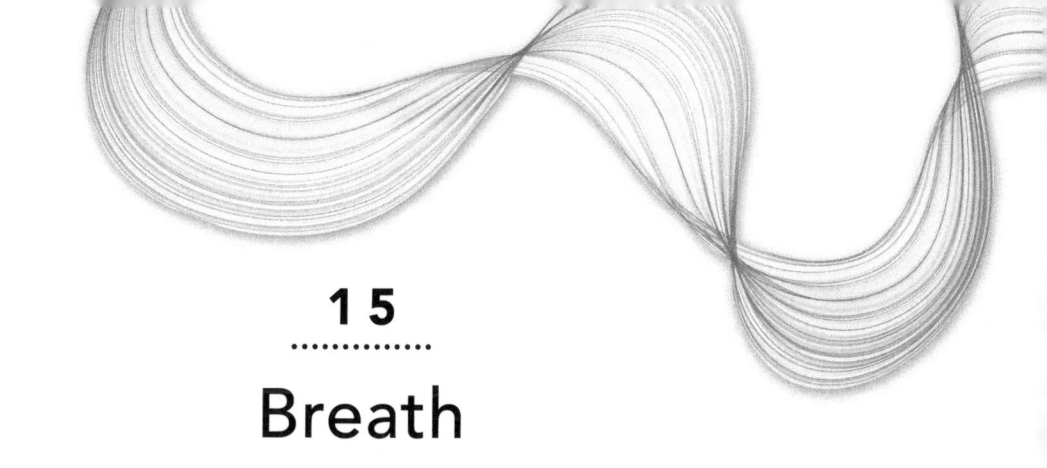

In the Zohar, breath is referred to as the kiss between heaven and earth. Breath is the uniting of body and soul, the physical and the spiritual. *Neshama*/נשמה is the Hebrew word for soul. Add a *yud*/י, the divine spark, to *neshama* and the soul comes to life with the word for breath, *neshima*/נשימה.

The breaths presented here enhance the practices that follow but they can also be practiced on their own. Energy practices are greatly enhanced by adding conscious breathing so feel free to use another conscious breathing method if you find it is more effective to do so.

1. **Adam Breath**

When *Elohim*, the God-force of creation, breathed into Adam, this first being came to life. The last thing we do when we exit our physical bodies is return this breath to God. Adam breath is calming. With it you experience the "big picture" by connecting every place the breath travels, within and without, to the goodness and love of life-sustaining God-force.

    How: Imagine your inhale is the exhale of God.

    Imagine your exhale is the inhale of God.

- *Optional: With your hand(s), trace the infinity sign of this connection with the center at your heart.*

2. **The Breath of Light**

The Hebrew word for air is avir/ אויר /spelled *aleph* א / *vav* ו / *yud* י / *resh* ר. Air/avir contains our life force. When we breathe, much as life-sustaining oxygen molecules separate from air, we can imagine that the *yud*(s)/ י as divine sparks, separate from the *avir*/ אויר.

Air = divine spark(s) + light

אור + י = אויר

What remains of *avir* is the word *aur*/ אור, light. We can radiate this light with every breath. We also channel divine sparks of *yuds* throughout our bodies.

How: Consciously inhale *avir*/ אויר. Follow the breath as it travels to the lungs/heart area. Imagine the *avir* separating there into *aur*/ אור and divine sparks of *yuds*/ י . Shine your light with the exhaled breath. Send the divine sparks wherever they are needed in your own body or possibly through the hands for healing. (Remember that *yad*, spelled the same as the letter *yud*, is the Hebrew word for "hand.")

3. *Aleph* Breath/The Breath of Love

Imagine yourself as an *aleph*/א, with its components:

Yud/Vav/Yud	יוי
	upper י/crown—heaven(K"BH)
א =	ו–heart (*Vav*=connector)
	lower י/feet—earth (*Shechina*)

י-י is a divine Name symbolizing the balance of heaven and earth, *K"BH* and *Shechina*. The ו/ *vav* of the א lies at the heart. The heart, as *vav*, connects the two *yuds*/י-י. It is where heaven and earth, *K"BH* and *Shechina* meet. The exhale and inhale of the breath can be represented by an infinity sign. The center of the infinity sign is the *vav* at the heart, the wellspring of love.

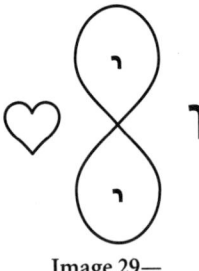

Image 29—
Heaven and Earth

1. Inhale the gifts of the heavens through the crown. Filter them through the love in your heart, *vav*. With your exhaled breath offer these gifts to the earth.

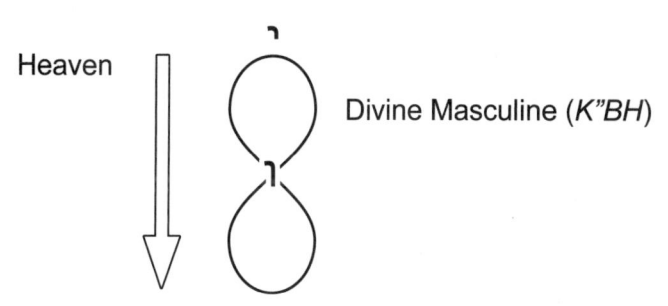

Image 30—Heaven Divine Masculine K"BH

2. Reverse your breathing pattern, receiving from earth, feeling the breath in the heart, releasing to heaven.

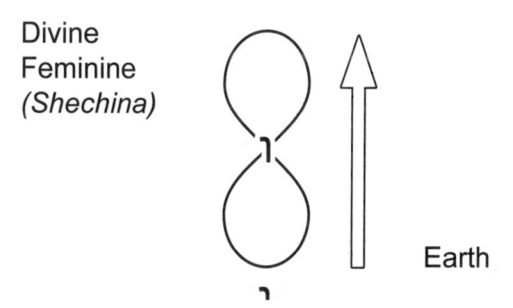

Image 31—Earth Divine Feminine Shechina

The Breath of Love

When you have practiced receiving from heaven and earth separately, **try to inhale from heaven and earth at the same time.** Exhale through the heart, which opens more and more with each breath.

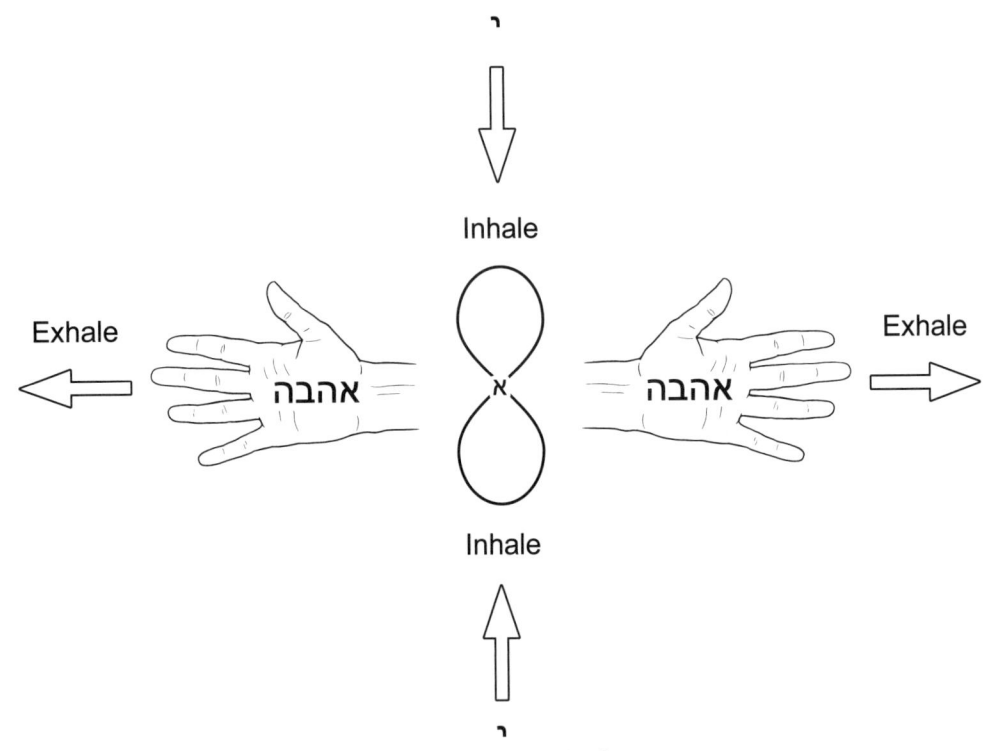

Image 32—The Breath of Love

You are embodying both the א and its *gematria*, 26.

When heaven and earth connect in the heart, the 26 of the א becomes 2 x 13.

gematria 13 = *ahava*/אהבה/love.

The arms and hands connect directly to the energy of the heart. As you exhale, send a current of *ahava* from the heart out each hand. Send this love anywhere that needs healing. The Breath of Love helps to amplify the effects of many of the practices that follow.

3. Creating balance: Alternate nostril breathing with the Name

Alternate nostril breathing has been practiced by yogis for thousands of years. It helps to connect the right and left hemispheres of the brain, balancing the masculine analytic side with feminine intuitive side. The results are extremely calming even after just a few rounds.

The Name YHVH/י-הוה reflects spiritual masculine/feminine balance. Visualizing the letters of the Name as you breathe adds a dimension to this pranayama (breath practice) that links body and soul.

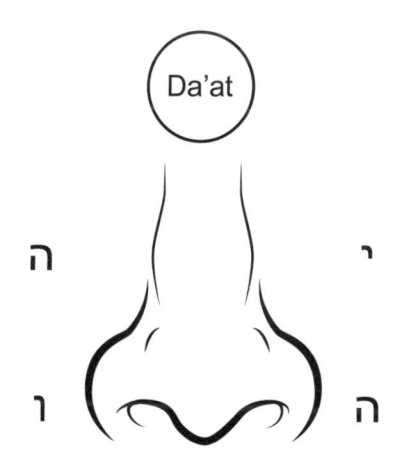

Image 33—Alternate Nostril Breathing with YHVH

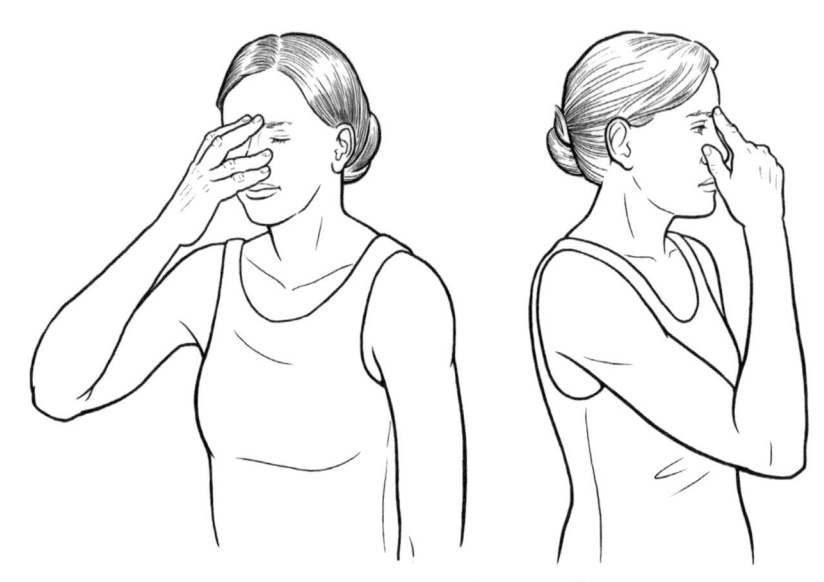

Image 34 and 35—How Steps 1 and 2

How: (1.) The index and middle finger of the right hand rest on the third eye, at the sphera of *Da'at*, between the eyebrows. (*Da'at* is the *sefirotic* link between masculine and feminine, and the right and left hemispheres.) Close off the left nostril with the ring finger of that hand.
(2.) Inhale through the right nostril visualizing the letter *yud*/י.
(3.) Close off the right nostril with the thumb.
(4.) Exhale through the left nostril visualizing the letter *hei*/ה. It is helpful that the letter *hei* makes the same sound as the exhaled breath—hhhhhh.
(5.) Inhale through the left nostril visualizing the letter *vav*/ו.
(6.) Close off the left nostril with the ring finger.
(7.) Exhale through the right nostril visualizing the letter *hei*/ה. Again the *hhh* sound of the exhale reinforces the visualization.

This is one round of breathing. Increase your capacity slowly. This pranayama is an excellent preparation for prayer or any spiritual practice.

Many years ago, as I was practicing alternate nostril breathing while visualizing the Name, I saw the letters flowing in infinity patterns and realized I was seeing the wings of a dragonfly. It may also help you to see the letters flowing this way:

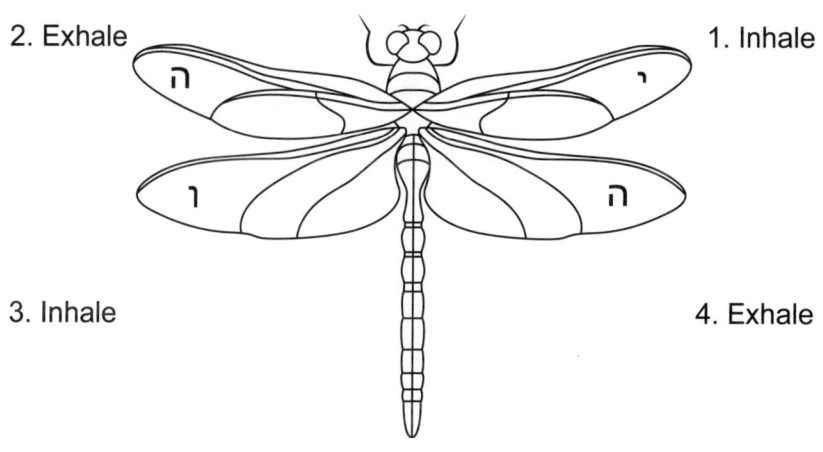

2. Exhale ה   1. Inhale י

3. Inhale ו   4. Exhale ה

Image 36—Dragonfly with Letters

16
The Hands

The hands are an extension of the energy of the heart. Compassionate touch that comes from the heart is the basis of ancient and modern healing methods such as Reiki, Healing Touch, jin shin jyutsu, Quantum-Touch, acupressure, and energy medicine. Compassionate touch is also the basis of the healing practice presented in part 3.

Image 37—The Hands

Hands have always held an important place in the Jewish/Kabbalah tradition. Psalms (8:4) refers to creation as the work of God's fingers.

In the ancient temple in Jerusalem, the priests would channel blessings to the people through their hands. While reciting a special invocation called the "priestly benediction," the priests held their hands at eye level and made the shape of the letter *shin*/ש with their fingers.[62] It is said that the light of the *Shechina*, the Indwelling Presence, would shine through the fingers of the priests as they recited this prayer. Those being blessed were instructed to close their eyes and lower their heads because of the intensity of the light. The priestly benediction is still recited by their descendants as a special ritual in some synagogues. Leonard Nimoy, Mr. Spock of *Star Trek* fame, was such a descendent and created the Vulcan salute, "live long and prosper," to replicate the hand shape the priests held when blessing the people. Although traditionally reserved for men, some synagogues allow women like myself, who are daughters of the descendants of priests, to formally transmit this blessing. However, because the ancient temple in Jerusalem no longer exists, *anyone with the proper intention* can direct blessings through the hands. The special power of the hands in the ש position will be presented in Part 3, but the nature of the hands themselves allows for healing in many positions.

Hands-on healing is described in ancient kabbalistic texts. For example, Sefer Yetzira relates fingers and hand parts to each of the *sefirot* and to the Hebrew letters. Different color visualizations that accompany them have also been described, though specific colors vary depending on the source. In addition, the fifteen Hebrew words of the priestly benediction which begins "may the Lord bless you and keep you" each correspond to a different section of finger.[63] These practices keep the healer totally focused in the mental arena and therefore will not be detailed here.

The Hebrew word for hand, *yad*/יד, is the same as the letter *yud*/יי. In the Zohar, the *yud*/י, the smallest letter, represents the divine spark, architect of all creation.[64]

....
62   Shin/ש, standing for the name of God, *Shaddai*/שדי, has feminine connotations from the same root as the word for breasts, *shadayim*.
63   Shamanic training with Rabbi Gershon Winkler.
64   Amid the Japanese-based Reiki symbols strangely sits the letter yud as well!

In Hebrew the name of something is not just a name. All of creation came to be because of the vibration of words and the letters they are made of. The letters hold the energy and essence of the thing.

Each hand is YD/יד

Y/י is symbolic of the divine spark

        and

D/ד/*dalet* means a "door"

So in essence, hands are the doors to the divine sparks.

Accessing the Divine Sparks

Imagine your hands as the upper and lower *yuds* of the letter *aleph*. Recall that the deconstructed *aleph*/א can be thought of as

         י *yud*

     ו *vav* (and)

י *yud*

The *vav*, as the center of the torso, both connects and separates the *yuds*. It lies between them with the heart at the center.

Image 38—Divine Spark Hands

The hands are a direct connection into the wellspring of love that lies within our hearts and the means to send this love out beyond ourselves.

Also recall that the *yuds* in the letter *aleph* represent Y/Y, י-י the divine name that combines YHVH and *Adonai*, symbolizing divine masculine and feminine.[65]

---

65 See page 49.

י-הוה אדנ-י

>Divine Masculine and Feminine,
>>Heaven and Earth,
>>>the tension of opposites.

We could not exist without the tension of opposites. We are electromagnetic beings. Our blood is charged with iron. Our cells, all life, depend on ionic positive and negative charges to move nutrients across cell membranes. The hands themselves exhibit positive and negative polarities that can be put to good use. Anywhere you place your hands on your own body or someone else's moves energy. Placing both hands directly on the body or in the energy field that surrounds it can act like jumper cables, reconnecting energies like an old-time switchboard operator, encouraging healthy communication and interaction.

Simple Methods for Healing with the Hands

1. The palm and top of the hand are magnetic opposites. Merely flipping the hands over and back can help relieve pain in an area of the body that is stuck from stress or injury by encouraging energy to move.

2. Your hands can transmit divine sparks of healing. When they are held together over a body, or moved in figure-eight patterns, the divine sparks pass between them and into the targeted area.

Image 39—Infinity Sign

3. Kabbalah and energy medicine also agree on the nature of right and left, which can have practical applications when working with energies such as pain.

The right hand is considered more masculine and outwardly directed (yang.) The left hand is considered receptive (yin) and thus more feminine.

Pain can be siphoned by placing the left hand over the afflicted area and draining the pain out of the body through the right. Shake off the right hand to release unwanted energy.

> 4. The energy of the radiant circuits, the light of our direct connection to soul and source, is especially effective in healing. My colleague Ellen Meredith has developed a simple way to access these special energies.[66] Extend the left index finger and plug it, like an electric prong, into whatever you consider to be a source of divine energy. In this variation, the radiant energy flows through the left index finger up through the heart and out the right hand onto the body for healing.

Kabbalah adds the symbolism of
    yud/יד = *yad*/יד
the letter *yud* = hand

They are the same word, differing only in the vowels that affect their pronunciation.

---

66 Ellen Meredith's website is www.listening-in.com.

Recall the chapter on the Name, YHVH. When YHVH is written vertically, the crown of the *yud*, its highest point, is our closest connection to the spiritual universe, *Atzilut*, the world of Infinite Light.

YUD ⇧ י

HEI ה

VAV ו

HEI ה

Image 40—Atzilut

The tip of the *yud* points directly to the unknowable realms of the divine.

How

Let the hand/*yad* symbolize the letter *yud*, and the left index finger represent the crown of the *yud*, its highest part.

Place your left hand in a comfortable position. Extend the left index finger and imagine you are plugging it into a source of divine radiance. Feel the energy entering your body through the fingertip and let it flow through the heart and out the right hand. With the right hand direct the energy flow to the body part in need of attention.

Clearing and Preparing the Hands for Energy Work

Not surprisingly, hands often pick up unwanted energy and that *shmutz* needs to be cleared.[67] It is good practice to wash the hands before and after working in your own or another's energy field. Rubbing the hands together and then shaking them vigorously will also help clear unwanted energy. In the absence of water or another clearing agent such as sea salt, imagine sending discarded energy into a "universal recycling bin." The traditional Hebrew blessing for washing the hands facilitates both cleansing and the transmission of healing energy:

בָּרוּךְ אַתָּה יְיָ אֱלֹהֵינוּ מֶלֶךְ הָעוֹלָם אֲשֶׁר קִדְּשָׁנוּ בְּמִצְוֹתָיו וְצִוָּנוּ עַל נְטִילַת יָדָיִם.

Baruch ata Adonai, Eloheinu melech ha'olam asher kid'shanu b'mitzvotav v'tzeevanu al nitilat yadayim.

Blessed are you Source of blessings,
who has commanded us on the washing of the hands.

In addition, before working with clients in my healing space, I place my hands in the shape of a ש/*shin*, the position of the priestly benediction on top of the four-letter Name inlaid in the wings of a stone dragonfly (as shown in image 36, page 125). I set my intention and ask that the healing come from the highest sources. I recite the traditional Jewish invocation of the archangels modified to include the presence of the *Shechina* over my head, in my essence, and beneath my feet.

I recite the *Sh'ma* (Chapter 20), and a personal Hebrew blessing of the hands that I composed, roughly translated as "Source of blessing, please bless my hands with the light of a pure and loving heart."

To close a session, I draw figure-eights of love over the client from head to toe and back up again while reciting *Ana B'Koach* (Chapter 24) and/or the priestly benediction (Numbers 6:24–26).

This is my personal practice for opening and closing a healing session. Feel free to modify the ideas presented in this chapter or perhaps create a heart-centered blessing that fills your individual needs.

Be conscious of the power of your hands and the sacred work they can do.

....
67 *Shmutz* is a colorful Yiddish word meaning grime, dirt, or impurity.

17
Boundaries

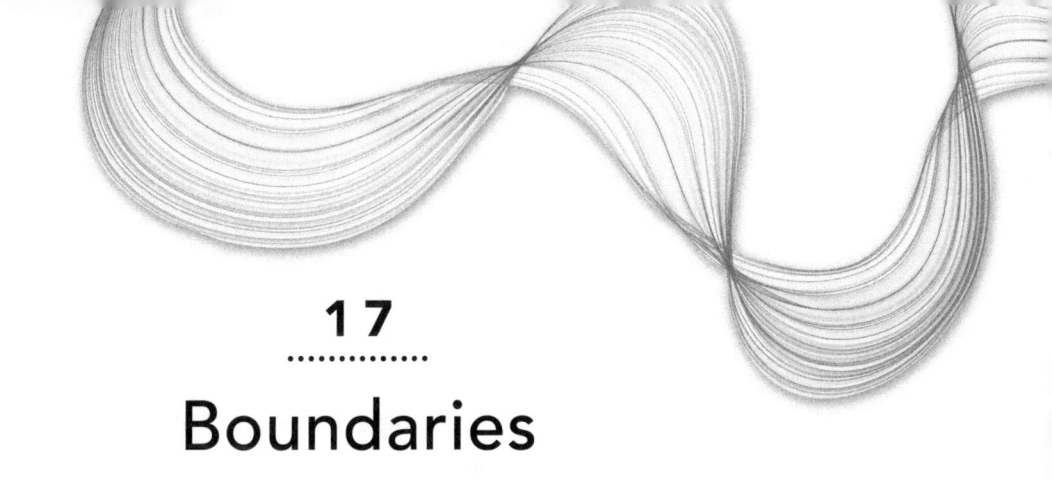

The practices in this chapter help to create and maintain safe and healthy personal space. Kabbalistic symbolism adds the power of divine protection. When the self feels safe, the power of the yin, and its higher counterpart, the divine presence, can blossom.

Boundaries are a necessary part of a healthy psyche. Many of us have unhealthy energetic boundaries. We take on the emotions of others, or unconsciously allow our energies to leak into situations that may not even directly concern us. Then we wonder why we feel drained. Boundaries are so important in Kabbalah that a section of the Zohar discusses in great detail the ramifications of their coming into being on the second day of creation. The ultimate kabbalistic vision is of oneness and unity, but it is only through having secure boundaries in ourselves that we can fulfill our individual missions and have true relationship and the intimacy of "oneness" with others. The addition of kabbalistic symbols in these boundary practices permeates and surrounds the energy body with divine love.

Kabbalah Zip-Up (KAZU)
Energy/Kabbalah Background
The Zip-Up is an Eden Energy Medicine technique that creates natural self-protection from both environmental toxins and unwanted human energies. The kabbalistic Zip-Up (KAZU) is a variation of this exercise which uses the infinity signs of love to create both boundaries and balance.

The Zip-Up protects the most receptive (yin) channel of the body, the central meridian. The Zip-Up also creates a boundary over the lower five chakras which lie directly on the central meridian, including the ever-vulnerable heart and solar plexus.

The central meridian corresponds to the central column of the kabbalistic Tree of Life as projected on a physical body. The central meridian is also a radiant circuit, and like each of the radiant circuits, contributes an essential attribute, a gift that is part of our essence. The gift of the central channel is love.[68]

On a spiritual level then, the KAZU protects the *sefirot* in the central column of the Tree. Because the Tree also has right and left columns, tracing horizontal infinity signs of love helps to balance these opposites as well. Balancing the right and left takes on even more significance because the left, feminine, side of the tree is the boundary-creator. The right (masculine) side seeks relationship and unity. Balancing right and left with a physical exercise helps bring stability to all the universes, including the spiritual body.

How: Place the hands over the heart and take a deep breath in and out. The visualization is similar to the Breath of Love in Chapter 15. The heart is at the center of an infinity sign that receives the energy of Heaven and Earth in the form of YHVH. In the heart, the *gematria* of YHVH, 26, divides into 2 x 13/*ahava* and *ahava*, and love flows out the hands.

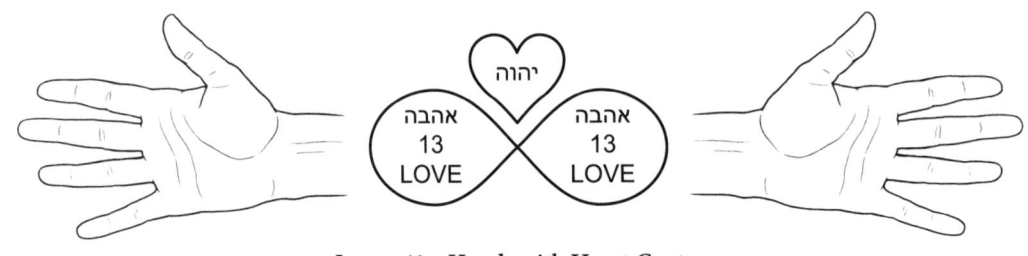

Image 41—Hands with Heart Center

---

68 As taught by Dr. Sara Allen, Energy Kineseology (EnKa) Conference, August 2016.

Activate the hands by imagining they are connected to an infinity sign of love centered in the heart.

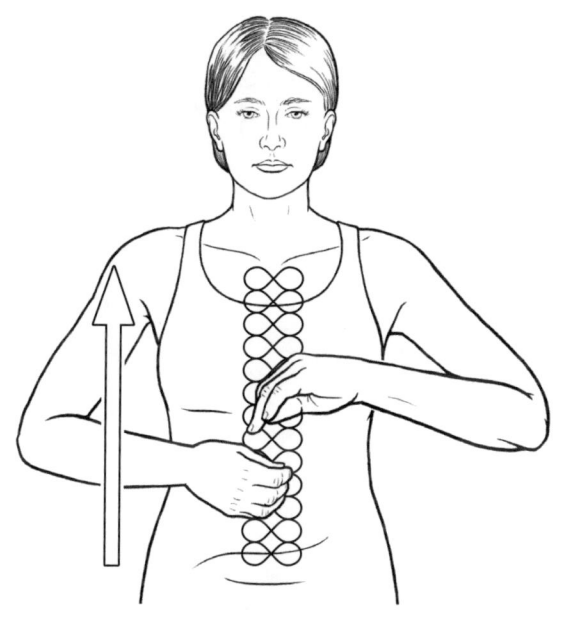

Image 42—Body with Hands in Front

Extend the arms down in front of the body. Draw small infinity signs of love by flipping your hands over and back up the center of your body to the mouth. It may help to imagine that you are connecting the right and left columns of the Tree or that you are conducting a mini-orchestra up the center of your body as it plays the music of love.

Draw several infinity signs over the mouth, sealing in the energy.

Image 43—Body with Hands at Mouth

The Kabbalistic Aura Protector

The kabbalistic Aura Protector (**KAP**) is based on Ellen Meredith's exercise for reinforcing the boundary of the aura.[69]

An aura of light surrounds all living beings. Interestingly, *aur*/אור is the Hebrew word for light.

---

69   Ellen Meredith's website is www.listening-in.com.

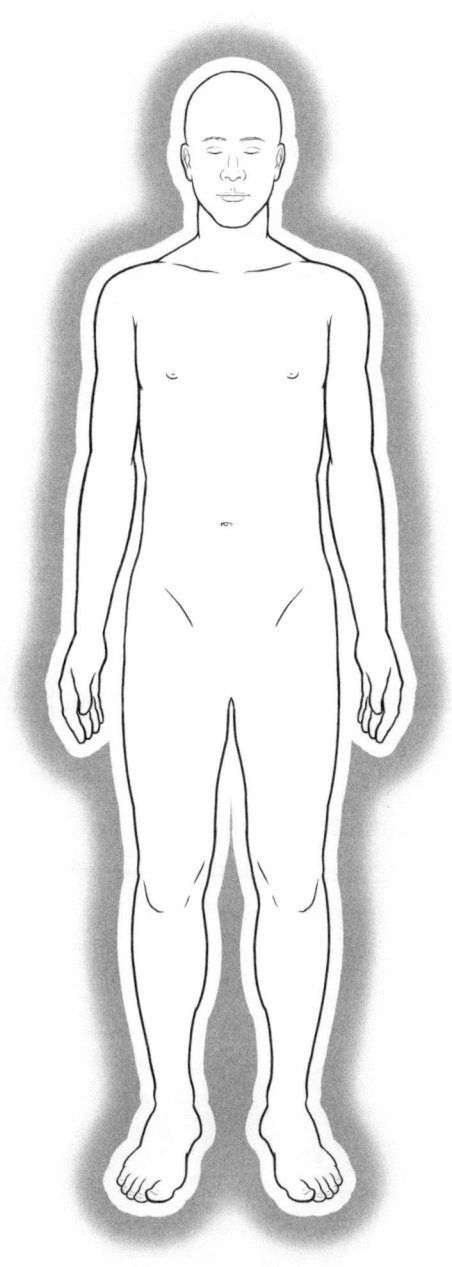

Image 44—The Aura

The aura is your personal energy field. It encases and protects the physical body extending some inches beyond the outstretched fingertips. It includes areas above the head and below the feet. Many people are susceptible to picking up emotions from others, and their auras absorb these unwanted energies like a sponge, often without their conscious awareness. The reverse is also true: if the aura has leaks or holes, needed energies can drain out. Both situations can cause physical or emotional depletion. Luckily, they can be managed in most cases with a simple exercise.

The edge of the aura forms a boundary between the *you* and the *not-you*, acting as a smart filter of sorts. Just as the cell membrane determines what enters and leaves a cell, the smart filter determines what energies come in and out of your field. If you imagine your body as a castle, the Zip-Up protects the front door. Strengthening the smart filter of the aura prevents uninvited energies from even crossing the moat to get to the door. You, and only you, should be in charge of the drawbridge into your personal space. Activating the smart filter protection by tracing infinity signs at the edge of the auric field and from the edge to the solidity of the physical body creates a safe space filled only with your energies and those you invite. A healthy aura creates balance between the inner life and the outer connection to the rest of the world. The energy field feels safe and secure.

How

As in the kabbalistic Zip-up, infinity signs of love create the KAP/smart filter boundary. What is not recognized as "you" is cleared from your field and you return to your true self, protected in a field of divine love.

1. Bring back your energy.

    Before securing the aura, open the palms. Reaching out on either side, slowly gather into your heart any pieces of yourself or your personal power you may have given away consciously or unconsciously.

    This includes any uncomfortable situation or anyone who triggered you negatively, anyone you blame or who caused you to act in a way that went against your gut feeling or sense of who you really are. When this process feels complete, pause for a moment and feel yourself centered and grounded.

Image 45—Bring Back Your Energy diagram #1

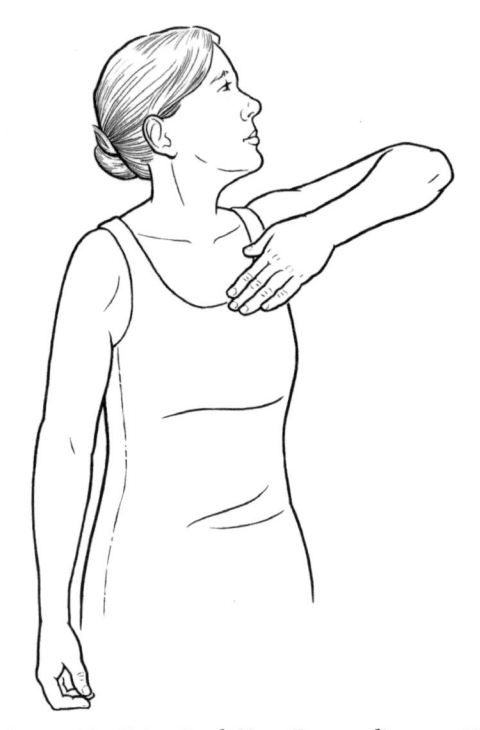

Image 46—Bring Back Your Energy diagram #2

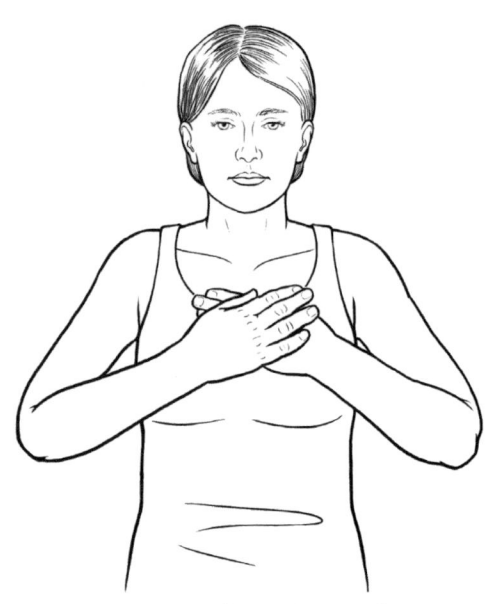

Image 47—Bring Back Your Energy diagram #3

142 Chapter 17

2. Activate the KAP/smart filter.

   Imagine your auric field, your personal space, surrounding you and extending about six inches farther than your hands can reach when fully extended. Call upon your higher self, your guides, angels, or personal spiritual assistants to help secure the edge of your auric field. They will create the boundary that lies beyond your fingers and assist you in securing areas of special vulnerability of which you may be unaware.

   You may choose to visualize infinity signs of love or divine sparks to activate the KAP. The physical movement is the same for either one.

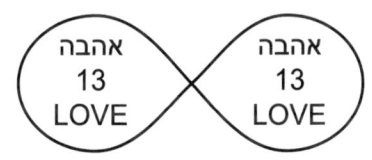

Image 48—Infinity Sign of Love

Infinity signs of love contain the equivalent *gematria* of YHVH (26), ahava/ahava, the same as the KAZU.

Image 49—Infinity Sign of Divine Sparks

Infinity signs of divine sparks contain י/י (Y/Y). Surround yourself with this divine balance of love.

With the arms extended draw small infinity signs of love or divine sparks by flipping the hands over and back, away from you and back again. Let the hands travel around you wherever they will, securing the KAP/smart filter with the help of your support team. When you sense that the edge of the field is secure, you may choose to bring the arms in closer to the body and fill the interior of the aura with more infinity signs. As you continue to draw the infinity signs of love or divine sparks you may enhance the visualization by adding a vibrant color to the infinity signs. Choose a color that makes you feel happy and safe. You may also add a verbal intention.

The intention can be a simple affirmation, such as "only love and goodness" or "invitation only." Affirmations should be short, worded positively, and expressed in the present tense. End by expressing gratitude to the members of the universal support team who assisted you.

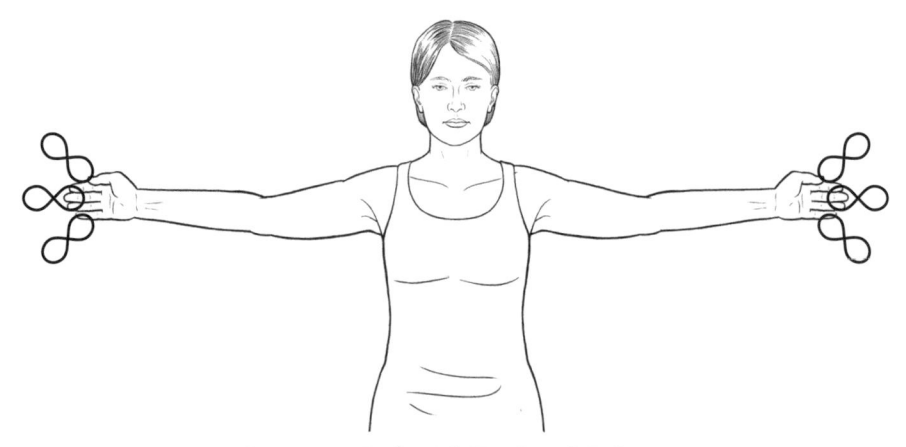

Image 50—Body with Hands with Infinity

In challenging situations, to further strengthen the aura, try reciting one the following safety-enhancing pronouncements as you draw the infinity signs:

1. Affirmation of self authority
2. Traditional Hebrew morning prayer of protection
3. *Hashkeevaynu*/הַשְׁכִּיבֵנוּ: traditional Hebrew evening prayer of protection recited each evening at bedtime
4. Psalm 91[70]

   1. **Affirmation of self-authority:**
      I am surrounded by safe and stable boundaries.
      I take responsibility for my life.

---
70 Items 2 and 3 can be found in most *sidurim*, Jewish prayerbooks: 2 in the *Shacharit* morning service, 3 in the *Ma'ariv* evening service. Psalm 91, in its entirety with oral recitation and traditional translation, can be found at http://www.mechon-mamre.org/p/pt/pt2691.htm.

My highest self determines what enters my field and what stays out.

I recognize my own emotions and allow them to flow through me without judgment.

May I be surrounded by and filled with love and healing light.

2. **Morning prayer of protection:**
   Source of blessings: May it be your will that I be protected today and every day from the insolence of others and arrogance in myself. Save me from vicious people, from evil neighbors, and corrupt companions. Preserve me from misfortune and the powers of destruction, harsh judgments, and ruthless opponents.

3. **Hashkeevaynu** (my translation of the appropriate verses):
   Allow us to rest peacefully and awaken with vitality. Surround us with peace, wholeness, and safety. Shield us from sickness, depression, hatred, violence, famine, and grief. Remove any blockages in our lives that prevent us from fulfilling our soul's mission, blockages we are aware of and those we are unaware of. Help us to transform our anger and need to inflict pain. Help us to move through our lives with vitality and integrity. Source of all blessings, please shelter us and all the peoples of the world in a field of peace. Amen.

4. **Psalm 91** is a powerful declaration of protection and is an excellent addition to the KAP. Here is my translation of the appropriate verses:
   Surrounding yourself with the protection of the One will shield you from unforeseen danger and disease.

   It will alleviate your anxieties, night and day.

   No evil will happen to you or harm your home.

   You will easily overcome difficulties, even those that appear insurmountable.

   Trust in the protection of the One and you will be safe.

18

The Belt Flow: The Rakia of Energy

The belt flow balances the energies coming through the crown with those traveling up the body from the earth. It is a physical reflection of the mystical connection and longing between Heaven and Earth. Use it to help maintain the internal balance of body and soul and bring ideas into manifestation.

In the beginning, there was only the ONE. There were no boundaries or separations. An ancient Chinese creation story tells of a great creator named Pongu, who used his physical strength to force apart the upper and lower waters and hold them apart until they were stable as the sky and the seas. In contrast, the Torah and the *Zohar* account for this separation of the waters through the vibration of speech.

Kabbalah Background

On the second day of creation, as written in Genesis, *Elohim*, the Creator persona of YHVH, spoke boundaries into existence by creating the *rakia*, or firmament. The *rakia* separated the "waters above from the waters below." Sky and ocean were divided from each other. Although no longer ONE, being water they could quickly blend into each other and, given a chance, could easily become ONE again. According to the symbolism of the Zohar, the *rakia* created a separation between YHVH as the divine masculine upper waters, and *YHVH Eloheinu*, as the divine feminine lower waters. According to the Zohar, the *rakia* and the waters above and below are symbolized by the letter *aleph* and its three components, *yud, vav,* and *yud*. We have looked at the *aleph* and the relationship of the components. The idea of the waters and the *rakia* adds an additional layer of symbolism.

> י   The upper *yud* = upper waters, the heavens, divine masculine *K"BH*.
>
> א ו   Between the waters is the letter *vav*. Vav, the word "and," creates balance by simultaneously separating and connecting the *yuds*.
>
> י   The lower *yud* = lower waters, the divine presence, the *Shechina*, partner to the *K"BH*.

The *yuds*, like the north and south poles of a magnet, are drawn to each other and try to reconnect. The boundary between them cannot be passive. It must continually allow for a dynamic reflection, tension, conflict, and balance between these forces.

Energy Background

Boundaries are reflected in our energy body in many ways. The belt flow is one of the radiant circuits, eight special energies of light. They are the first energies to emerge in the fertilized egg or zygote, and represent to some degree, the soul that enters the body at birth and departs from it at death. The belt flow runs around the belly like an equator. *It corresponds to the position and function of the rakia in the creation story.*

After conception, even before the fertilized egg divides, the first radiant circuits emerge, creating a continuous flow of life force potential around the zygote. Eventually, this circuit of life force develops into the main masculine (yang) and feminine (yin) energy channels of the body. The yin central meridian (item 51) is also called the conception vessel. It runs up the front of the body from the perineum over the soft and vulnerable belly to the mouth. There in the mouth, the central channel completes the circuit by connecting with its yang partner, the governing meridian (item 52). The governing meridian runs up the back, from the tailbone up along the spine over the top of the head where it connects to the central channel in the mouth. In an adult, this circuit becomes the microcosmic orbit, a powerful meditation channel Taoists have used for millennia.

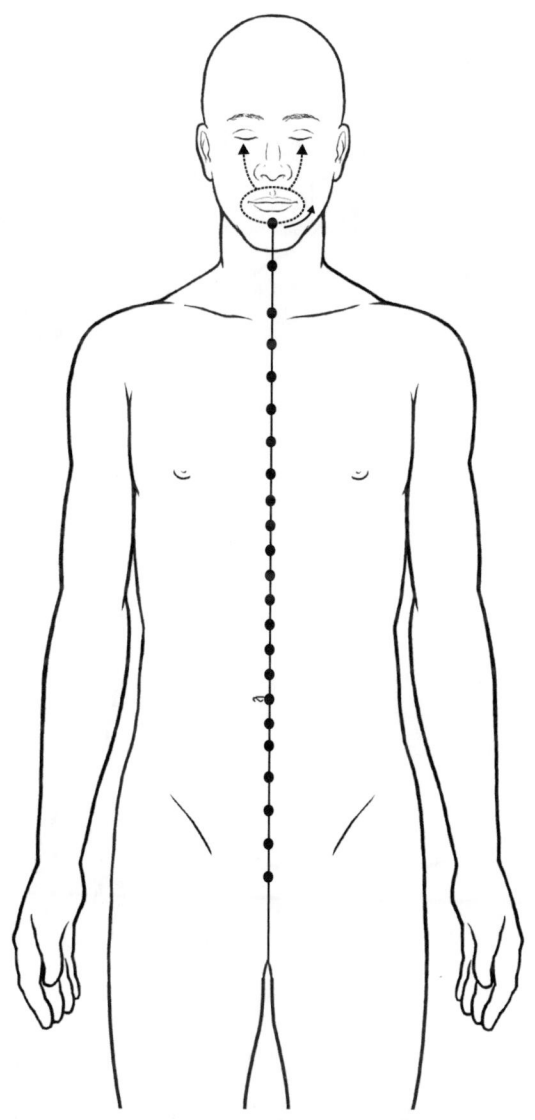

Image 51—Central Meridian

The Belt Flow: The Rakia of Energy 149

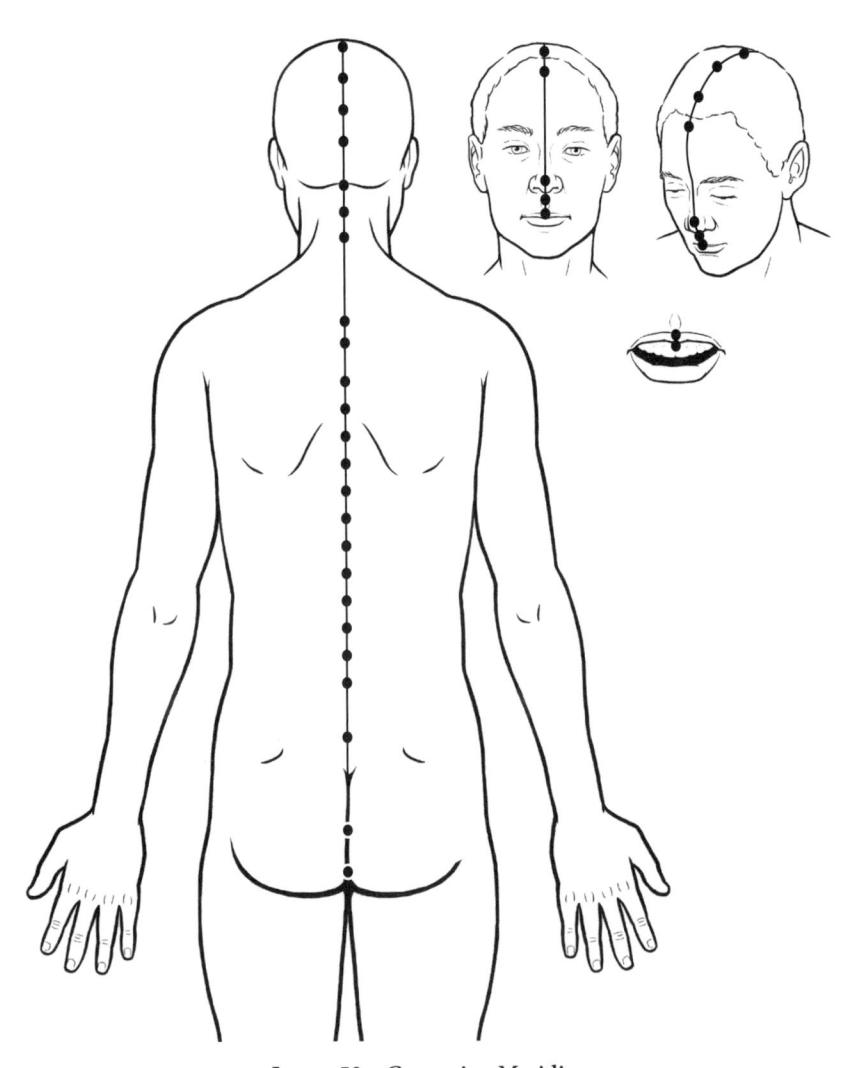

Image 52—Governing Meridian

150 Chapter 18

The microcosmic orbit is a re-creation of the original united life force that exists in the zygote before it begins to differentiate and split into two cells. And as below so above... this energy orbit is a reflection of circular orbits as we find them throughout the universe. Symbolically it re-creates the pre-*rakia* universe of Genesis when everything was still united as ONE.

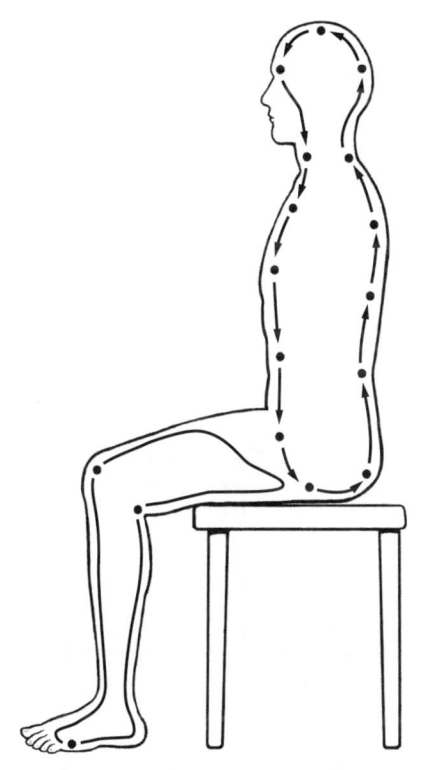

Image 53—Microcosmic Orbit

When the zygote splits into two cells, a radiant circuit called the belt flow creates a horizontal band, like an equator, around this original orbit. The one continuous orbit of the zygote then separates into the two connected channels that will become the central and governing vessels.

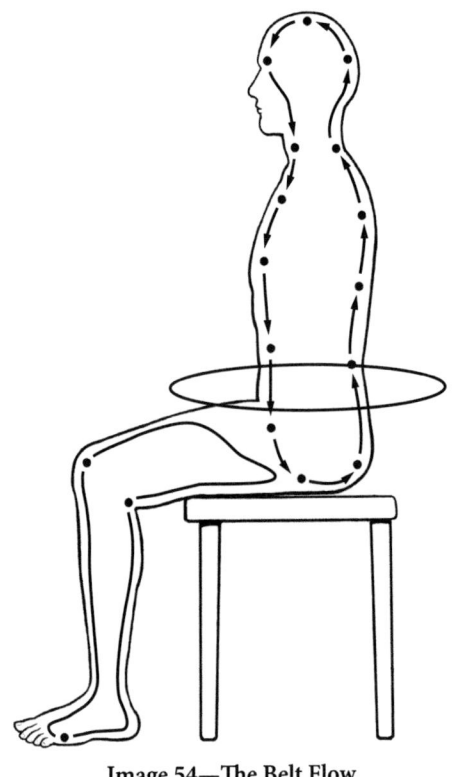

Image 54—The Belt Flow

In her book *Fabric of the Soul: 8 Extraordinary Vessels*, Dr. Hubatch describes the belt flow:

> The governing and conception vessels represent the front (yin) and back (yang). In addition, in general, the yang meridians enter through the head, above, and come down. The yin meridians enter through the feet (below) and flow up to meet them. The belt flow employs the balance and stability between the cosmic

forces of heaven above and earth below to maintain yin/yang balance in the body. Heaven relates to the mind and earth to the physical and emotional bodies. The belt flow loosens and tightens to regulate the balance between these two life forces. In this way the belt flow supports the balance between "heaven and earth." The Chinese symbol for this flow called dai, 帶, represents a belt, separating and harmonizing "heaven and earth" (Quote marks are from Dr. Hubatch, 14).

The belt flow exercise is an Eden Energy practice that clears and activates the belt channel, allowing the mind to connect with the physical body. Without this connection, ideas remain unmanifested dreams. It takes the connection of ideas to the physical body, to earth energy, to manifest our dreams into reality.

These two ideas together, belt flow and *rakia,* become the *rakia* flow. Energy medicine and Kabbalah weave together, creating a physical exercise with a spiritual context. The belt flow is a physical reflection of the connection and longing between Heaven and Earth. It creates stability between them. The belt flow as *rakia* is a place of divine connection and balance between the *Shechina* representing Earth and the *K"BH,* symbolic of Heaven. It is reflected in our bodies as healing the relationship between yang and yin, masculine and feminine.

    masculine/6 +
        feminine/7 =
            13 =
                Love/*Ahava* and Oneness/*Echad*

Rakia Flow

The *aleph* visualization infuses the belt flow with love.

Imagine yourself as the letter *aleph*, א, with its components: the upper and lower *yuds* and the *vav* separating and connecting them. The *vav*, as *rakia*, lies horizontally and separates the body above the waist, the upper *yud*, from that below the waist, the lower *yud* י.

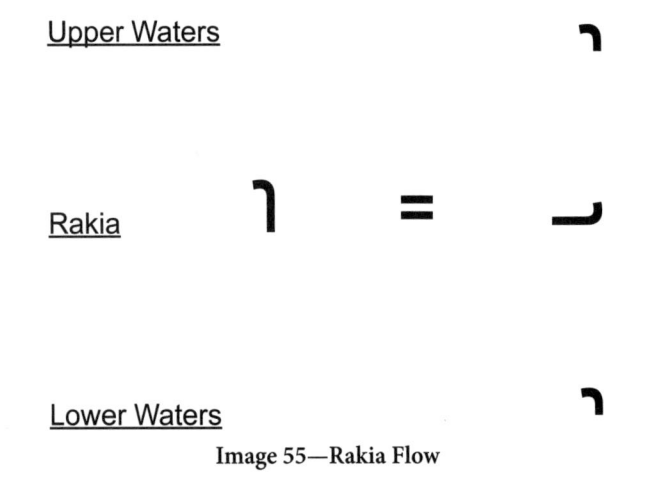

Upper Waters   י

Rakia   ו   =   ـا

Lower Waters   י

Image 55—Rakia Flow

1. The mingmen acupressure point is the origin of the belt/*rakia* flow and a major storage area for life force energy. The mingmen point lies directly behind the navel on the back. Rub, scratch, or stretch this point a bit to activate the flow.

2. Use the thumbs to drag the hands slowly around the waist, from the middle of the back around to the front of the body.

3. Cross your arms and sweep the energy from the belly, down the legs and off the feet.

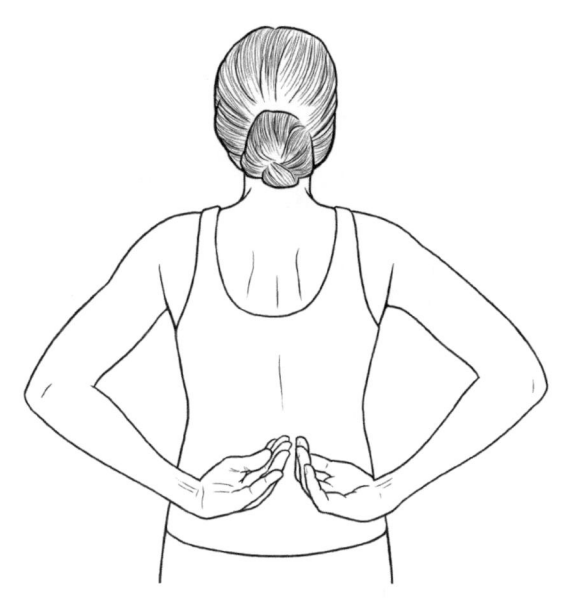

Image 56—Rakia Flow diagram #1

Image 57—Rakia Flow diagram #2

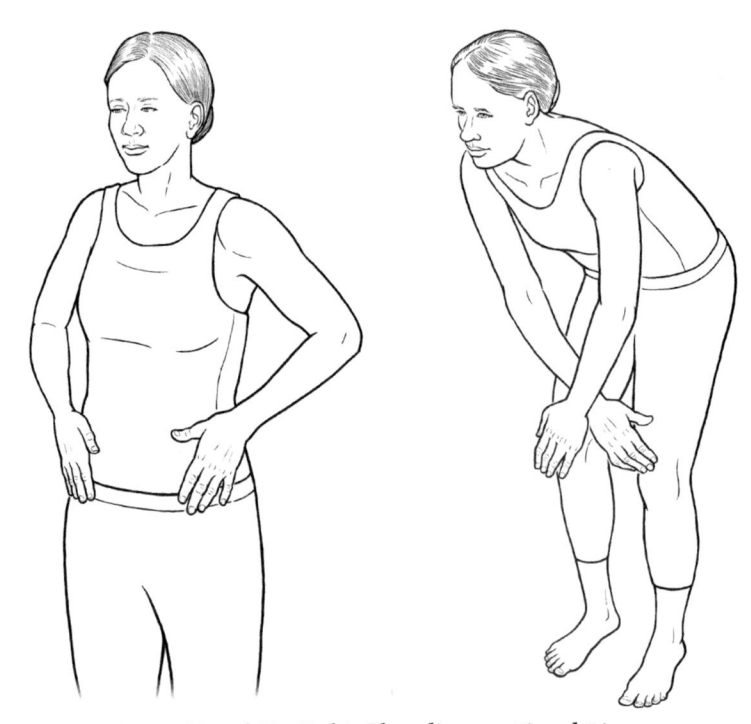

Image 58 and 59—Rakia Flow diagram #3 and #4

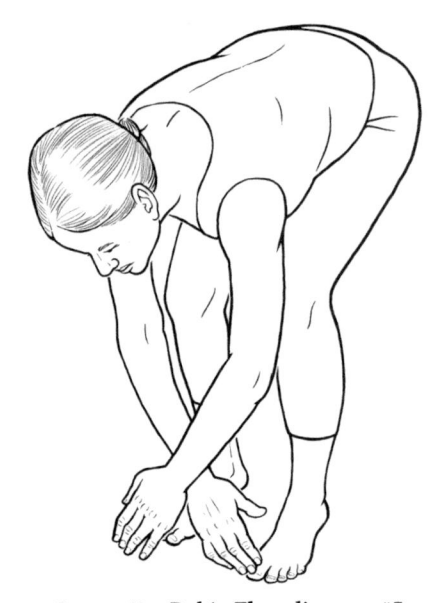

Image 60—Rakia Flow diagram #5

Visualize the clearing of the *vav* channel around the belly so that the two *yuds*, though separated, can maintain their attraction to each other and their balance. Remember the *gematria*:

א/*aleph* = 26

26 = 13 + 13 = 1. 13 = *ahava*/love.

Send love through the hands as you work with the *rakia*/belt flow.

19

Connecting Heaven and Earth

Connecting heaven and earth is a physical embodiment of the letter aleph/א. Aleph equals ONE. In the Breath of Love (aleph breath, chapter 15), love flows out from the heart through the hands. In connecting heaven and earth, the hands receive the energy from above and below and channel it to the heart creating wholeness, balance, and a reflection of the divine marriage and cosmic Oneness.

We *are* the connection between heaven and earth and this exercise is a powerful embodiment of that widely-held belief. Variations of connecting heaven and earth are found in many ancient traditions. It is part of the practice of qi gong and is even depicted in drawings from ancient Egypt. It was adapted by Donna Eden as an energy medicine exercise and is part of the daily energy routine she recommends.

Practicing connecting heaven and earth provides many positive benefits to the energy body:

It connects the life force, also called *ruach* or chi, of the yang field, heaven, to the yin life force of earth.

It grounds and centers the physical body and helps to balance heart and mind.

It helps to release unwanted emotions, flushing old energy out of the body, stimulating fresh energy to flow.

It helps move stuck energy out of the joints.

It expands the auric energy field that surrounds the body.

It activates spleen energy, which helps keep both the immune system and the blood healthy.

Connecting Heaven and Earth

The basic energy exercise

The exercise is usually done standing, but if that is not possible, please sit.

Open the energy flow

1. Breathe deeply in through the nose and out the mouth. With feet flat on the floor, place open hands on thighs. Feel your connection and grounding to the earth through the soles of the feet. Imagine energy flowing up the body.

2. Massage and stimulate the top of the head with the fingers to encourage the flow of energy through the crown.

3. Inhale, resting the hands over the heart. Exhale and feel the heart open.

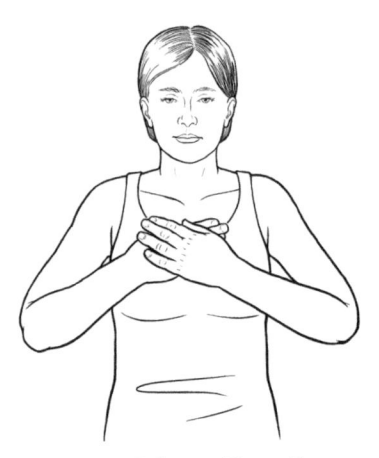

Image 61—Palms at Heart Center

4. Inhale through the nose as you stretch one arm up and the other down with flat palms.

Image 62—Stretch Arms with Palms Flat

5. Hold the breath. Look at the top hand, stretching and reaching. Imagine the energy flowing in through the top hand traveling through the heart and out the bottom hand.

6. Exhale, returning both hands to rest on the heart.

7. Repeat steps 4 through 6 on the other side.

Image 63—Right Arm Upward

8. With both hands resting over the heart, exhale through the mouth.

Optional: Repeat the exercise looking *down* this time, imagining the energy flowing up from the bottom hand, through the heart and out the top hand. Switch hands and repeat on the other side.

9. Hang over the legs and slowly roll up. Use this opportunity to surround yourself with infinity signs of love. Flip your hands over and back, drawing eights of any size throughout the auric field.

Background for Kabbalistic Visualizations

The physical practice is identical to that just described. Kabbalah adds the א symbolism.

The deconstructed letter *aleph*/א, has three components:

	Yud/י upper hand
א	Vav/ו torso(heart)
	Yud/י lower hand

Remember that the letter *y(ud)* is also the word for hand *y(ad)*. The hands represent the *y*'s of the *aleph*.

Embody the shape of the *aleph*.
The hands represent the upper and lower *yuds*.
The hand that reaches up is the upper *yud*/י .
The hand that reaches down is the lower *yud*/י .

Aleph also symbolizes the YY/י-י name of God. The top *yud*/י represents the *K"BH*. The lower *yud*/י represents the *Shechina*.

The *v(av)*/ו, meaning "connector," is represented by the heart, the center of the torso. It separates the *K"BH* and *Shechina*, but is also the space where they come together.

Inhale

The top hand Y/י stretches up up to heaven, receives and draws the divine light of the *K"BH* down. The bottom hand Y/י stretches to Earth, receives and brings up the light of the *Shechina*.

Connecting Heaven and Earth 163

Exhale

Rest the hands at the heart, the *vav*. Allow the heart to receive this balance of heaven and earth deeply. There in the heart, Y meets Y, and two opposite divine forces, facilitated by the boundary created by the *vav*, mix and dance. The three components of the *aleph* reunite. Like the *aleph*, they are ONE. The Oneness radiates from the heart creating balance and wholeness throughout the body. Send this light to every cell of the body, illuminating and healing areas of darkness.

Because connecting heaven and earth overlaid with *aleph* is an embodiment of divine marriage, it is a form of physical blessing. The union of Earth/*Shechina* with Heaven/*KB"H* is the mystical intention of *Shabbat* and of all Jewish blessings. Blessing is a conscious gratitude, a connecting of heaven and earth possible in every moment. Consciously reciting or embodying a blessing, being present in the moment to do so, is an act of *tikun olam*, repair of the world. Repair of the world begins with restoring balance in ourselves and this exercise is a powerful step in that direction.

Variation: The Doors of the Heart

The word for hand, *yad*/יד, is made up of the same two letters as the letter *yud*/יד: Y/י/*yud* and D/ד/*dalet*.

YD = YD   יד = יד

The letters hold the energy and essence of the thing.

Y/י is symbolic of the divine spark and

D/ד/*dalet* means a "door." [71]

So in essence, hands are the doors to divine sparks.

....

[71] YHVH, the sacred four-letter Name, is also referred to as Dalet/ד because the *gematria* of ד is four.

Remember that the hands are extensions of heart energy.

As you stretch out your arms in the exercises, imagine that the word YD/יד extends from the spark/Y of the hand, to the door/D of the heart.

The *yuds,* the divine sparks in your hands, connect to the *dalets,* the doors, in your heart. At the end of Connecting Heaven and Earth, when the hands rest over the heart, breathe deeply, and imagine the divine sparks you have just gathered flowing from the hands through the doors of your heart. There, the light of the sparks illuminates your inner being and when the doors open outward the divine sparks you have gathered radiate out to light the world.

20

Sh'ma and the Kabbalistic Hook-In

The addition of radiant circuit energy to the *Sh'ma* prayer creates a visceral feeling of connection to both the infinite and finite that centers in the heart.

> *It is significant that the Torah presents man and woman together as comprising the image of the Divine (Genesis 1:27). This clearly implies that male and female together form the image of God.*[72]
> —Rabbi Aryeh Kaplan

Many cultures and religions embrace the ideal of universal Oneness. In Judaism, the *Sh'ma* prayer is the declaration of unity and **the** statement of faith. Its six words are the first prayer children are taught. It is to be recited privately and in public prayer services each morning and night. Its words are traditionally the last to be recited on the deathbed. Many Jewish martyrs including the great kabbalist Rabbi Akiba have died sanctifying God with the *Sh'ma* on their lips.

There are many interpretations of the Hebrew:

שְׁמַע יִשְׂרָאֵל יהוה אלֹ‌ֵהינוּ יהוה אֶחָד
Sh'ma Yisrael Adonai Eloheinu Adonai Echad.

---

72 Rabbi Aryeh Kaplan, *Innerspace*, 67.

The widely used prayerbook translation of the *Sh'ma* is:

Hear O Israel, the Lord our God (*Adonai Eloheinu*), the Lord (*Adonai*) is ONE.

(Remember that when YHVH appears in prayer, it is pronounced *Adonai*.)

In chapter 8, "The Unpronounceable Name," the symbolism of YHVH as the transcendent and unknowable Name was presented. *Eloheinu* means our *Elohim*. Because *Elohim* is the only Name of God appearing in the Genesis creation story, and the *gematria* of *Elohim* is the same as "the nature," the name *Elohim* and its variation YHVH *Elohim*, associate with creation, the feminine, the *Shechina* and multiplicity.

In *The Secret Doctrine of the Kabbalah*, the late scholar, Leonora Leet states:

The esoteric meaning of the Sh'ma appearing most prominently in the Zohar and consistently repeated throughout the later history of the Kabbalah it that it affirms not a simple divine unity but a divine unification, Yichud, one involving a femininely conceived God who is immanent in multiplicity, YHVH Elohim, and a masculinely conceived transcendent God beyond all qualification, YHVH. The Zohar (2:216a) expresses this most simply in the statement: "This is the mystery of Hear O Israel, God is our Lord. God is One." The mystery is that the two are united as one.

This meaning is more clearly conveyed through the following translation of the Sh'ma:

Hear: [O] Israel,
YHVH *Eloheinu* [and] YHVH [are] ONE. [73]

A shorthand for this idea is found in the letter *aleph*. *Aleph*/one, holds within it the unification of the divine masculine (upper *yud*) with the divine feminine (lower *yud*). Together the three components of the *aleph*, *yud*/*vav*/*yud* add to *gematria* twenty-six, the same as YHVH. (See the end of chapter 10, "Aleph/א Redux.")

---

73 Leonora Leet, *The Secret Doctrine of Kabbalah*, 69.

I was pondering this concept in services one Sabbath morning and became very curious about the *Sh'ma*. I started counting the letters of the prayer. Would there be twenty-six? Well, no. There are twenty-five letters in the *Sh'ma*, not 26. *But if you count the letters from either end, the thirteenth letter, the one in the middle is the letter aleph. Aleph* is ONE, the symbol of unification. *Aleph* as *gematria* is twenty-six, divisible into 13 + 13.

13 = LOVE/אהבה/*Ahava*

שְׁמַע יִשְׂרָאֵל יהוה אֱלֹהֵינוּ יהוה אֶחָד

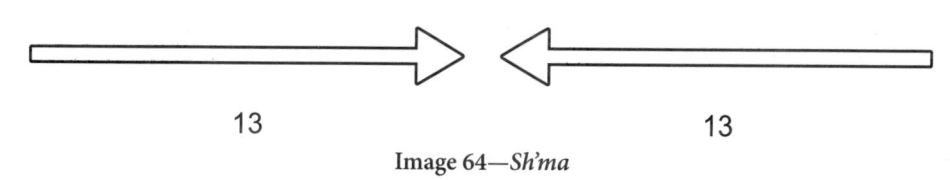

⟶   ⟵

13   13

Image 64—Sh'ma

In either direction 13 + 13 is created by the letter *aleph*, ONE!
The letters of the *Sh'ma* create an infinity sign of LOVE! [74]

Energy and the Sh'ma

The hook-in exercise, based on Eden Energy's Hook-up, connects the most fundamental masculine and feminine aspects of ourselves, the central and governing meridians. Because these channels are radiant circuits, coming directly from the level of the soul and divine light, this exercise can act as a beautiful physical accompaniment to the *Sh'ma*, the most revered declaration of Oneness.

---

74   The words of the *Sh'ma* and the paragraph that follows it in the prayer service are found in Deuteronomy 6:4–9. That the *Sh'ma* is a declaration of LOVE is found in its placement in the service. The prayer immediately preceding the *Sh'ma* begins with the word *ahava*/love and ends with a blessing for love. The first word of the paragraph immediately following the *Sh'ma*'s declaration of Oneness is *V'Ahavta*, you shall love, and centers that love in the heart (6:6).

The *Sh'ma* is a statement of divine unity, affirming that the *K"BH* (YHVH) and *Shechina* (YHVH *Eloheinu*) are ONE. Leet goes on to state that we are One with the divine unity. All is ONE.

In our lives, we become "ONE" at the moment of conception. The fertilized egg, the zygote, is a single cell that downloads life force to spark further development. To this end, two special energies of light assist the entrance of the soul: the central (conception) vessel and the governing vessel. These two "sparks" will create the energy fields for masculine (yang) and feminine (yin) to differentiate. As the zygote begins the process of division, a front and back form. The front of the body becomes the feminine, soft belly of yin. The back becomes the masculine yang, reflecting the dynamic power of the spine and spinal cord.

In our fully-formed bodies, the yin central vessel runs straight up the center of the belly from the perineum to the back of the throat. Some say it connects directly into the earth. On its journey up the front of the body, the central meridian runs directly through chakras including the heart.

Its yang counterpart, the governing vessel, begins at the tailbone. It rises up the spine, traveling up over the head, over the crown chakra and down to the upper lip. It meets the central meridian at the back of the throat. These two channels connect to create the dynamic microcosmic orbit that circles the body. This circuit sends energy to all the meridians, the radiant circuits, and even beyond, as it enlivens the aura surrounding the body.

Keeping masculine and feminine energies in harmony grounds and stabilizes the whole energy body, and the balance enhances feelings of connection to oneself and others. When we are deep in meditation, prayer, or joy these channels connect to each other and to the other energies of light. As the radiant circuits fill the body with their light, we feel expansive, totally connected, both to ourselves and to the universe. We are truly lit up.

When you are "in the zone," the central and governing channels create a tunnel of light that surrounds and encloses the physical body, connecting up into the cosmos and down into the earth. The hook-in reminds these radiant energies that they were once a unified part of source light.

The Energy Exercise

Place the middle finger of one hand in the navel and rest the other middle finger at the third eye (the space between the eyebrows). Gently press the fingers in and up. Breathe slowly in through the nose and out the mouth three or four times. You may feel the energies connect, possibly with an accompanying yawn or sigh.

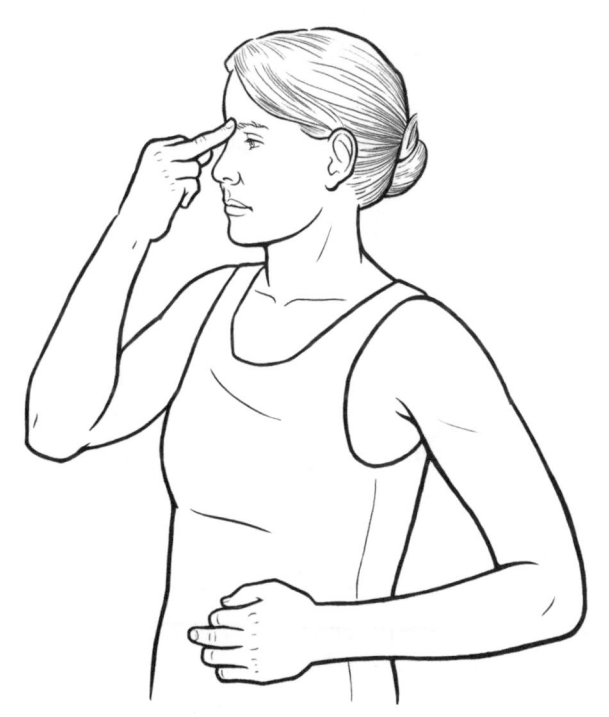

Image 65—Energy Exercise

Kabbalistic Visualization

The *Sh'ma*, as it is written, can be envisioned as the infinity sign of love and oneness for there are thirteen (representing *ahava*, love) letters, including the *aleph*/א, when counted from from both directions.

שְׁמַע יִשְׂרָאֵל יהוה אֱלֹהֵינוּ יהוה אֶחָד

1. Close your eyes and direct the vision inward. The third eye here represents the *sefira* of *Da'at*. *Da'at* is the channel between mind and heart, and holds the balance of all opposites. The navel is where we are connected to our ancestors and the wisdom of the ages.

2. Press your fingers in and up at *Da'at* and at the navel and imagine that these two points are the centers of each side of an infinity sign of love (13 + 13 = 26 = 1). The two sides connect at an *aleph*/א which lies over the heart.

3. As you Hook-In recite the *Sh'ma*, or an alternative personal affirmation of Oneness. Breathe deeply in through the nose and out the mouth.

4. Continue hooking-in as you slowly recite the words. Visualize the infinity sign of love/Oneness you are creating. One side extends up from the earth and the other down from heaven, meeting in your heart. The microcosmic orbit of light, your original state of oneness, is turned on as cosmic Oneness. Heaven/*KB"H* and Earth/*Shechina* connect to each other and to your essence, your heart.

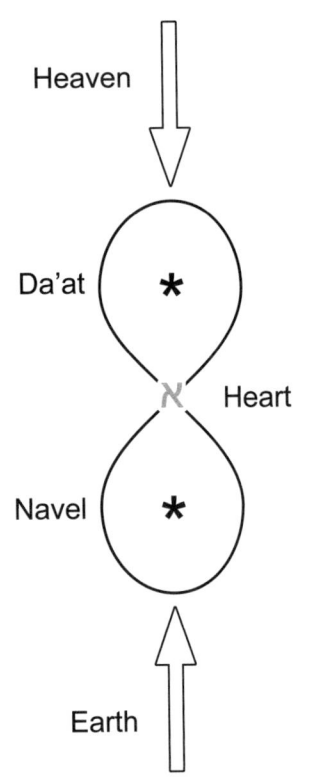

Image 66—Sh'ma Hook-In

Baruch Shem

It is traditional to whisper the six-word *Baruch Shem* prayer after saying the *Sh'ma* or a Holy name, such as the forty-two-letter Name in *Ana B'Koach* (chapter 24). The six words of the *Sh'ma* reflect the ultimate unity of Heaven and the *Baruch Shem* reflects them back from the multiplicity that is Earth. The words contain the reassurance that, although Oneness is the ultimate goal, we were created to celebrate the gifts of our individuality. As in the Tree, the word *Malchut* in the *Baruch Shem* can be interpreted as the physical world of creation.

The radiant circuit called the bridge flow connects body and spirit, individuality to unity. It is activated by drawing three hearts around the heart, symbolizing mind, body, and spirit. As you whisper the six-word *Baruch Shem* prayer, draw three hearts around the heart, imagining sparkling light coming out of your hands.

בָּרוּךְ שֵׁם כְּבוֹד מַלְכוּתוֹ לְעוֹלָם וָעֶד
Baruch Shem K'vod Malchuto L'olam VaEd.
Blessed is the Name of the Holy One.
Malchut is Forever.

Do not be surprised if you experience a visceral power surge.

Healing

I am grateful to Reb Rachmiel Drizin for teaching me this healing after I incurred the strange traumatic injury to my neck at the start of my journey many years ago. I have added the energy component to the power of the words.

Refer back to Leet's translation of the *Sh'ma*, which proclaims the unity of the Creation (us), YHVH *Eloheinu*, with the Creator YHVH:

"YHVH *Eloheinu* [and] YHVH [are] ONE."

Repeat the three words of unification:

Adonai Eloheinu Adonai   יהוה אֱלֹהֵינוּ יהוה

At the same time, either: trace infinity signs flipping the hands over and back, over the affected body part(s), encouraging them back to a state of wholeness at every level; or trace the three hearts of the bridge flow, as described above, over the affected area, connecting it to the intertwined light of body, mind, and spirit.

21

A Physical Practice of *Devekut*

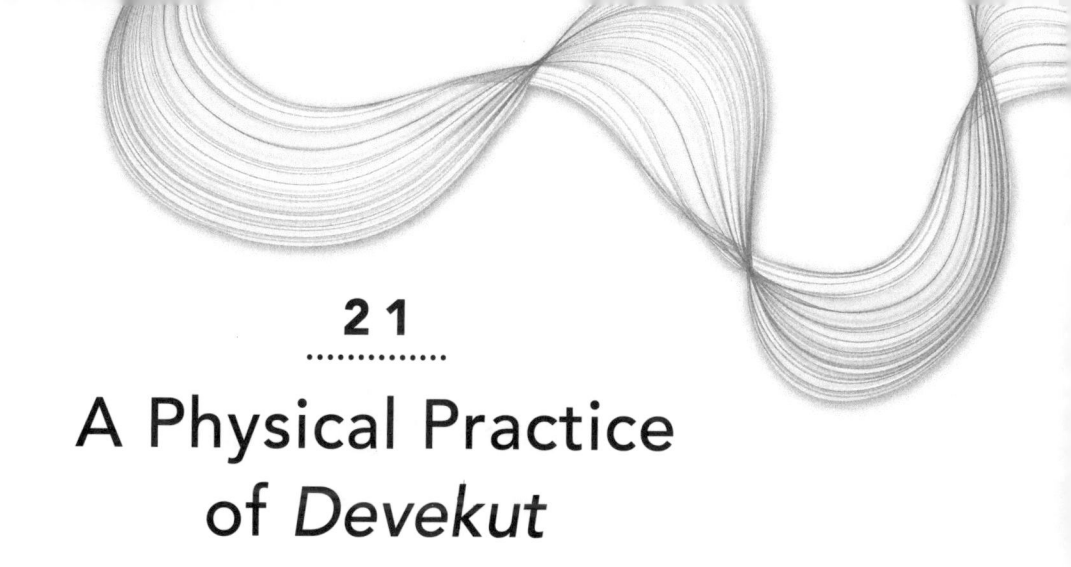

This practice provides a way to feel connected to God by embodying the letters of the tetragrammaton in a yoga-like flow. If standing is not possible, the letter shapes can also be made sitting or lying on the back. Please modify according to your physical limitations.

The physical body is the home of the divine presence, the *Shechina*. Recognizing and nurturing this God-spark in ourselves and others strengthens the "vessel" of our Tree and the more en"light"ened we become. *Devekut*, cleaving to God, was practiced by the Ari and his group for this purpose.

Their practice of *devekut* was entirely mental, consisting of specific meditations and prayers. Chaim Vital, in *Sha'arei Kedusha*, The Gates of Holiness, details this practice, based on teachings of the Ari and others. In one form of *devekut*, intense focus over long, long periods of time on the name YHVH/י-הוה was intended to bring the kabbalist closer to the "light", to the higher vibration of Source. Sometimes, other divine names would be visualized as woven between the letters of YHVH/י-הוה. Meditation on these Name combinations was a practice called unifications, or *yichudim*.

The following is a physical practice for creating *devekut*.

Although the Name cannot be pronounced, It can be embodied through assuming the shapes of the letters of the Name י-הוה, something like yoga poses. The mind and physical body work together with the breath. In the process we weave the self to both heaven and earth, the spiritual and the physical.

As you assume each pose, visualize the letter you are creating. Try to inhale through the bottoms of the feet and top of the head at the same time (Breath of Love, chapter 15). Exhale love through the heart. This practice also takes into account the masculine/feminine balance of the Name as seen in the Tree, specifically in the *Partzufim*.

Y	H	V	H
father	mother	son	daughter
י	ה	ו	י

Father

Inhale

י

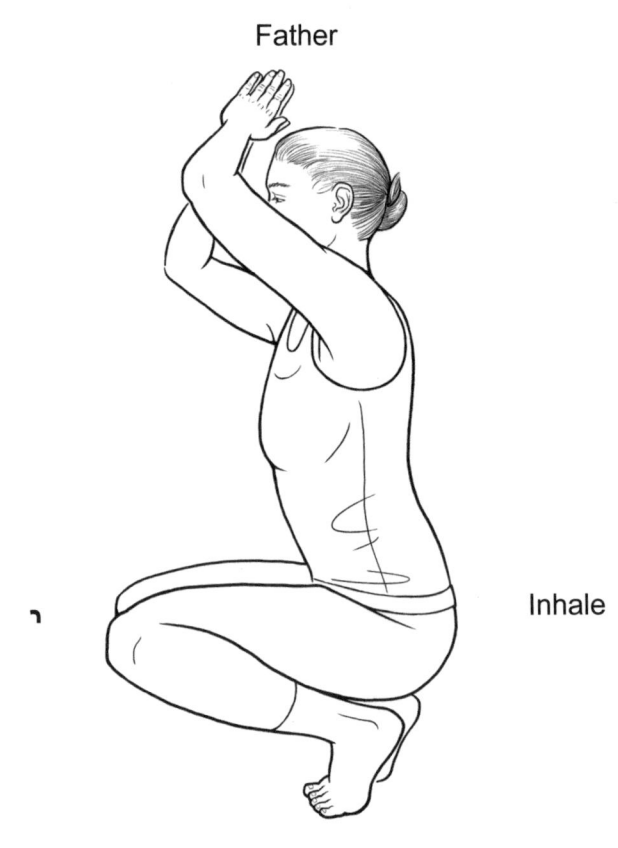

Image 67—Father Inhale

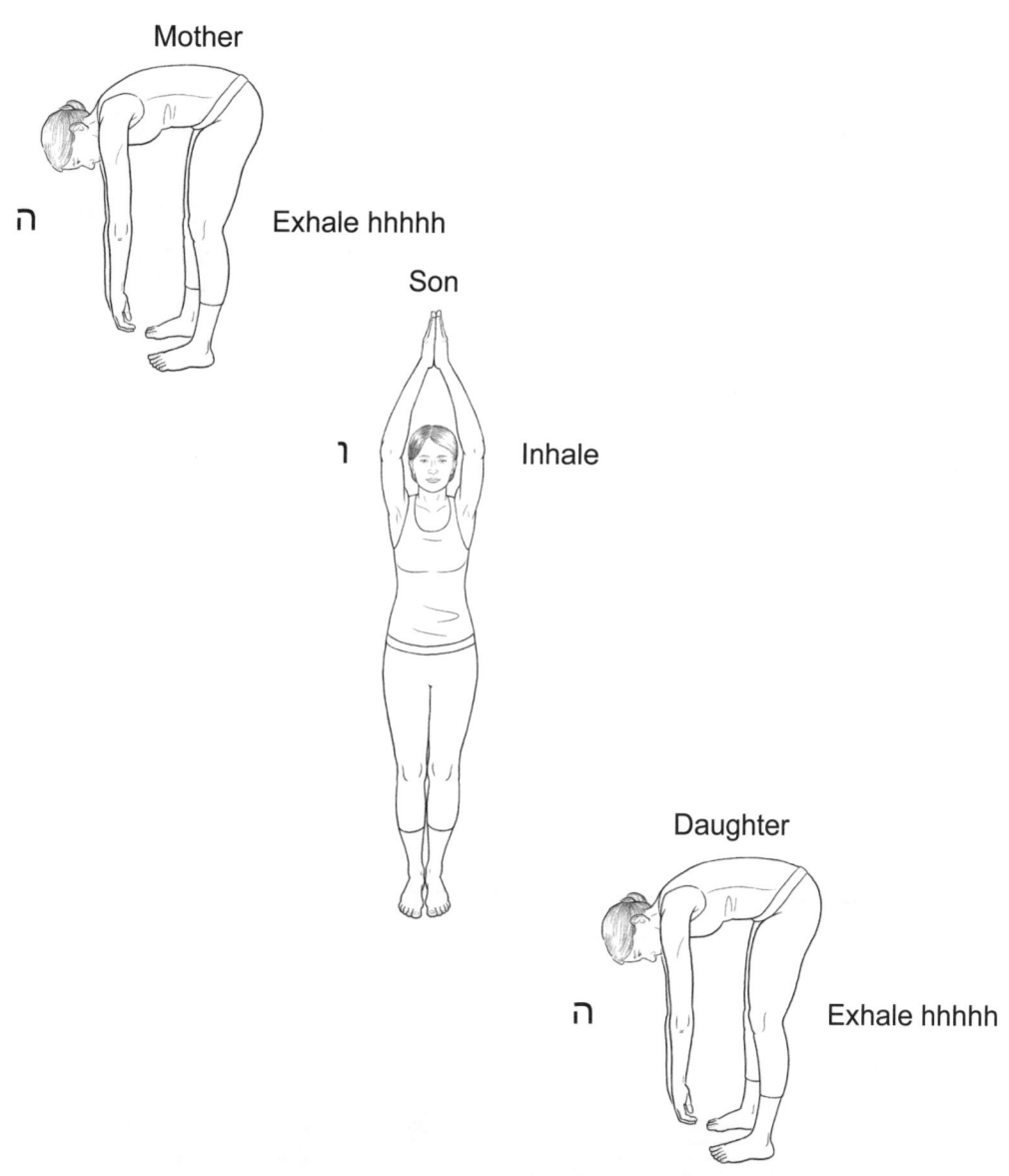

Image 68—Mother Exhale hhhhh, Son Inhale, Daughter Exhale hhhhh

The Y/י and V/ו represent the masculine letters: these postures require effort. Inhale as you bend the knees deeply into the *yud*/י shape, raising the arms. Inhale as you reach the arms up in the *vav*/ו shape, connecting to heaven. The H/ה and H/ה represent the

A Physical Practice of *Devekut* 177

feminine letters. Let your head be heavy, relax into the poses, and hear the sound of the *heil* ... ה ... HHHHH ... in the exhaled breath.

As you move through the letters of the Name, the transitions between the letters can be of your choosing.

It is said that the Torah was written with black fire on white fire. The black fire represents the letters of the Torah. The white fire is the parchment that provides the background space so the letters can be seen. The letters of this practice are the black fire. The transitions as you move between the letters are the white fire. You create the white fire in the moment. It is Presence. It represents the journey unique to each of us.

In the spaces, the white fire, you can insert a symbolic posture, a full breath, personalize the movement in the moment, or practice as a continuous flow.

Further Practice

One form of the practice of unifications called *yichudim*, consisted of weaving the YHVH Name with other Names of God and meditating on them. You can adapt this practice by weaving your own Name, in Hebrew or English, between the letters of YHVH. Create appropriate body shapes that are comfortable for you. Here is an example: weaving my name Devi דוי in between the letters of YHVH: Y-D-H-E-V-V-H-I.

י -ה-ו-ו –ה- ד י

You can also weave an intention into the Name such as love, hope, or gratitude in Hebrew or English. For example: YHVH+ love/*ahava*/אהבה, or YHVH+ gratitude/*todah*/תודה.

A good source of information on letter shapes is *Aleph-Bet Yoga: Embodying the Hebrew Letters for Physical and Spiritual Well-Being* by Stephen A. Rapp and Tamar Frankiel.

22

Infinity Eyes: Connecting to a Higher Knowing

Image 69—Infinity Eyes

Open my eyes so I may behold גַּל עֵינַי וְאַבִּיטָה[75]

This practice makes use of the poetry of *midrash*, traditional interpretations of the Torah. The images invoked are symbolic yet personal. Energy techniques and kabbalistic visualizations unify the letters of the Name. The light created by the unification can then illuminate inward to the self and outward as far as the imagination allows. Be sure to stay grounded whenever you practice.

---

75   Psalm 119.

Kabbalistic Background

In the Tree of Life, the *Partzufim* of *Abba* and *Ema*—the Father and Mother—are responsible for the passage of ideas into consciousness.[76] In the imagery of Kabbalah, a spark, the seed of an idea, is transmitted from *Abba* to *Ema*. *Ema* becomes "pregnant" with the spark which can then be birthed down the Tree into the physical world of manifestation.

If placed on the body of *Adam Kadmon*, the original enlightened human, these archetypes represent the right and left brain. *Abba* and *Ema* are also represented by the first two letters of the Name, YHVH/י-הוה.

Abba is represented by the *Yud*/י
   and
Ema by the first *Hei*/ה

Abba and *Ema* are always together, and they can be visualized as connecting back-to-back or face-to-face. Back-to-back is a superficial union requiring no effort, although a union nonetheless. Our everyday thoughts and ideas are brought into manifestation through the back-to-back relationship. The face-to-face union on the other hand, is a deep, intimate, intertwined marriage that, according to Kabbalah, brings in the lights of higher consciousness.

As previously discussed, the Israelites carried the Ten Commandments with them in a portable sanctuary, the *Mishkan*, throughout their desert journey. Inside the *Mishkan*, the Ten Commandments were secured in the Ark of the Covenant. The Ark was guarded by the images of two golden cherubs said to have been entwined face-to-face in a loving embrace.[77] In the Book of Numbers (7:89) it is written that God's voice, the di-

---

76   The *sefirot* of *Chochma* and *Bina*, make up the *Partzufim* of *Abba* and *Ema*. See chapter 4.

77   Although there are many interpretations as to the appearance of cherubs, the sages of the Talmud state that the cherubs of the Ark had the faces of children (*Chagiga* 13b, *Sukah* 5ab). The symbolism of love comes from the Talmudic writings of Rav Katina in B. *Yoma* 74. Rav Katina wrote that when the Israelites would come to the Temple, they would see the cherubs intertwined with each other. They were told "Behold, the love of you before God is like the love between man and woman."

vine presence of the *Shechina*, emanated from between the cherubs. When the ancient Temple in Jerusalem was built by King Solomon, the Ark was transferred to the Holy of Holies. According to *midrash,* the embracing cherubs remained there guarding the Ark until the Temple was destroyed. When the *Shechina* went into exile with the conquered Jews, the cherubs no longer faced each other. Instead, they sat back-to-back, awaiting Her return.

According to the Torah, humans were created in the image of God. Like the *Mishkan*, our bodies are sanctuaries, personal dwelling places for the divine presence. Often we lose sight of our divine inner light, the presence of the *Shechina* in ourselves and others. One way to reconnect to the divine presence is to visualize the marriage of *Abba* and *Ema*, opposites forming a unity. The symbolic marriage *of Abba and Ema* creates a sacred space for the cherubs to reunite in face-to-face embrace. When the cherubs reunite in our personal *Mishkan*, the light of higher consciousness can flow from between them.

This idea is symbolized by *Abba* and *Ema as* first two letters of YHVH.

יה

The process of reuniting the cherubs involves a deep archetypal healing of the Mother/*hei*/ה with the Father/*yud*/י. According to legend, when the *Shechina* returns, the first *hei*/ה, the Mother/*Ema*, will turn to face the *yud*/י, the Father/*Abba*. The י will fill in the open space in the ה creating the letter *chet*/ח, representing a *chuppah*, wedding canopy.

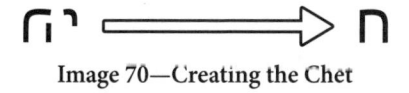

הי ⟹ ח

Image 70—Creating the Chet

The cherubs then reunite in this sacred space, under the *chuppah* created by the face-to-face union of *Abba* and *Ema*. The *chuppa,* in this practice, rests at the third eye, which here represents the "quasi *sefira*" of *Da'at*, literally "knowing."

Da'at

Da'at lies between *Abba* on the right and *Ema* on the left in the central column of the Tree, directly below *Keter*. *Keter*, the crown, is the most direct link to the infinite light of Source. This level is unfathomable to us. Whatever light is revealed to us is channeled through *Da'at*.[78] *Da'at* is the *sefira* of transformation. *Da'at* is not only the link between *Abba* and *Ema*, the higher masculine and feminine archetypes, but also contains the full complement of the masculine and feminine forces of the Tree within it. It has the potential to hold, balance, and integrate the tension of all opposites and paradoxes, as symbolized here by the infinity sign. The verb form of *da'at* "to know," *la'da'at*, is used in the Torah to describe intimate sexual relationships. The masculine/feminine unifications envisioned by this practice are total and equal: metaphorically face to face, aligned from head to toe. According to the Zohar, such unions create the highest possibility of *tikun olam*, repair of the world through the light of higher consciousness. *Da'at* is the doorway to this light.

Da'at also creates the path of connection between mind and heart. Most of us are *Da'at* challenged in the sense that we live mainly in our heads rather than our hearts. Part of this practice is an opening and healing of *Da'at*, creating a clear path for *Ruach Hakodesh*, divine inspiration, to enter our hearts and provide clarity for our lives.

Infinity Eyes as *Devekut*

Devekut, cleaving to the Name to bring in *Ruach Hakodesh,* was a well-known kabbalistic practice (introduced in Chapter 21). The thirteenth-century kabbalist, Isaac of Acco, wrote that the secret to *devekut* was to cleave to God not just with the mind but with the body as well. To this end he advised seeing the Name over the eyes. Infinity Eyes is this form of *devekut*: the Name YHVH/י-הוה is visualized as infinity signs, horizontal eights, drawn around the eyes.[79]

---

78 There are two aspects of *Da'at*—the lower form, *Da'at Tachton*, connects the mind and heart. The higher form, *Da'at Elyon*, balances the left and right hemispheres of the brain.

79 Remember that the letter ח, standing for *chuppa*, is also the number eight and the shape of the infinity sign.

In Summary

Imagine that you, like the *Mishkan* of old, have cherubs guarding the sanctuary of your body and soul. When the union of *Abba* and *Ema* creates the *chuppa* at *Da'at*, your personal cherubs reunite under it in a face-to-face embrace. From between them flows the letters of the most sacred Name YHVH. The four letters entwine, creating frames of golden spectacles, a *devekut* of divine light with which to view inward to the self and outward as far as the imagination allows. This is an act of self-healing, and a *tikun* that can impact repair of the world.

Energy Background

In order for the energy body to function with maximum vitality, energies need to be communicating and connected in a balanced way. Figure eights/infinity signs serve to both connect and balance energies. Tracing eights over the energy body in any direction encourages the body's innate healing wisdom at every level. The more infinity patterns there are in the energy field, the greater the power of the life force energy.

The foundational energy practice presented here is called "eighting the eyes." It brings balance to the energy body in several ways.

1. Slowly circling the eyes in horizontal figure eight/infinity sign patterns creates long-lasting connections between all the body's energies. Eighting the eyes can replace the repatterning exercise called the homolateral cross-crawl [80] which may be physically challenging or even ineffective in certain people.

2. Eighting the eyes can help to reverse brain scramble, improve focus, and balance the right and left hemispheres of the brain.[81]

3. Eighting the eyes is part of a daily energy routine to strengthen the eyesight.

---

80 Described in Donna Eden's book, *Energy Medicine*.

81 Similar to Wayne Cook Posture and Cook's Hook-Up described in Donna Eden's book *Energy Medicine*. This is an observation from my work with clients.

How

Use the left index finger to slowly trace large horizontal eights, infinity patterns, around the eyes. It may be helpful to imagine that you are drawing the frames of very large glasses. Keep the eyes closed throughout. Remember to breathe deeply and slowly. Repeat six to eight times or more. There is no need to reverse direction. When you feel comfortable with the physical movements continue to the kabbalistic visualizations.

Kabbalistic Symbolism and Visualization

Unification, also called *Yichud*/Oneness, is the spiritual essence of *Da'at*. Because *Da'at* has the capacity to bear the tension of opposites, it acts as the center of the infinity sign, between *Abba* and *Ema* at the third eye.

The unification of the letters of YHVH takes place in two steps. First the V and H, representing Heaven and Earth, come together at the heart. They form the foundation for the union of Y and H, *Abba* and *Ema*. The marriage of *Abba* and *Ema* creates the *chuppa* at *Da'at* under which the cherubs embrace. There, at the third eye, the four letters of the Name emerge in golden light from between the cherubs.

Unification of the Letters of the Name

1. Heaven and Earth: *Vav*/ו with *Hei*/ה

    YH<u>VH</u>/וה-י

    in the name YHVH:

    In Kabbalah, these letters of the Name can be symbolized in several other ways:

- Soul and Body

- K"BH and *Shechina,*

- Z"A and *NOK,*

- 6 masculine + 7 feminine = 13/*ahava*/love.

Choose a pair of symbols that resonates with you. In the practice, visualize those symbols coming together, balancing, dancing, and filling the heart.

2. *Yud*/י and *hei*/ה/*Abba* and *Ema*/<u>YHVH</u>/יהוה

    In this special coupling the *h(ei)*/ה of *Ema* turns to face the *y(ud)*/י of *Abba*. Together as equals, face to face, they form the letter *chet*/ח and create a golden *chuppa* at *Da'at*.

    Visualize this golden *chuppa* between your eyebrows.

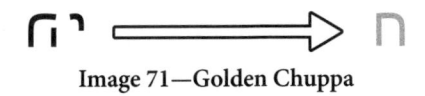

Image 71—Golden Chuppa

- The hands connect the four letters of the Name at *Da'at*:
  Y/י and H/ה from the third eye
  and
  V/ו and H/ה from the heart.

- Surrounded by the harmonious unification of the letters, the cherubs of your personal *Mishkan* are called to reunite under the *chuppa*. In the intimacy of *Da'at*, a higher knowing, they turn to face each other once again in a heart-to-heart, loving and equal embrace.

- The golden letters of the name YHVH/הוה -י flow out from between the cherubs.

- As you trace big eights around the eyes, the four letters, י-ה-ו-ה, dance and intertwine in the path, creating dynamic golden YHVH spectacles. Your eyes are framed by moving letters of the Name.

- Stop at this point and experience the sensations. When you are ready, continue with one or more of the suggested meditations.

The Kabbalah/Energy Practice

First Union: Heaven and Earth/V and H

1. Grounding to the Earth

Place both hands over the heart and take several deep breaths. Imagine the bottoms of the feet opening to receive the nurturing energy of Earth, *Malchut/Shechina*.[82] Feel this grounding energy rise easily up the legs and belly. Let the energy open any places that are blocked as it flows up the body and fills the heart. During the rest of the practice, periodically reconnect with this stabilizing flow.[83]

2. Connecting to Heaven: Heaven Rushing In

Inhale deeply. Maintain connection with the flow of earth energy. Open your arms wide, extending them overhead. Imagine divine radiance entering your head, fingers, and hands. It may help to imagine this radiance as beautiful feelings such as gratitude, hope, faith, compassion, joy, etc. Your hands may start to tingle or get warm. When you are ready, gather this energy from above and bring it into the heart to meet the earth energy.[84]

Visualize the symbols you chose balancing, dancing, and filling the heart. Maintain awareness of their unification in your heart and when you feel ready, continue.

3. Second Union: *Ema* and *Abba*/Y and H

---

82 For a grounding review, see chapter 14.

83 If you would like to add conscious breathing, inhale from earth (*Malchut*) and heaven (*Keter*), simultaneously. Exhale through *Da'at* at the third eye as the letters are released. The inhale is similar to *aleph* breath.

84 There is an energy vortex at the heart called "heaven rushing in" waiting to receive this beautiful gift of infinite love and connection.

Image 72—Palms on Temples

Place the palms gently on the temples as the fingers lie flat over the right and left side of the head. Inhale and exhale normally but consciously.

Image 73—Smooth Behind the Ears

With your fingers, smooth slowly behind the ears several times, from the temple to the jaw. With respect and gratitude, invite the Mother/*Ema* and Father/*Abba* aspects of your higher self to the practice. For example, *Ema* may embody such qualities as softness, gentleness, self-acceptance and nurturing. *Abba* may embody strength in a protective embrace.

Return your palms to the side of the head as before. As you hold your fingers there, visualize the *hei*/ה of *Ema* turning to face the *yud*/י of *Abba*.

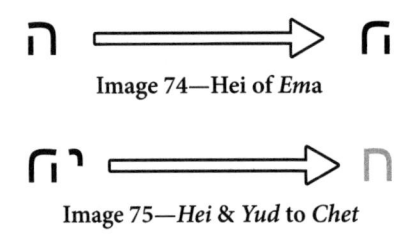

ה ⟹ ה

Image 74—Hei of *Ema*

הי ⟹ ח

Image 75—*Hei* & *Yud* to *Chet*

See the creation of a letter *chet*/ח by the alignment of *Ema* and *Abba* in a total face-to-face connection. Take several deep breaths in through the nose and out the mouth. Visualize the *chet*/ח slowly turning gold. The ח sits right over the third eye, between the eyebrows, at *Da'at*. Rest the left middle finger on *Da'at*/the union of Y and H/יה, and the right hand on the heart/the union of V and H/וה.

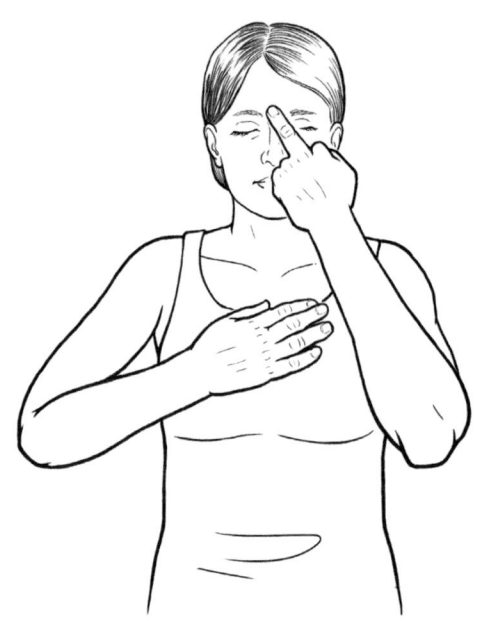

Image 76—Fingers at Third Eye and Heart

Visualize the connection of all the letters of the Name through the connection of mind and heart.

Invite the cherubs to enter the golden *chuppa*. See them there in *Da'at*, entwined once more in loving embrace. The powerful love[85] generated by their reunion can be visualized as the unified name YHVH/הוה -י emanating from beneath the *chuppa*.

Accessing the Flow of Light

Start and end with the left index finger in *Da'at* at the third eye and the right hand over the heart. Close the eyes. Imagine the letters of the Name ה -ו- ה- י emanating through the *chuppah* in a stream of golden light. With the left index finger trace infinity loops of this golden light around the eyes. Imagine the letters intertwining, joyfully weaving around and through each other as you trace their path of light.

The letters continue to pour out as you trace. The golden light grows stronger and stronger as you add more layers of letters. The letters frame the eyes and illuminate the vision with a higher consciousness.

If desired, continue with one or more of the following.

Meditation 1: Looking Inward

Place the left hand on the forehead over *Da'at* and the right hand over the heart.

The entwined golden letters ה -ו- ה- י continue to circle the eyes. With your eyes framed by the letters, focus your vision into the body through the portal of *Da'at*. See your deepest self illuminated by the divine light that projects inward. Your inner vision may take you to a place of shadow, a dark place that longs to be brought into awareness. Use the light and power of the Name to heal this place by revealing what is concealed and then freeing the sparks of insight hidden there. When you have finished, journal if desired.

---

85   Recall the *gematria* of *ahava*/love = 13. Two cherubs = love + love = 13 + 13 = 26. The *gematria* of YHVH is 26. The letters of YHVH flow from between the cherubs.

Meditation 2: Higher Guidance

Place the left hand on the forehead over *Da'at* and the right hand over the heart.

This meditation can also be used to make difficult choices from a level of higher consciousness. Hold your question under the *chuppa*. The golden light of the letters emanating from *Da'at* can open a channel to divinely-inspired inner knowing. Set an intention to being guided at the highest levels.

Receive the answers with confidence.

Meditation 3: The Shiviti Spectacles of Equanimity

It is a practice, especially in the Sephardic tradition to embody the words of King David (Psalms 6:8):

שִׁוִּיתִי ה' לְנֶגְדִּי תָמִיד

Shiviti Hashem l'negdi Tamid.
I have placed God before me always.

Plaques inscribed with this verse, called *shivitis* (shee vee tees) for short, are used as a reminder of this intention.

The Ba'al Shem Tov, founder of the Chassidic movement, interpreted this verse to mean:

I have equanimity: YHVH is before me always.

Equanimity is the attribute of mental calmness, composure, and evenness of temper, especially in challenging situations. Equanimity, according to Chaim Vital in *Shaa'rei Kedusha, The Gates of Holiness,* is necessary in order to attain the influx of divine light, the enlightenment of *Ruach Hakodesh*.

Use the visualization of the intertwined letters: י-הוה as *shiviti* spectacles. As you imagine the letters actively surrounding the eyes, experience their impact when your eyes are open. Practice seeing the Name before you like a visual mantra of equanimity. In everyday life, there are many opportunities to use the *shiviti* spectacles. The golden letters will surround anyone and anything you project them onto. They are a constant reminder of God's omnipresence.

Meditation 4: Surrounded by the Love of YHVH

Continue to trace large eights of the intertwined golden letters around the eyes. As the letters flow from between the cherubs, they spill forth and begin to surround the head and then the whole body. With both hands, continue spreading and intertwining the letters by tracing golden infinity signs of any size in any direction all around the body. The eights fill the aura, spiraling and dancing. Feel yourself surrounded by the golden light of YHVH/י-הוה in the form of infinity signs of love and oneness. You are safe and protected. Take a few moments to experience the sensations. This visualization can also be added to the aura boundary protection exercise (KAP) presented in Chapter 17. Stay grounded. Offer thanks.

Meditation 5: Expanding the Vision

Seeing through the Divine Name can transform both your internal life and external reality.

The entwined eights of YHVH/י-הוה continue to generate from between the cherubs under the *chuppa*. As the letters frame the eyes they begin to spill forth. They fill the aura as in Meditation 4 and extend out beyond it. The eights connect to the eights of others creating a web of balance and harmony. The ancient flower of life symbol (see page 77) is a helpful way to visualize the interconnection of all beings. Because the eights are made of the Name YHVH, each eight has a gematria of twenty-six. Each segment of the infinity sign therefore has a value of thirteen, love. The connections are golden infinity signs of YHVH = love + love.

No matter how many loops and connections there are, they are all love and they always add to ONE.

13 + 13 = 26 ~ YHVH
YHVH is ONE

23
The Light Weave

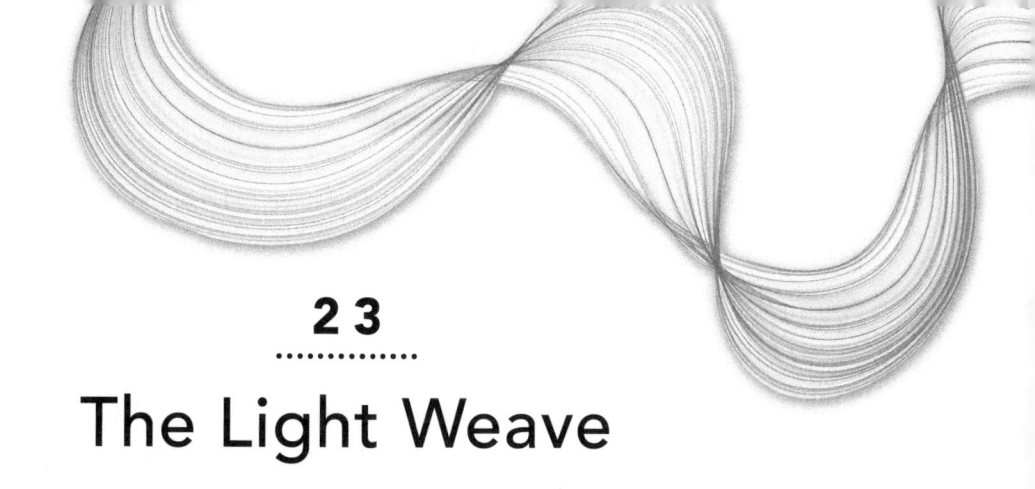

One of the goals of kabbalistic meditation and prayer is cleaving to God (*devekut*) in order to bring down the divine light of higher consciousness for the good of all. Many years ago, I was demonstrating this practice for my kabbalistic healing teacher, Dr. Prinzivalli, as we sat in a hotel lobby. After showing her the basic energy exercise called the Celtic weave, I repeated the practice adding the kabbalistic symbolism presented here. She remarked that the addition of the divine names spread light to everyone in the lobby.

> *Deep inside each of us a light is burning.*
> *No one's light is the same as anyone else's.*
> *There is no person who does not have a light.*
> *It is our responsibility to reveal the light of this candle publicly*
> *Together creating a great torch to illuminate the entire world.*
> —excerpted from the poetry of the great mystic,
> Rav Avraham Kook (1865–1935)

The Ari, Rabbi Isaac Luria, used a term called *yichudim* (unifications) to indicate the weaving of the letters of certain names of God, usually with YHVH/י-הוה in order to bring in the light of higher consciousness. Kabbalists would meditate on the intertwined letters of Divine Names for hours, even days, to glean the truths forthcoming from this practice. Rabbi Ariel Bar Tzadok describes such a practice of *yichudim* in a meditation for unification with divine light.[86] The light is the light of spirit illuminating our consciousness. The Light Weave adds physical movement to the purely mental focusing Rabbi Bar Tzadok describes.

Background

There are many names of God used throughout the Torah. Kabbalists associate different names of God with the four worlds of the physical/emotional/mental/and spiritual. Woven together as they are in this practice, these same names, also represent a concise symbol for the evolution of all masculine and feminine relationships. In addition, meditation on these specific names has the power to clarify the vision of what we want to enfold in our lives.[87]

Four Worlds/Four Names

Spiritual
YHVH/י-הוה: the most exalted Name of the Eternal Oneness. This Name is visualized, not pronounced.

It represents the kabbalistic world closest to Source, *Atzilut,* meaning nearness.

Mental
EHIYEH/א-היה: the Name pronounced to Moses at the burning bush (Exodus 3:14), where God spoke the phrase "Ehiyeh asher ehiyeh"

אֶהְיֶה אֲשֶׁר אֶהְיֶה
I will be what I will be,

beyond time or space. We can interpret this Name as "being present" and here it represents the power of the **MIND**, and the kabbalistic world of *Briyah*.

....
86 Rabbi Ariel Bar Tzadok, *Walking In the Fire*, 258–263.
87 Sarah Yehudit Schneider, Still Small Voice Correspondence School: Zohar Class, 6/5/16.

Emotional
***ELOHIM*/א-להים**: In Genesis, the first book of the Bible, God says "Let there be LIGHT." *Elohim* is the Name used in that verse and in the rest of the creation story. *Elohim* has the same *gematria* as **Nature** (*Hateva*) and here represents the **emotions** and the light we can shine through a loving **heart**.

The emotions are the world of *Yetzira*.

Physical
***ADONAI*/א-דני**: the name usually substituted for the unpronounceable YHVH/י-הוה, represents the **physical body**. The unpronounceable vibration of YHVH/י-הוה is manifested into the physical world by the vibration of saying *Adonai*. Voice vibration serves as the vehicle connecting the worlds of the spiritual and physical. Manifestation cannot occur without physical grounding. So here, *Adonai* can also represent the physical manifestation of our life's mission and corresponds to the kabbalistic world of *Assiya*, action.

Why Light?
When the numerical values of each of these names—*Ehiyeh*(21)/*Elohim*(91)/*Adonai* (65) is combined with the numerical value of YHVH (26), they add up to 250. In Kabbalah, words that have the same *gematria* are deeply related. Two hundred and fifty is the numerical value of the word *ner*, נֵר meaning candle or light. In Proverbs (20:27) is the verse:

> *The spirit of man is the candle of the Lord.*
> נֵר יהוה נִשְׁמַת אָדָם

Energy Background
The Light Weave is based on Donna Eden's Celtic Weave exercise. According to Eden, who sees energy clearly, the Celtic Weave connects the energies of the mind, emotions, and physical body. It creates a dynamic spiraling infinity sign through and around the body weaving together all the energy systems down to the crossover patterns of the

double helix of the DNA. It also enlivens and strengthens the aura of energy that surrounds the body.

The hands are activated by rubbing them together and are held in turn on the thighs, in front of the heart, and at the sides of the head. These correspond to the physical/thighs, emotional/heart, and the mental/head.

Large horizontal infinity patterns are traced back down the body, where the energy is then "scooped up" in the hands, released over the head, and allowed to flow down the front and back of the body.

Kabbalah Addition

As you come up the body, each hand placement activates a Divine Name and its corresponding world:

Thighs: *Adonai*/א-דני (*Assiya*/physical body)

Heart: *Elohim*/א-להים (*Yetsira*/emotions)

Sides of the head: *Ehiyeh*/א-היה (*Briya*/mind)

The arms then move back down the body, tracing horizontal infinity patterns, weaving the three Names/worlds together. The palms then turn up to gather the combined energy of all three. The open palms are raised over the top of the head connecting to the most Holy Name YHVH/י-הוה at the *sefira* of *Keter*/crown. There the three interwoven Names you have brought up weave with the letters of YHVH/י-הוה and the divine light from the world of *Atzilut*/spirit infuses through the three lower worlds. You are surrounded inside and out with physical *yichudim*, unifications with divine names. The Light Weave calls forth and strengthens the divine light within and radiates the light out to everyone you encounter. After you become familiar with the practice, try adding the Breath of Light from chapter 15.

The practice is usually done standing, but if that is not possible, please sit. Intention is key. Physical movement and mental focus work together. Choose the mental construct that works best for you of the choices given.

The focus can be on a Name,

the kabbalistic world it represents,

or the letter *aleph*/א, which is the first letter of   Adonai/א-דני

Elohim/א-להים

and   Ehiyeh/א-היה

Try the exercise with these alternate visualizations to discover what works best for you.

Image 77—Hands on Thighs

The Light Weave Practice
Come up the body, activating the Names.

1. Activate the hands by rubbing them together vigorously and shaking them off. Place them on your thighs. Ground the physical body. Feel the sensation of earth energy rising up the legs through the bottoms of the feet, holding you gently and securely. Feel energy coming back down through the legs into the earth. Slowly and deeply inhale through the nose and exhale through the mouth.

    say *Adonai*/א-דני

    or think: *Assiya*/physical body

    or visualize the letter *Aleph*/א

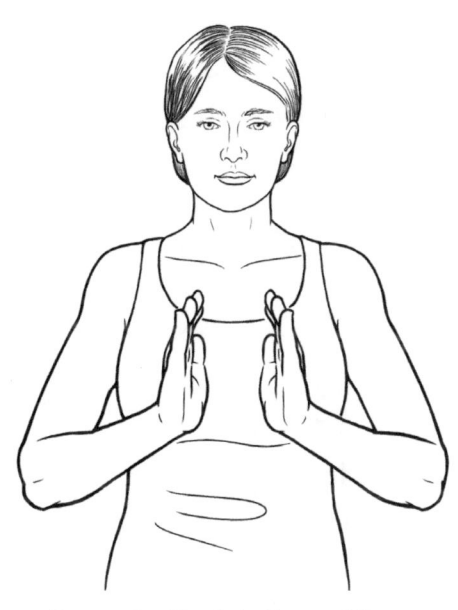

Image 78—Hands in Front of Heart

2. Rub your hands together and shake them off. Hold the hands, with palms facing each other, about eight inches apart in front of your heart. You may feel energy connecting through your hands as heat, vibration, or another sensation. Slowly and deeply inhale through the nose and exhale through the mouth.

    say: *Elohim*/א-להים

    or think: *Yetzira*/emotions

    or visualize the letter *aleph*/א

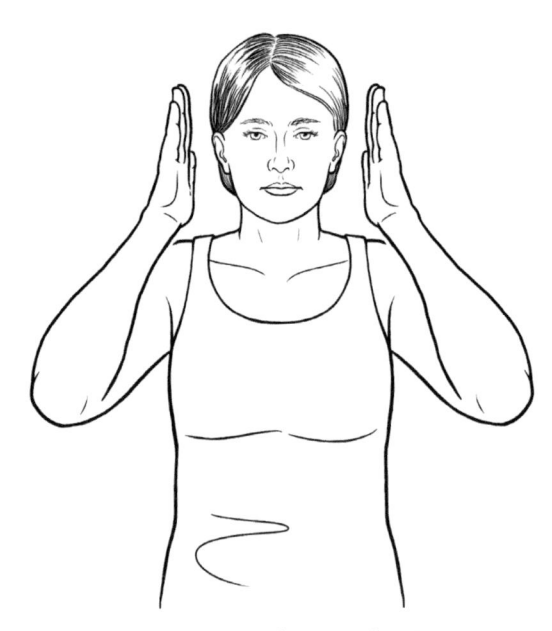

Image 79—Hands Cupped at Ears

3. Rub your hands together and shake them off. Hold them a few inches from the ears. Deeply inhale through the nose and exhale through the mouth.

    say: *Ehiyeh*/א-היה

    or think: *Briya*/the mind

    or visualize the letter *aleph*/א

Come back down the body, tracing horizontal infinity patterns as you go.

Inhale through the nose, bringing the elbows together. Exhale through the mouth, crossing your arms in front of your chest and then swinging them out to the side.

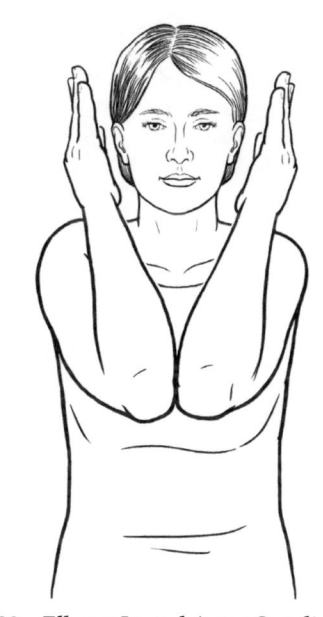

Image 80—Elbows In and Arms Out diagram #1

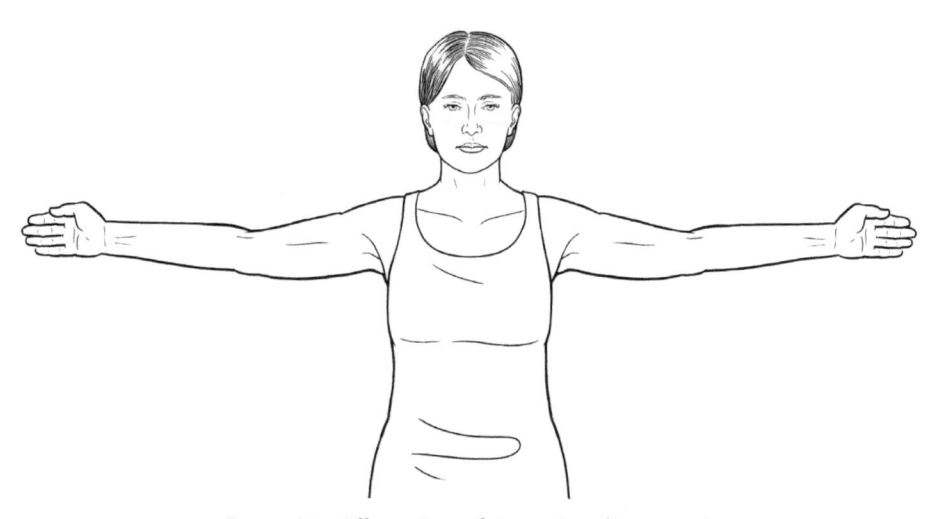

Image 81—Elbows In and Arms Out diagram #2

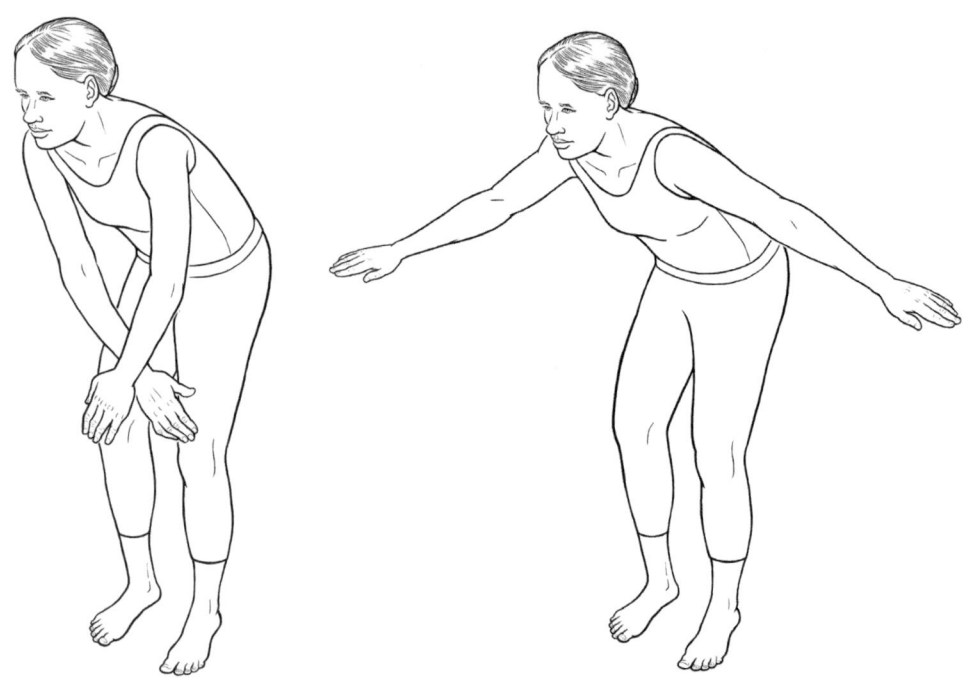

Image 82 and 83—Cross Arms, Arms to Side diagram #1 and #2

Inhale through the nose, crossing the arms in front of the knees. Exhale through the mouth, swinging the arms out to the side.

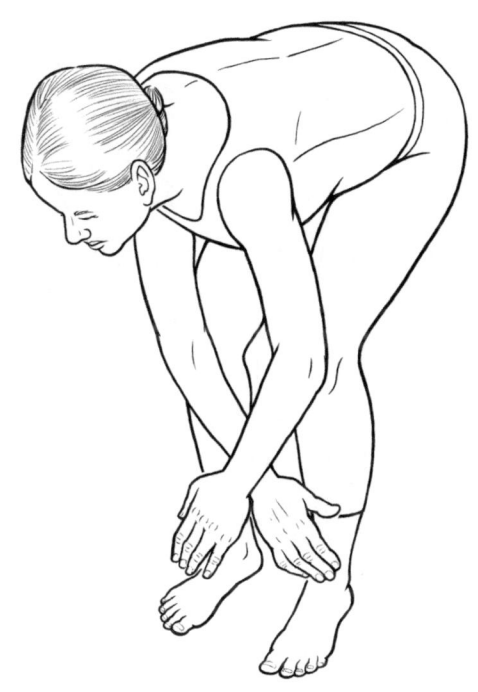

Image 84—Cross Hands at Ankles

4. Inhale through the nose, crossing the arms in front of the ankles. Exhale through the mouth, swinging the arms out to the side.

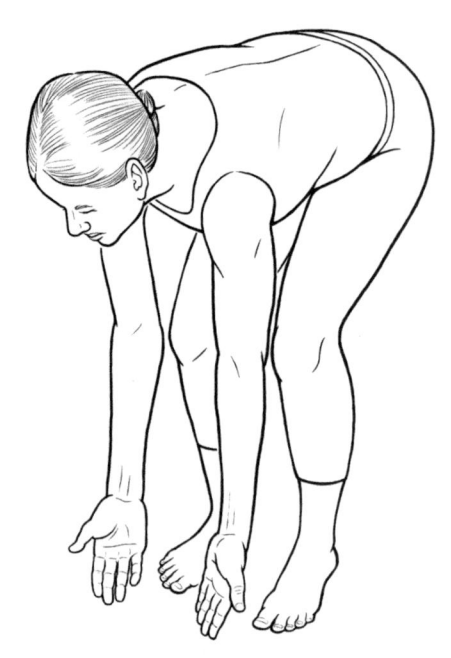

Image 85—Palms Up at Feet

5. Turn the palms face up. Slowly roll up, raising the arms, gathering the energy of the Divine Names and the worlds they represent.

Image 86—Stretch Arms over Head

6. Stand tall, with your hands above your head. Connect to the Name YHVH/י-הוה and the world of *Atzilut*/spirit. Inhale and fill the hands with the letters of the Name YHVH/י-הוה.

7. Turn the palms face down, exhale deeply through the mouth, and release the energy you have gathered. Shower yourself with light. Visualize the letters of YHVH woven with *Ehiyeh*, *Elohim*, and *Adonai*.

Guided by your hands, the integrated energy of the four Names cascades gently down the body from *Keter*, weaving through the worlds of *Briya*/mind, *Yetzira*/emotions, and *Assiya*/physical.

Your whole body is enveloped by the light of the four interwoven Names, *gematria* 250, the candle נר/*ner* of God. As the Names weave down through the worlds, the divine light fills them all. You become a body of spiritual light. Take the time to fully experience any thoughts or sensations.

Focus the light in any way you are called to, for self or others. You may choose to share the light with anyone who needs its power, or for the general *tikun*/repair of the world. To do so, flip your hands over and back, drawing large infinity signs from your field out to a specific person you imagine or with the intention that the light bring illumination and healing wherever it may be needed.

24

Connecting to the Cosmos with the Forty-Two-Letter Name

We have explored the relationship of six/*vav*/masculine and seven/*zayin*/feminine as thirteen/*ahava*/love. This love connection extends from the divine union of Z"A and Shechina, down to the harmony of all opposites within ourselves. Now it is time to look at another expression of six and seven, their product, forty-two. The forty-two letter Name of God is said to connect to the primordial forces of the universe. The practice presented in this chapter helps to harmonize one's energies with these cosmic forces. Realigning oneself in this way is especially auspicious at fall or spring equinox times or to usher in the Sabbath. "The forty-two letter Name is the mechanism for the elevation of all worlds,"[88] so is it just a coincidence that in *The Hitchhiker's Guide to the Galaxy*, forty-two is said to be the secret of the universe?

Kabbalah Background

The number forty-two has many mystical connotations. The process of creation, as presented in Genesis, begins with the word *yehi*, meaning "let there be," as in "let there be light." The conclusion of the creative process comes when *Elohim* sees all of creation to

---
88 Rabbi Yizchak Ginsberg, inner.org, "The Name of 42-Letters."

be *tov*, "good." The gematria of *yehi* is twenty-five; of *tov*, seventeen. Together, *yehi* and *tov* encompass the entire creative process with their sum of forty-two. When God appeared to Moses at the burning bush, and Moses asked His Name, he was told, "*E'heye Asher E'heye*," translated as "I will be as I will be."

The numerical value of the name אהיה/*E'heye* is twenty-one:

א	Aleph	= 1
ה	Hei	= 5
י	Yud	= 10
ה	Hei	= 5

The name *E'heye* is repeated twice for a total *gematria* of forty-two.

Forty-two is also reflected in the story of the exodus from Egypt. Before the Israelites were able to be fully free and enter the promised land, they made forty-two stops, known as the Forty-two Journeys (described in the book of Numbers, chapter 33). According to the Baal Shem Tov, founder of the Chassidic movement, these journeys represent the forty-two stages every soul undergoes in a lifetime, from the moment of birth until it leaves the body.

We will focus, however, on another aspect of forty-two, the forty-two-letter Name, the prayer that encodes the Name called *Ana B'Koach*, and the divine union symbolized by the prayer.

The intention of blessing in Kabbalah is to create a divine union between heaven and earth, the *KB"H* (the *Kadosh Baruch Hu*, Holy One Blessed be He) and the *Shechina*, between the spiritual and the physical. To that end, this Aramaic formula is declared before the beginning of any blessing:

L' shem Yichud Kud'sha Brich hu u'Shechinatay…
לשם יחוד קודשא בריך הוא ושכינתיה...

For the sake of the unification (*Yichud*) of the *K"BH* and His *Shechina*…

The *K"BH* is represented in the Tree of Life by *Ze'er Anpin (Z"A)*, also called the Six. The *Shechina* is represented in the Tree by *Nukva*, also called the Seven or the seventh *sefira* of *Z"A*. Their union then is six times seven, which equals forty-two. The forty-two-letter name of God symbolizes their union. Each letter of the forty-two-letter Name comes from a mystical coupling derived from intricate transformations of letters in the Genesis creation story.

Like the four-letter Name YHVH/יהוה, the forty-two-letter Name cannot be pronounced. In order to access it, Rabbi Nehunia Ha-Kanoh, in the first century, created a forty-two word prayer, *Ana B'Koach*. Each letter of the Name, in order, is the first letter of each word in the prayer. Thus, the *Ana B'Koach* prayer is an acrostic for the forty-two-letter Name.

Especially in the Sephardic tradition, *Ana B'Koach* is recited in morning and evening prayers. Significantly, it is also recited on Friday evenings as the sixth day meets the seventh, right before another mystical prayer, *Lecha Dodi*, which welcomes the Sabbath as the beloved bride of the *K"BH*.

Both the forty-two letter Name and the structure of *Ana B'Koach* reflect the creation story. There are seven lines in *Ana B'Koach*. Each line has six words. The *six words* in each line symbolize the six days of active creation, and the *seven lines* symbolize the Sabbath. According to Genesis, creation encompassed six days of outwardly focused energy. As the sixth day drew to a close, creation ceased, and the first Sabbath was ushered in. Sabbath, the *Shabbat*, is a time of receptivity, rest, and inward reflection. It is a personification of the divine feminine, the *Shechina*, in sacred time. The six days of work are balanced by having just one day of renewal.

At eighteen minutes before sunset on Fridays, it is traditional to light candles to welcome the Sabbath. According to *midrash*, stories that help interpret the Torah, this marks the moment when creation ceased. The flames of the two identical pure white candles represent the reunion of the *K"BH* with the Sabbath Bride, the *Shechina*. The candles stand side by side as they are blessed, as if united under a *chuppa*, the wedding canopy of their joined lights. This reunion is also symbolized by the forty-two-letter Name, as six, the *K"BH*, is reunited with the seven, *Shechina*. You may also recall the significance of 6 + 7; 6 + 7 = 13, the same *gematria* as the word for love and the word for one. It is a time for unity within ourselves and with others. In a mirroring of the divine marriage, of becoming one, Friday evenings are a traditional time for sacred lovemaking.

Sabbath is a celebration of both the oneness of the divine union and the integration of our own aspects of masculine/doing verses feminine/being. On Saturday evening, as the *Shechina* prepares to depart, a single braided candle with at least **two wicks** is lit. The candle, colored rather than white, symbolizes that throughout the **Sabbath** day, the energies of the beloveds have intertwined in joy and love.

Image 87—Braided Havdalah Candle

Ana B'Koach can be used for both healing and meditation. It is mystical formula of duality becoming unity, as reflected by the divine union. There are many layers of symbolism and the specific correlations vary depending on the source.

Each of the seven lines corresponds to a:
- Planet
- Day of the week: starting on Sunday, ending at *Shabbat*

- *Sefira* of the Tree: starting with *Chesed* and ending in *Malchut* (*Shechina, Shabbat*)
- Direction: right/left/front/behind/up/down/inward

Four of these directions also correspond to where the archangels are traditionally imagined:

Michael: right
Gavriel: left
Uriel: front
R'phael: behind

Abbreviation

Each line of six words can also be abbreviated into two three-letter words made from the first letter of each of the six words.

These two-word acrostics are also used for prayer, healing, and meditation.

Energy/Kabbalah Background

The foundation of the practice is an energy exercise called "The Seven Spirals" created and taught to me by Ellen Meredith.[89] Seven Spirals is a vehicle for creating balance between Earth and Heaven. It realigns the physical body to the universal rhythms of the cosmos and the soul's truth. It also helps to assimilate the new energies of awakened consciousness.

Performing the Seven Spirals clears energy all around the body. As the energies clear, they come more into sync with rhythms of the universe. Stress is removed, encouraging the different energy patterns to communicate in vital infinity crossing patterns. Personal power becomes strengthened and centered.

---

[89] www.listening-in.com.

The Seven Spirals and *Ana B'Koach* are an uncanny match. In the Seven Spirals, the hands trace circular shapes, spirals, next to the body in each of the six traditional directions: up and down, right and left, back and front.[90] The seventh spiral is drawn facing the body. Clockwise and counterclockwise spirals are actually ancient Jewish mystical symbols.[91] Counterclockwise represents cleansing, the undoing of anything that stands in the way of our peace and wholeness. Clockwise symbolizes an influx of life force energy. In energy medicine, spirals are routinely used in this way to clear chakras and bring in fresh energy. In my clinical work I often recite the *Ana B'Koach* at the close of a session as I trace spirals and infinity patterns over the client. The unifying nature of the prayer helps to integrate energy balances that have been reestablished in the session, especially in the chakras. The Seven Spirals are in effect clearing the chakras of your relationship with universal energies in all directions, and then realigning and balancing these forces with those inside the body.

Sacred direction ceremonies are common to many indigenous cultures. For example, South American shamans and Native American tribes use invocations to the directions serve to connect to the energy of the earth. According to Sefer Yetzira, the six directions are the foundation of the Tree of Life. In Jewish tradition, a direction ceremony is performed in celebration of Sukkot, the fall harvest festival.

---

90 The correlation of the six *sefirot of Z"A* to the six directions is discussed in Sefer Yetzira, chapter 1, 13.

91 Spirals are part of a group of seven mystical symbols or seals called the "Earth Chambers" which are found in ancient manuscripts. Adam baal Shem, in *Toldot Adam* 158, attributes them to the Rambam, Rabbi Moshe ben Maimon.

Image 88—*Lulav* and *Etrog*

Palm, myrtle, and willow branches are bound together in a *lulav*, held in the the right hand (male) and ritually shaken up, down, right, left, front, and back. The seventh direction, inward, is symbolized by the fragrance and shape of the round *etrog*, citron fruit, held in the left (feminine) hand.[92]

This exercise is also an embodiment of the *Magen David*. It creates a six-pointed, three-dimensional Jewish star. Your heart, representing the *Shabbat*, rests in the center.

As you trace the Seven Spirals add *Ana B'Koach* by reciting the prayer or its translation line by line, or silently meditating on the energetic messages the acrostics convey.

How

The order of the six directions is traditional, based on the six lines of the prayer. The seventh and final direction in Seven Spirals is always inward to the heart. This corresponds to the seventh and last line of *Ana B'Koach* which symbolizes our inner God-presence, the *Shechina*.

---

92 The six parts of the *lulav*, according to my training with Rabbi Gershon Winkler, represent the six *sefirot* of *Ze'er Anpin (Z"A)*. The straight palm branch represents *Yesod*, the spine, the three sprigs of myrtle the triangle formed by *Chesed, Gvurah,* and *Tiferet*. The two willow branches represent the two legs, *Netzach* and *Hod*. The *etrog* is *Malchut*. If you find yourself in a *Sukkah* without a *lulav* try the Seven Spirals/*Ana B'Koach* practice.

Lines 1–6

Hold either palm facing away from you about eight inches from the body. Circle the hand eight times in one direction, clockwise or counterclockwise. When you have finished, reverse direction and trace eight more spirals in the opposite direction. It does not matter if you begin begin circling clockwise or counterclockwise. For example, for the first line of the prayer, draw eight spirals with the right hand counterclockwise on the right side of the body and then eight more clockwise, still on the right side.[93]

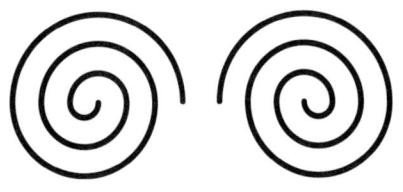

Item 89—8x Circles

The hand position changes with each line:

Line 1. right side/palm faces right/*CHESED*

Line 2. left side/palm faces left/*GVURAH*

Line 3. front/palm in front of the body facing away/*TIFERET*

Line 4. back/hand is behind the body as far as comfortable with palm facing away/*NETZACH*

Line 5. up/palm is above the head facing up/*HOD*

Line 6. down/You cannot actually draw spirals beneath your feet, so draw circles in front with the palm facing down. As you draw, simply imagine the spirals beneath you/*YESOD*

Line 7

The seventh line corresponds to *Malchut*, the physical world and the *Shechina*. It grounds the forty-two-letter Name into the heart. As you trace spirals as in lines one through six, use both hands, palms facing in toward you and over the heart.

---

[93] It may help to recall the *Karate Kid* and Mr. Miyagi's "wax on, wax off" instructions.

Add *Ana B'Koach* to the Seven Spirals exercise either by reciting the prayer, aloud or silently, or its translation line by line. Choose between the original Hebrew (transliteration provided) or the accompanying translation.

An alternative is to meditate on the energetic message conveyed by the *sefira* associated with each line, which are listed above.

Suggestions for:

1. Reciting the line in Hebrew or English
Hebrew: Draw one spiral for each of the six words and then add two more cycles, making eight.
Repeat the line aloud or silently after you change the direction your hand is circling. This creates a natural rhythm of eight so you are not consciously counting.

English: The English translations, created specifically for this practice, each have eight words per line. Draw one spiral for each of the eight words. Repeat the line drawing spirals in the opposite direction.

2. Meditating on the energy of the line
Stay connected to the intention and energy of each line with your breath. This will help you determine when to intuitively change direction.

The Seven Spirals of *Ana B'koach*
Practice either standing or seated

With palm facing away, about eight inches from the body, circle the hand(s) eight times in one direction (i.e., counterclockwise) and then eight times in the opposite direction (i.e., clockwise).

Image 90—Palm Facing Away from Body Right

1. Draw eight spirals on the **right** side of the body.
    Recite:
    אנא בכח גדלת ימינך תתיר צרורה
    Ana B'Koach gedulat yemincha tatir tserura
    By the power of Your mercy, untangle sorrows.
    or
    Think:
    Kindness, compassion

Image 91—Palm Facing Away from Body Left

2. Eight spirals on the **left** side of the body.
   Recite:
   קבל רנת עמך, שגבנו, טהרנו, נורא
   Kabel Rinat Amcha Sag'venu Ta'ha're'nu Norah
   Awesome One, accept our joy, elevate, cleanse us.
   or
   Think:
   Clear my blockages

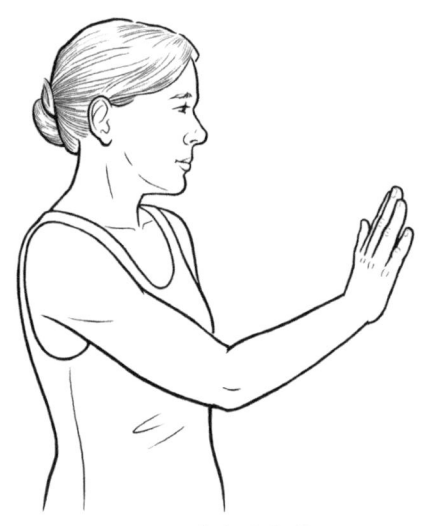

Image 92—Spirals in Front

3. Eight spirals in **front of the body.**
   Recite:
   נא גבור, דורשי יחודך כבבת שמרם
   Na Gibor Dorshei Yechudcha Kevavat Shamrem
   Almighty One, please guard your faithful seekers closely.
   or
   Think: Harmony, beauty

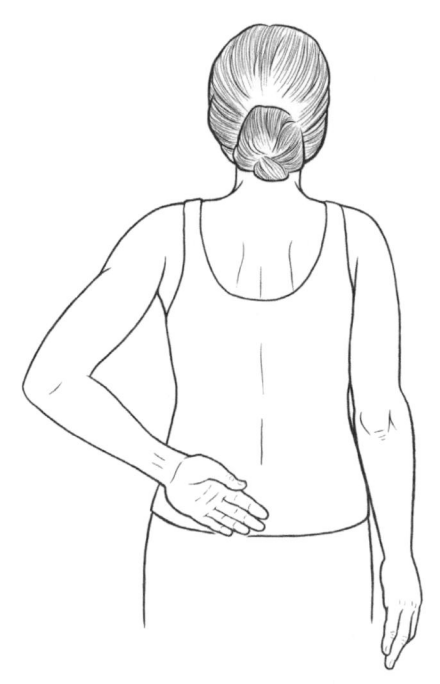

Image 93—Spirals Behind

4. Eight spirals **behind the body.** (Wherever you can reach, remember palm faces away)
   Recite:
   ### ברכם, טהרם, רחמי צדקתך תמיד גמלם
   Barchem Taharem Rachmei Tzidkadcha Tamid Gamlem
   Justice giver, bless, purify, reward us with compassion.
   or
   Think: Endurance, self-mastery

Image 94—Above the Head

5. Eight spirals **up above the head**.
   Recite:
   חסין קדוש, ברוב טובך נהל עדתך
   Cha'seen Ka'dosh B'rov Tuv'cha Na'chel A'da'te'cha
   Sacred Protector, guide us to holiness and kindness.
   or
   Think: Surrender to a greater purpose, humility, gratitude

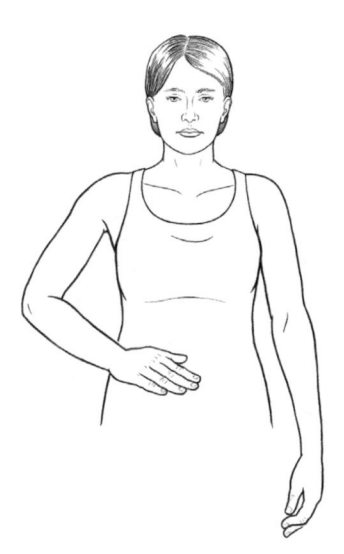

Image 95—Spirals Down

6. Eight spirals **below the body.** (Imagine the spirals beneath your feet.)
   Recite:
   יחיד גאה, לעמך פנה, זוכרי קדשתך
   Ya'chid Ge'eh L'Am'cha P'Nai Zoch'ray Ke'du'sha'te'cha
   Infinite One, receive those who acknowledge your holiness.
   or
   Think: Intimacy, connection

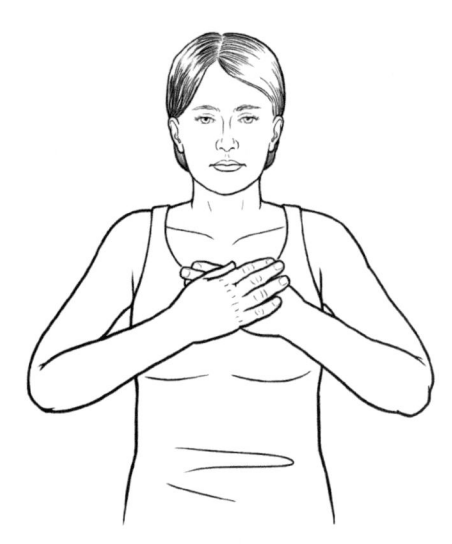

Image 96—Palms Toward You

7. **Turn palms toward you.** Eight spirals **in toward the heart.**
   Recite:
   שועתנו קבל ושמע צעקתנו עייד תעלומות.
   Shavatenu Kabayl U'Shma Tza'a'ka taynu Yodayah ta-alumot
   Mysterious One, hear and accept our deepest secrets.
   or
   Think: Be in the present moment

222 Chapter 24

It is traditional to whisper the *Baruch Shem* prayer after saying a Holy Name.

בָּרוּךְ שֵׁם כְּבוֹד מַלְכוּתוֹ לְעוֹלָם וָעֶד

Baruch Shem K Vod Malchuto L Olam VaEd.

Blessed is the Name of the Holy One.
Malchut is forever.

Seal in the effects of the seven spirals combined with the power of the Forty-two-letter Name. Open the hands overhead, and connect to the energy of your spiritual nature: gratitude, love, hope, goodness. Feel the hands and fingers tingle as they fill with these sparkling vibrations.

Image 97—Cupped Hands Over Head diagram #1

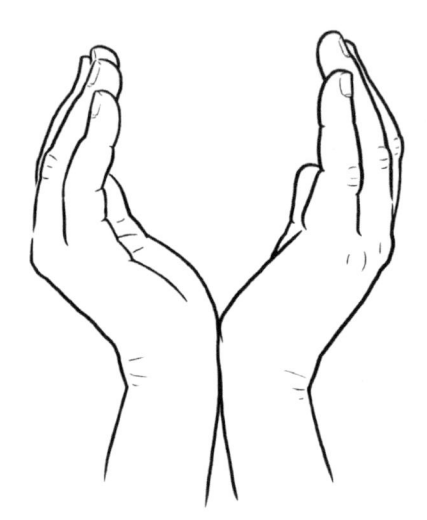

Image 98—Cupped Hands Over Head diagram #2

As you whisper the six-word *Baruch Shem* prayer, draw infinity signs of this sparkling light all around yourself. The infinity signs can be large or small in any place or direction. Sense your cosmic alignment and and yet how grounded and solid you feel. Your body may have goosebumps, feel warm, or have another visceral reaction, so spend a few moments quietly integrating the effects of the practice.

Note:
An alternative when whispering the *Baruch Shem* is to draw the three hearts of the bridge flow as described in chapter 20, "*Sh'ma* and the Kabbalistic Hook-In."

25

Energizing Blessing

Raising the Sparks in Food

The Ari taught that the prime path of enlightenment is through the conscious blessing of food.[94] Blessing food is a mindfulness practice. It forces you to pause and be conscious of what you are about to eat, even if you are very hungry and find it hard to resist tasting that first bite.

All food is a union of heaven and earth, and Hebrew blessings reflect this idea. Food is light energy from the sun transformed by the earth through photosynthesis and the food chain. When we eat, the light becomes renewed within us. Heaven and earth unite in us through the process of assimilation. In Kabbalah, when food is blessed, the divine sparks in food, which is physical, are elevated to the level of the spiritual and eating becomes sacred.[95] Every cell in our bodies is nourished and sustained by the energy of food that is blessed.

Rabbi Moshe ben Aderet, in the 1200s, wrote that acknowledging God as the source of blessing draws divine energy into the world. Blessing food helps to release and elevate concealed divine sparks in the physical world and at the same time draws divine energy down to us.

---

94 Rabbi Aryeh Kaplan quoting Chaim Vital's *Sha'areh Kedusha* in *Meditation and Kabbalah*, 227.
95 In *The Hidden Messages in Water*, Masaru Emoto shows the profound effects of blessing and love on water. Water is the main component of both us and our food.

Blessings provide a verbal formula for repairing the world through the balance of opposites and divine marriage. As you may recall, all Hebrew blessings in the kabbalistic tradition, begin with the intention, "for the sake of the unification of the masculine divine principle/*Kadosh Baruch Hu* with the feminine divine principle/*Shechina*." [96]

לשם יחוד קודשא בריך הוא ושכינתיה

Le'shem y'chud kudsha bri'chu u'shechinatay

Then the formal blessing begins with the phrase:

Blessed are You, God,

    Baruch Atah YY,

ברוך אתה יי

YY/י-י, pronounced *Adonai*, is also a unification of divine masculine and feminine, as in the combined name

    YHVH/*Adonai* [97]

י-הוהאדנ-י

Unification is the intention both at the beginning of a blessing and at the end. Examine the *gematria*:

At the beginning of a blessing:

The *gematria* of the combined name YHVH/*ADONAI* is:

YHVH	=	26
Adonai	=	65
total		91

....
96   Refer to chapters 24 and 117. This phrase is in Aramaic, an earlier form of Hebrew.
97   Explained in chapter 8, "The Unpronounceable Name."

At the end: Those who hear a blessing reply, "**Amen.**"
The *gematria* of *Amen* is:

א	A	Aleph	=	1
מ	M	Mem	=	40
נ	N	Nun	=	50
Total				91

91 = 91

The *gematria* of *Amen* is equal to that of the combined Name.

The blessing is sealed with unification at the end when all who have heard the blessing say *Amen*.

Blessing acknowledges that nourishment of the physical body with the light energy of food is a divine unification and a sacred act from start to finish.

The Energy Component

In modern times, even the freshest organic produce may have been harvested days before it reaches us. Donna Eden, who clearly sees the energy in food, notes that processed and microwaved food has lost most of its vitality. Energizing and blessing food can restore the original energy our bodies need for maximum health. Donna often relates the story of one her students, a poor, sickly man who lived in a gas station and only ate from the vending machines. When Donna taught him the energy protocol below, and he started energizing the food in his very unhealthy diet, his vitality returned.[98]

In addition, foods testing "no" can be reversed to "yes" by the addition of an energy blessing.[99]

---

98 Personal communication.

99 In my energy medicine classes we have performed an interesting experiment. We periodically test foods, such as dairy and gluten, to see what is compatible with our different energies. One day we tested an old piece of white bread, which tested negative for everyone. As a group we then blessed the bread in our own modalities. Applied kineseology testing showed that the bread no longer weakened anyone. We repeated the experiment on a different day with similar results. I have also observed the power of blessing food in my clients with food sensitivities.

Energizing food can include the traditional Hebrew blessing for bread, the *Motzi*, or another blessing of your choice. The *Motzi* is offered over bread at the beginning of a meal and includes everything that will be eaten.

The Energy *Motzi*

A Hebrew blessing called the *Motzi* is traditionally offered at the beginning of any meal that includes bread. The energy *Motzi* combines this blessing with a method of revitalizing the energy in food, as taught to me by Donna Eden. The *Motzi*, its transliteration, and English translation are provided. Choose one or feel free to choose or compose an alternate that resonates with you.

1. Connect to the radiance of heaven by holding your fingers together in a pyramid over the food (bread). Say:

Image 99—Fingers Together

For the sake of the unification of the *K"BH* and the *Shechina*
I recite the following:
לשם יחוד קודשא בריך הוא ושכינתיה
l'shem yichud kudsha bri'chu u'shechinatey

2. With your left hand draw **counterclockwise** circles over the food. Say:

Image 100—Counterclockwise Circles

Blessed are You, *Adonai*
ברוך אתה יי
Baruch atah adonai

3. With your right hand draw **clockwise** circles over the food. Say:

Image 101—Clockwise Circles

Energizing Blessing 229

Creator of the universe,
אלהינו מלך העולם
Eloheinu melech haolam

4. Draw figure eights, vertical infinity signs, from the bread up to heaven and down from the bread to earth.

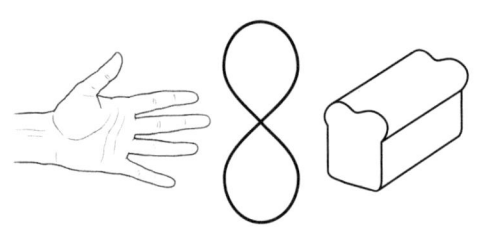

Image 102—From Bread to Heaven

Say:
Who brings forth bread…
המוציא לחם
hamotzi lechem

5. Using either hand or both, draw infinity signs to the food and back to you.

Image 103—Connect the Food to You with 8s

Say:
…from the earth.
מן הארץ
min haaretz

If it is your practice to verbalize a different prayer or grace of your choice, do so as you perform steps one through five, connecting your thoughts and intentions, through words, to the physical world.

26
Blessing Water

Any discussion of the balance of heaven and earth would be remiss without including water. Earth is the water planet. Following are ideas for infusing divine radiance into water. Water is associated with the feminine, so blessing water is also a blessing of the feminine.

Water is our mother. Our bodies begin life in the water of the womb. Water sustains us throughout our physical lives. It is time to regard water in a new light, a light of higher consciousness.

Water Energy

The water element in Chinese medicine is the essence of yin, the feminine. The characteristics of water are the basic characteristics of yin energy: wet, cold, dark, receptive. Water receives without judgment, absorbing almost any mineral it encounters. In the five-rhythm system of Chinese medicine, water also represents winter, the darkest time of the year and the beginning of the cycle of life. In winter, everything lies below the surface waiting, like a fetus in the water of the womb, to be born (again) and begin. Like the melting snow brings the return of life in spring, the energy of the water element feeds and nurtures all the other elements.

Water and Kabbalah

In Kabbalah the feminine and water are also linked. The *Shechina*, symbol of the divine feminine, is sometimes referred to as water. It was the water of Miriam's well[100] that sustained the Israelites on the desert journey of forty years.

Water is represented in the Tree by the letter *mem*/מ. *Mem*/מ is called a "mother letter" and stands for *mayim*/מים/water. If the Tree is imagined on a woman, *mem*/מ lies in the area of the womb. It forms the horizontal connection between the *sefirot* of *Netzach*/control, endurance and *Hod*/gratitude, surrender.

The *gematria* of *mem* is forty, the number of weeks of human gestation. M(em) is the sound of a baby suckling at its mother's breast. The prefix "mamma" means breast, and the "M" sound is the found in many languages in the word for mother.

Why Now?

Water absorbs and water reflects. Major disruptions of water energy reflect the chaotic state of our world today. Water has absorbed the energy of conflict and hatred, imbalance and negativity for so long that we now have a "water crisis." Water wars exist. Water shortages foster hatred between neighbors. We cannot take an abundant supply of clean fresh water for granted, even here in the United States. The intensity of droughts, tsunamis, glacier melt, and subsequent rising of ocean levels is speeding up at an alarming rate. Repercussions such as the decline of the sea as a food source will affect all of us. I believe that adding radiance to water through blessing will help to heal both the earth and us all, for we too are primarily water.

Blessing Water

Blessing may actually alter the structure of water. Masaru Emoto's photographs in *The Hidden Messages in Water* (published in 2005, a *New York Times* bestseller) showed that positive messages radically changed water into beautiful crystalline shapes, even at a distance. Although not embraced by the scientific establishment, his findings were and continue to be very compelling.

---

100   Miriam the prophetess was the sister of Moses.

The purpose of many Hebrew blessings is to acknowledge the pleasure of experiencing the physical wonders which fill our world and not take them for granted.[101] There are blessings to recite upon seeing trees blossom in the spring, for seeing a rainbow, and for witnessing natural phenomena such as lightning, thunder, deserts, mountains, even sunrise. Other blessings, such as the one presented for bread, cover our gratitude for all manner of food and drink.

Waters fits into both of these categories. So where is the blessing for water?

According to tradition water is included in the following group:

"All foods that do not fall into ... specific groups get the blessing *shehakol*. This category includes animal products: meat, chicken, fish, and eggs; water and all other drinks (except for wine, which has its own separate blessing) and soups; and miscellaneous foods like mushrooms, candy, et cetera."[102]

The blessing is:

בָּרוּךְ אַתָּה יְיָ אֱל הֵינוּ מֶלֶךְ הָעוֹלָם שֶׁהַכֹּל נִהְיֶה בִּדְבָרוֹ:

Baruch atah Adonai, Eloheinu Melech Ha'Olam shehakol nihiyeh b'd'varo.

Blessed are You, YHVH, Creator of the universe,
by Whose word all things came to be.

Although this blessing is traditional, I believe that water is too important to be lumped in a miscellaneous group. Water is essential to life and should be blessed in a way that reflects our love, respect, and gratitude. Love, respect, and gratitude are the energies of radiance. We can infuse these the same qualities into our own unique water essence.

The words of traditional blessings are fixed and unchanging. Water changes constantly. It naturally moves and flows, so the water blessing can be fluid as well. Fluidity, like water, reflects the moment.

---

101   A category called *Birchot HaNehenin*, blessings of enjoyment.
102   see www.chabad.org/library/article_cdo/aid/278538/jewish/Basic-Blessings-on-Food-Guide.htm. There is one preexisting blessing that includes water: "Blessed are you O Lord our God who created the oceans." There are also prayers said at fixed times of the year for rain and dew.

Blessing Water   235

I have been thinking about a water blessing for many years. In 2010, I created and participated in a day-long symposium called "Reconnecting to the Divine Feminine." It was held in Highland Park, Illinois, at the Infinity Foundation, and it featured presentations from myself, my teachers, and an eclectic set of colleagues. My presentation was on creating a blessing for water.

Those assembled each composed a personal blessing for water. We did Connecting Heaven and Earth.[103] Then, all together, we blessed a large container of water, showering it with radiant infinity signs and our individual blessings and intentions. I had asked the participants to bring containers with them and they filled them with the water we had blessed. Some drank it, sending the blessings inside to their cells. Some watered flowers, or used it to clear the energy of their homes. Some water was poured into nearby Lake Michigan. The intention was that wherever the water was poured the blessings would spread, multiply, and heal. We realized that we could each bless water whenever we chose to.

Wording

Following are some suggestions for creating water blessings in the moment. The energy exercises provide a background of intention for reciting and directing a verbal blessing. As we strive to elevate the energy of the feminine, remember that because water is associated with the feminine, blessing water is essentially a blessing of the feminine.[104]

For Drinking Water

If you are drinking the water, blessing it can light up every cell of your body as it connects to your own water nature. If possible, place the hands on or over the water vessel and say:

Source of blessings, please bless this water. May it sustain my body now and this planet always. May I, like water, feel safe to receive.

---

103 See chapter 19, "Connecting Heaven and Earth."
104 Traditional blessings begin with the words *baruch atah adonai,* "blessed are you, YHVH." It is interesting that the root of of the word *baruch*/blessing is *brecha* "pool" or "wellspring," which relates all blessings to water.

For Cleansing

Bathing or showering in radiant water is sublime. The water seems to sparkle and bring light to the skin. It elevates the experience of merely cleansing the body to the union of body and spirit.

As you feel the water on your body open the hands and say:

Source of blessings, thank you for the warmth and purity of this water and the pleasure this (shower, bath, ocean) is giving me. Bless the cleansing of my body and soul so that I may freely express my highest self.

Natural Phenomena

Watching the mist rise from a powerful waterfall, boating on a clear mountain lake, soaking in a natural hotspring, or the thrill of a magical sunset over the ocean can naturally fill you with radiance. You can also bring in radiance with your intention wherever you may find yourself. Take several deep breaths to help sense the moment fully. Open the heart. It may help to imagine someone you love dearly, or a time when you were happy and filled with "lightness." Feel the radiance of heavenly love enter the heart. The light of this radiance travels out the hands. You can also imagine either the infinity signs of love or the infinity signs of divine sparks (Y/Y) releasing from the hands. You may experience tingling, goosebumps, or other sensations, signaling that you have "connected."

You are ready to transmit your blessing. Direct your hands to the water and say:

Source of blessings, thank you for the wondrous gift of this water. May its beauty elevate my spirits and bless all who encounter it.

Blessing the Water in Your Body

Blessing Your Divine Essence

You can bring radiance to your water essence by connecting your hands at the second chakra (womb). This is also the path of the mother letter *mem*.

Spread the fingers gently over the belly.

Palms are over the hip bones.

The pinkie tips rest in the groins.

The middle fingers rest on the pubic bone about an inch in from the ends.

The thumbs connect at the navel.

Breathe deeply and say: *Thank you, blessed water, for sustaining me, healing me, and freeing my body from impurities.*

Connect with radiance and then possibly use either the Breath of Light (chapter 15), the infinity signs of love, or the infinity signs of divine sparks (Y/Y) to send the radiance out your hands into the belly. Emoto's experiments showed that positive messages radically changed water, so send blessings and affirmations to your water body.

Pregnancy

Bless the water surrounding and sustaining the fetus as above. Add the following or similar: "May the water of this womb bring radiance and blessing to the life within it."

Activating the *Mayim* Sparks

Recall that מ/*mem* is the "mother" letter representing the element of water/מים/*mayim*.[105] In the Tree, when projected on a physical body, the מ/*mem* water channel runs approximately around the belly. On the first and second day of creation as recounted in Genesis, the upper and lower waters were separated, creating heaven and earth. The upper waters of heaven symbolize the (divine) masculine, the lower waters of earth, the (divine) feminine. Balancing and connecting the upper and lower waters by using the word for water, *mayim*/מים, is the symbolic essence of the reconnection of physical and spiritual.

---

[105] ם is the form of letter *mem* when it comes at the end of a word.

In Kabbalah, the letters of the word reflect its essence. *Mayim* is also our essence. Deconstruct the word *mayim/mem-yud-mem* into

- מ *mem*/masculine/upper waters
- י *yud*/divine spark
- מ *mem*/feminine/lower waters

In this practice, the water within us symbolically separates into its componant letters. One wave of *mems* connects to our heaven/masculine aspects and the other wave of *mems* to our earth/feminine aspects. The mem waves return, masculine and feminine come together, and some oppposite aspects become integrated and whole. The divine sparks, *yuds* within water and thus within us, are strengthened by the *tikun* created by every harmonious pairing.

How

Place one hand over your belly with the palm covering the navel. Place the other hand directly behind it on your back with your palm covering the mingman point. Between your hands lies the center of your power. Take several deep slow breaths. Sense your internal ocean and the abundance of mayim, with its many *mems* and *yuds,* under your hands.[106]

---

106 The word *mayim* literally means "from the ocean."

Blessing Water 239

Visualize *mem*s separating from the central *yud*s of the word *mayim*. The *yud*s remain under your palms. Some *mem*s flow up the body connecting to heaven, while other *mem*s flow down connecting to earth. The *mem* waves are like ocean waves flowing slowly out to sea and back again. The *mem* waves surround you and rhythmically flow away from your hands in opposite directions, either toward the head and beyond and or to the feet and below and then return to the shore of your belly.

The *mem* waves from above return laden with bits of heaven/masculine energy the water has absorbed. The *mem* waves from below carry bits of earth/feminine energy. When the waves meet at the *yud*s under the hands, masculine and feminine, representing all opposites, have an opportunity to attract and come into harmony with each other. Whenever a pair of opposites integrates, we become more whole. The *tikun* of masculine and feminine activates the *yud*s and the divine sparks grow brighter and stronger each time the *mem*s return.

When you feel ready, place both thumbs in the middle of the back and drag your open hands around the waist several times, gathering the activated sparks and sweeping them to the front of the belly. Scoop up the *yud*s with your hands, float your arms overhead, open the hands and shower yourself with sparks of light. If desired, add an affirmation acknowledging your essence as divine light and bless the water that is you.

For Healing

Because we are mainly water, the visualization can be used anywhere on the physical body that needs special attention. Place your hands over the affected area, on or above the body. The *mem* waves will travel out from there and return to your hands with their bounty. Imagine that the sparks created and activated by the union of opposites under your hands are sparks of healing. The sparks create a field of oneness and love which encourages reintegration of a challenged area. Visualize any disease being carried away by the *mem* waves as they recede. Gather the divine sparks from under your hands and sprinkle their light where it is needed. In your own words, bless the water as an instrument of healing.

מממממממ

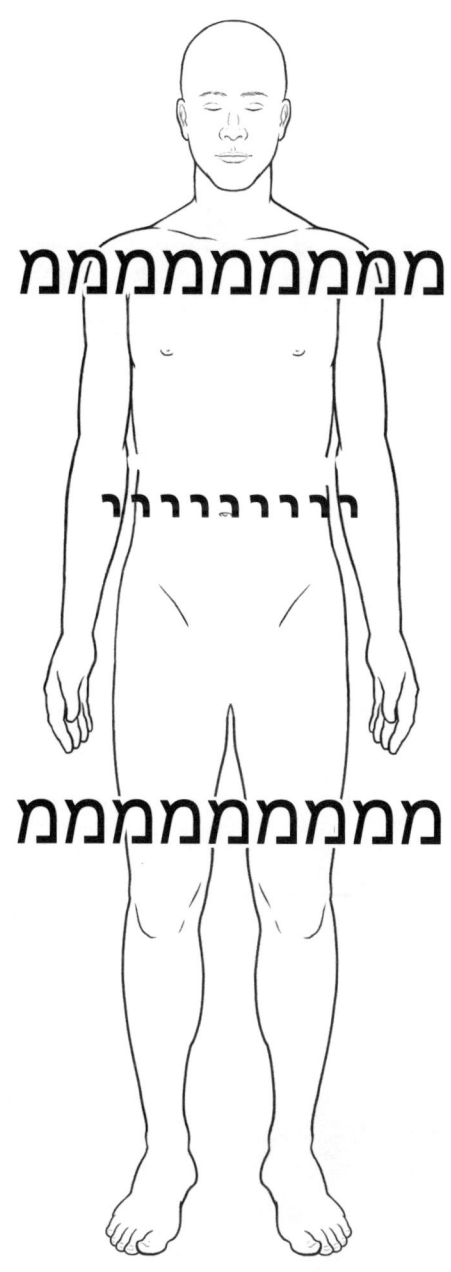

הררררררר

ממממממממ

Image 104—*Mayim* Man

27
The Shalom/Infinity Meditation

In Chinese medicine, stress is expressed through the fire element. The element of water is said to control the element of fire. A balance with the water element can convert a destructive, raging fire into a warm and soothing bath. Following is a similar concept using kabbalistic imagery.

In the Tree of Life, twenty-two paths, corresponding to the twenty-two letters of the Hebrew alphabet, form channels that link the ten *sefirot*. Of these, three are horizontal channels that connect the *sefirot* opposite each other on the right and left sides.[107] The letters found in the horizontal channels are called Mother letters and represent the elements of fire, air, and water.

---

107 *Chochma* and *Bina* are connected by the horizontal path of *shin*/fire; *Chesed* and *Gvurah* are connected by *aleph*/air; *Netzach* and *Hod* are connected by *mem*/water.

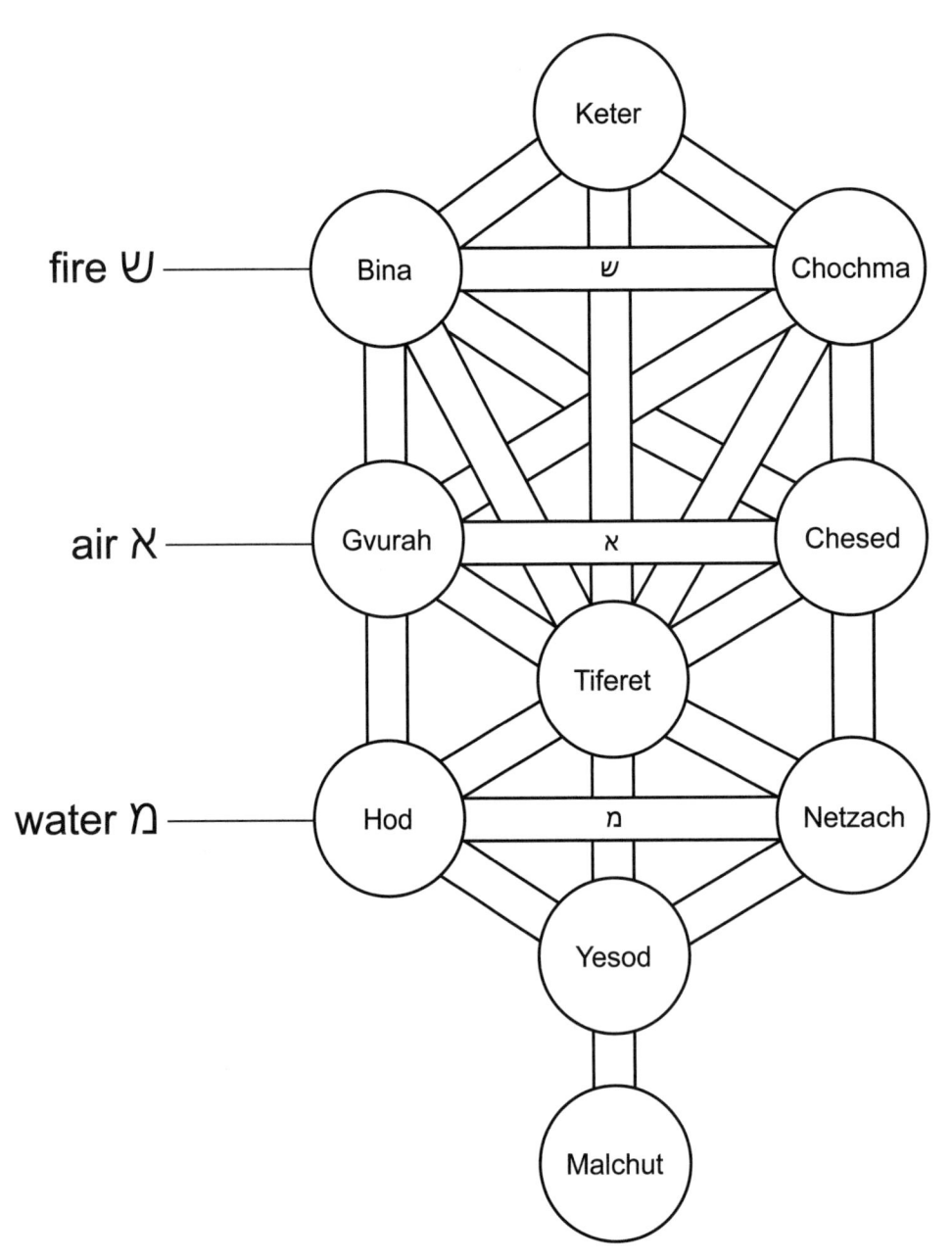

Image 105—Tree of Life with Mother Letters

Two of these elements are opposites:
Fire *shin*/ש,
   And
Water *mem*/מ

Shin/ש makes the sound **SHHH**, the sound of fire. *Shin*/ש represents passion, emotion, and because of its position in the Tree, the power of the mind. Fire is heat, yang, masculine.

The word for fire is **אש/*aish*.**

Mem/מ the symbol for water *mayim*/מים, and is found on the Tree in the area of the belly, which is also the domain of the second chakra. This area represents the waters of the womb, nurturing, flow, ease and the "gut" reactions of intuition. *Mem* makes the sound *mmm*, a sound of relaxation, of mama, of a baby nursing. Water is yin, feminine.

The Tree is the blueprint of creation and so provides a guide for examining different parts of ourselves. We all have masculine/feminine, fire/water aspects. The Hebrew word for heaven is שמים/*Shamayim*. Symbolically then, in heaven, the opposites of fire and water coexist peacefully. As above so below: we neither want to burn up in our passions nor drown in the depths of our own emotions, but find a warm bath of balance between them. To this end the two sounds, SHH and MMM, are often used in kabbalistic meditation to create balance.[108]

In this practice, the secret of balancing these two opposites: masculine and feminine, fire and water, is found in the word *shalom*, peace. *Shalom* comes from the root *shalem*: *shin*/ש, *lamed*/ל, *mem*/מ, meaning wholeness. *Shalom* begins with fire and ends with water.

....
108   Meditating on these sounds and their role in prophesy is discussed in Sefer Yetzira, chapter 2.

In the three root letters of *shalom*, the opposites of fire and water meet at the letter *lamed*. *Lamed* is the first letter of the word for heart, *lev*/לב (*lev* sounds a bit like love). The energy of the heart is the most powerful in the body. The heart has the wonderful ability to hold opposites, balancing and mediating between them to create peace and wholeness. The letters of *shalom* truly reflect its essence.

The following practice uses an infinity sign to create *shalom*/peace, and wholeness by balancing fire/*shin* ש and water/*mem* מ, as symbolic of all our parts that need balance, through the power of the heart, *lamed*/ל.

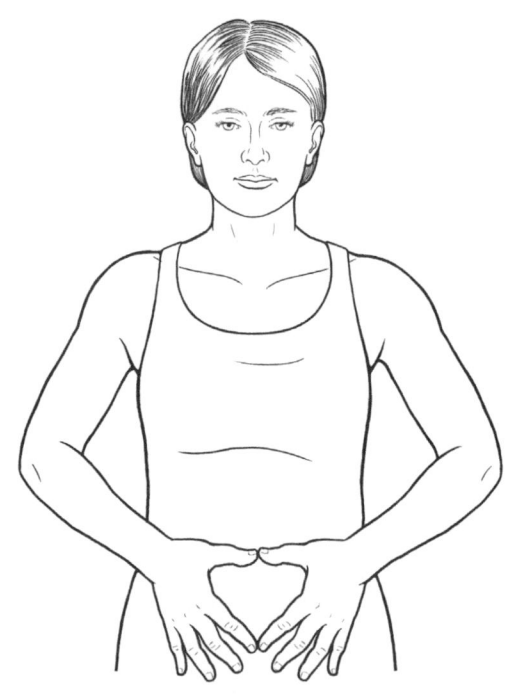

Image 106—Triangle Over Lower Belly

Water מ

Connect the thumbs on the navel and the spread fingers over the groin and pubic bone, making a triangle over the lower belly. Close your eyes. As you exhale, fill the belly with the MMM sound. Imagine the entire area as a clear, crystal blue, beautiful river. Feel the river flowing between the hands and then let it flow to every cell of the body, purifying, releasing stale patterns.

Continue exhaling with the MMM sound and picture the river flowing to a part of your back, belly, legs, or other body part that wants some attention. Let the purifying waters linger there, gently but firmly extracting whatever lies buried and is ready to be released. As the MMM of the crystalline water washes away old patterns that no longer serve you, observe closely to see if you can identify what is being released. When the cleansing feels complete move on to the *shin*.

Image 107—Hands on Forehead

Fire ש

Place your thumbs on the temples and let your fingers gently rest on the forehead above the eyebrows. Make sure the elbows are supported and comfortable. Your hands cradle the right and left brain and the main stress points of the body. The main stress points are located halfway between the arch of the eyebrows and the hairline.

As you exhale, make the sound SHHH and feel the *shin*, passion, the power of the mind's focus, enlivening between your hands, burning red. Feel the heat of the red fire burning off unwanted thoughts or stories that may be stuck in the mind. Observe closely to see if you can identify what is being released and when the process feels complete, move on.

Heart ל

Place the right hand on the forehead imagining the **red fire** of *shin*.

Place the left hand over the belly, imagining the **blue water** of *mem*.
   With either or both hands, slowly draw infinity signs between the forehead and the belly with *lamed/ל*, the heart, at the center. See the **red fire** of *shin* and the **blue water** of *mem* slowly blend as fire and water move closer the heart. At the heart/*lev*, **water** and **fire** are in such harmony that they appear **violet**.
   Bathe in the **violet light** of balance, harmony and wholeness. Imagine the **fire/water** infinity sign, animating every cell. See the cells glow violet.

Lev, the love of the heart, allows opposites to coexist and dance together without losing their individual identities. Together in the center of the heart they create something new and beautiful in its own right, **violet**. The heart can be a space of love, acceptance, presence, and *shalom/shleimut*, feelings of wholeness and inner peace. Acknowledge the opposites of fire/masculine and water/feminine within yourself and the beauty of their relationship. Know that the balance and wholeness you create is a *tikun*, a repair that goes beyond the self, influencing the energies of all those around you.

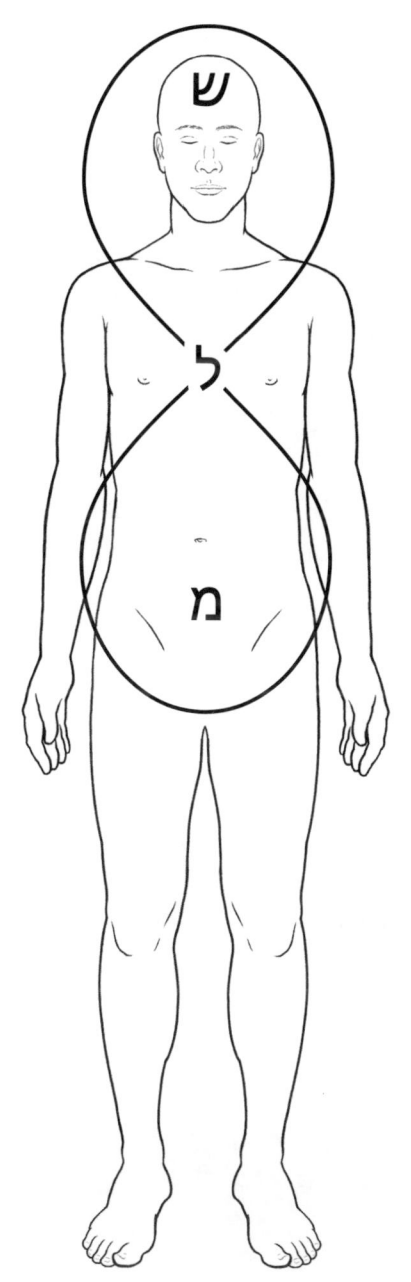

Image 108—Heart Fire

The Shalom/Infinity Meditation 249

28

Shabbat

The mystery of Shabbat is the unification of the Shechina and the K"BH, the masculine and feminine aspects of the Infinite One. Shabbat is a celebration of this divine marriage through a balance and harmony we can emulate in ourselves.

Shabbat, the Jewish Sabbath, begins on Friday evening and ends on Saturday night. In the Genesis creation story, each day ends with the words, "and there was evening and there was morning." Therefore, in the Jewish calendar, days begin and end in the evening. In the story, the process of creation ended as the sun set on the sixth day and on that evening a seventh sacred day of rest and renewal began. In our post-creation world, this pattern is emulated each Friday evening when the traditional workweek ends and the Sabbath (called *Shabbat*, from the Hebrew word for seven, *sheva*) begins.

The onset of Shabbat is symbolized by the return of the *Shechina*, as bride, queen, beloved. The kabbalists of Safed, singing, praying, and reciting psalms, would go out to the fields to greet her. Even today, the custom is to turn west to the setting sun to welcome her as she arrives.[109] The Zohar describes in beautifully poetic language how the *K"BH* waits for her as well as how, when the two are finally One, they are both surrounded in supernal holy light. The *K"BH* as Creator and *Shechina* as the Creation spend Shabbat blissfully merged in divine marriage. In the physical world, many categories of work are expressly forbidden in order to sanctify this oasis in time.

This beautiful passage from the Zohar (135a) is found in many *siddurim* in the Friday evening service that ushers in Shabbat. It is a poetic description of the arrival of

---
[109] This occurs during the last verse of the welcoming hymn, *Lecha Dodi* ("Come, My Beloved").

the *Shechina* and her reunion with the *K"BH* (here called the holy King, Oneness). The *K"BH* as Creator and *Shechina* as the Creation spend the day united in divine marriage.

> *The mystery of Shabbat is Shabbat herself: Shechina is called Shabbat when she is united with the mystery of Oneness. During the prepations for her arrival, the Shechina is liberated from all forces of evil and harsh judgments, leaving her free for intimate union with the supernal holy light. When Shabbat arrives she merges into Oneness, adorned with many crowns by the holy King. Her face glows in heavenly light while receiving a crown of Shabbat prayers from earth, from the holy people... happily blessing Her, joy on every face... Shabbat blessings and peace begin to flow.*[110]

Shabbat traditionally begins with ritual candle lighting. The candles symbolize and sanctify the reunion of the *K"BH* and *Shechina*. They are lit at eighteen minutes before sunset, the time, it is said, when creation ceased.[111] At this moment a powerful wave of candlelight travels around the world following the setting sun. The two candles are identical and white, reflecting the equality of the *K"BH* and *Shechina*. and the sacredness of their union.

The eighteen minutes between candle lighting and sunset, marking the joyful return of the *Shechina*, can be the most charged moments of the week. This time is an opportunity to both celebrate and emulate the Divine Union in ourselves and strengthen our own vessels to hold more light. To this end, candle lighting time is a particularly powerful time to practice Kabbalah/energy exercises.

Candlelighting Practices

Here are some suggested practices to accompany candlelighting. Try some or all. If you have other candlelighting rituals please include them.

---

110 Excerpted and adapted from the following sources: *Siddur Tehillat Hashem*, trans. Rabbi Nissen Mangel (New York, Merkos L'Inyonei Chinuch, 1978), 133–134; *Siddur Sim Shalom*, trans. Rabbi Jules Harlow (New York,Rabbinical Assembly, 1985), 278.

111 Candle lighting times specific for your location can be found at www.chabad.org. There is also an app with this information called Shabbat Times.

1. Before lighting and blessing the candles, practice the *Ana B'Koach*/Seven Spirals exercise in chapter 24. This connection to the forty-two-letter Name symbolically unites the six days of creation and the seventh, *Shabbat, the K"BH and Shechina*, and sets an energetic framework for welcoming the Sabbath by harmonizing all the directions.

2. Practice connecting heaven and earth (chapter 19) and feel your heart and every cell resonating with the power of this connection.

3. After lighting and just before blessing the candles observe the flames. The flames look like *yud*s, and the two flames together create the divine Name *yud/yud*, י-י, also a union of divine masculine and feminine. Stare at the flames for a few moments and you will see the infinity shape the flames create. Trace infinity signs of love between the flames themselves, between your heart and the flames, and then around your entire body.

4. Bless the candles, adding any customary practices.[112]

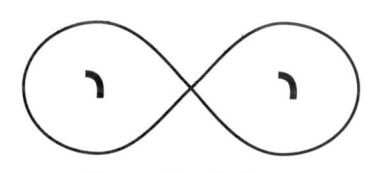

Image 109—Infinity Sign with Yuds

5. Candlelighting provides an opportunity to use the Shiviti spectacles (Infinity Eyes, chapter 22) Continue to face the candles with the eyes still covered by your hands. Imagine that the space between the candles, where the light of the flames meets, is the center of an infinity sign connecting them. Feel that point resonating with the golden *chuppa* at your third eye. Experience the ∞ of the YHVH spectacles coming from you as a reflection of the infinity signs of י-י created by the candle flames and vice versa. Stay in this meditation for as long as you like.

---

[112] The traditional candlelighting blessing for Shabbat is:
בָּרוּךְ אַתָּה יְיָ אֱלֹהֵינוּ מֶלֶךְ הָעוֹלָם אֲשֶׁר קִדְּשָׁנוּ
בְּמִצְוֹתָיו וְצִוָּנוּ לְהַדְלִיק נֵר שֶׁל שַׁבָּת.
Baruch ata Adonai, Eloheinu melech ha'olam, asher ki'di'sha'nu b'mitzvotav v'tzeevanu l'had'leek ner shel Shabbat.
Blessed are You, Source of blessings, Who commands us to light the Sabbath candles.

6. Open your eyes slowly, returning from the realm of spirit into the physical body, and maintaining your connection to both realms. The Hook-In *Sh'ma* can be added here to help connect grounding and centering to the sacred (see chapter 20).

7. End with the hands over the heart, breathing deeply in the nose and out the mouth.

Sacred Sexuality
An Energy/Kabbalah Practice for Shabbat Evening
This practice strengthens the bonds of intimacy between partners and also strengthens and expands the vessel of their relationship.

An Extra Soul

To prepare for Shabbat after a week of intense study, the kabbalists of the Ari's circle would purify themselves on Friday afternoon in the *mikva* (ritual bath). Afterwards, they would welcome the Sabbath, sometimes going out into the fields to greet the *Shechina*. It is said that the *Shechina* arrives with an extra soul called the *neshama yiteira* נְשָׁמָה יְתֵרָה for each of us to enjoy. There have been many discussions throughout the ages of what this "extra soul" might be. One kabbalistic explanation is that the *neshama yiteira* is an actual part of one's unique soul light that enhances the pleasures of Shabbat.

After prayer, the men of the Ari's circle would return home to enjoy a festive dinner with their families. *Shabbat* was the one day that pleasures of the body, such as eating and sexuality, were not just allowed but celebrated. Such pleasures were celebrated because on *Shabbat* the *neshama yiteira* expanded physical pleasure from the realm of the mundane into the level of the spiritual.

Specifically on *Shabbat*, sexual intimacy was regarded as an emulation of the divine marriage. The kabbalists of the Ari's circle honored their wives on Shabbat as embodiments of the *Shechina*, and sexual intimacy was part of their Friday evening tradition.

Without the spiritual component, the presence of *Yah*/י-ה in a relationship, man and woman are simply אש/fire, and passion can quickly burn their union into ashes. When י-ה is present, the *hei*/ה can face the *yud*/י creating a *chet*/ח, the first letter of *chuppah*, the holy container in which their passion can be contained and elevated.

Sexuality as Healing/*Tikun*

As mentioned in chapter 1, we are now in the Hebrew year of 5778, coming to the end of the sixth millennium. Each of the seven days of the creation story in Genesis correspond to a specific sefira. Similarly, each millennium is related to a specific *sefira*. For example, *Chesed* marked the first day of creation and the first thousand years. Through the millennia we have been moving down the Tree coming closer and closer to *Malchut* as the manifestation of a cosmic Shabbat, the full expression of the *Shechina*. We are now, in 5778, at the lowest *sefira* in Z"A, *Yesod*, coming ever closer to the border of *Malchut*. *Yesod*, representing the phallos of *Adam Kadmon*, is the place where the resolution of masculine/feminine balance will either be successful, or it won't. Truly uniting the six of Z"A to the seven of *Malchut/Shechina* would create the ultimate thirteen of love and Oneness. My Zohar teacher, Sarah Yehudit Schneider, refers to sexual healing as the last frontier of *tikun olam*, for this connection requires elevating the physicality of sex to the realm of the spiritual.[113] Sexual healing is a *tikun* within the realm of possibility for each of us, and our efforts matter.

A Beautiful Teaching

Remember that in Kabbalah, the letters of a word carry its essence.

The word for Man (איש/*eesh*), is made up of the word for

fire/אש/*aish* + the letter *yud*/י

MAN = Fire + *yud*

The word for Woman (אשה/*eesha*), is

fire/אש/*aish* +the letter *hei*/ה

WOMAN = Fire + *hei*

י-ה is a sacred Name of God, *Yah* = *yud*/י/*hei* + ה

---

[113] Recently formed movements and groups such as #MeToo and Time's Up are making progress in this *tikun* by revealing and healing a societal aspect of masculine/feminine imbalance.

Shabbat 255

The Practice

The Zohar describes sacred sexuality in great detail. Some sections were guarded so carefully that they are still in the process of being translated. The following Kabbalah/energy exercise is not in the Zohar, as far as I am aware. It is a way to weave your energies with the energies of your partner in an aligned face-to-face, head-to-toe connection. According to the Ari, this is the highest level of intimate relationship.[114] Like Eastern practices of tantra, kabbalists believe that sexual relationships can be both spiritual and transformational. The following practice can be a prelude to sacred sex, but it can also provide healing through deep and intimate energetic connection without a sexual component.

Energies need to be in communication with each other in order to function with maximum vitality. In healthy individuals this communication is often reflected in an abundance of infinity patterns throughout the energy body, including the surrounding auric field. Similarly, the more infinity shape connections exist between two people, the stronger and deeper is their energetic relationship. In this Kabbalah/energy practice, rhythmic infinity-shaped movements, first with the hands and then with the entire body, unite and ignite the spiritual and sexual energies.

The partners imagine their individual Trees of Life linked through a shared central column. Together, they focus on the *sefirot* of that central column: *Da'at*, *Tiferet*, *Yesod*, and *Malchut*. Unlike tantric practices that move up the body, this practice moves down, to activate, strengthen and expand *Malchut* into a vessel that protects and surrounds the partners. Because of the balance created between the partners, the central column becomes a conduit for higher consciousness that can help to heal whatever issues arise in the relationship.

The sacred sexuality practice can be done at any time. However, if it is actually Shabbat, you may choose to visualize the *neshama yiteira* (the extra layer of Shabbat soul) as a river of light that intensifies the light emitted by the letters.

---

114 Sarah Yehudit Schneider, *Kabbalistic Writings on the Nature of Masculine and Feminine*, chapter 3.

Individual Preparation

Start by bringing balance to your own Tree. Balance the *sefirot* of the right and left columns with each other by tracing horizontal infinity signs of love and oneness. Begin at the head. Trace the infinity signs from side to side, down the body and back up again. Use one hand or both. Balancing the right and left columns of your Tree will activate its central column to connect through the practice with that of your partner.

Imagine that the infinity signs penetrate through you so that they simultaneously cover your back. Tracing or imagining horizontal infinity signs on the back activates the radiant circuit called the bridge flow which helps to connect body and spirit.

With Your Partner

This practice is an extension of Infinity Eyes from Chapter 22, so you may want to review it. Sit in a comfortable seated position across from your partner, close enough to touch. You may choose to verbalize your intention for the practice. Place your left, receiving, hands over your own hearts and rest your right, giving, hand over your partner's left. Close the eyes and take some deep breaths together, in the nose and out the mouth.

Activating *Da'at*

Open your eyes. Gaze gently at your partner's third eye, the space between the eyebrows which represents *Da'at*.[115] *Da'at* is the realm of sacred sexuality, the source of pleasure, and in the Torah refers to knowing one's partner totally. Feel the special intensity of your connection at *Da'at*.

Stay close enough to your partner to be in physical contact, perhaps cross-legged, touching at the knees. Keep your left hand on your own heart and with the right, trace infinity signs between your heads at the level of *Da'at*. Imagine a *chuppah* at the center point between you.

Note: In Infinity Eyes, a *chuppa* is created at the *Da'at* visualized between your own eyes. In that practice, the golden letters of the four-letter Name flow out from between

....
115 The physical location of *Da'at* is subject to interpretation. Although sometimes placed in the area of the throat, for this practice, as in Infinity Eyes, it is visualized at the third eye.

Shabbat 257

the cherubs who reunite under the chuppa of your personal sanctuary (*mishkan*). In this partnered practice a *mishkan* for two is created, and the letters of the Name YHVH flow from the shared *chuppah* resting between you. Remember that the *gematria* of YHVH is twenty-six, the same as love/*ahava*/13 + love/*ahava*/13. In addition to the power of the letters themselves, the flow of Y/H/V/H generates an ever-growing bond of love between the partners throughout the practice.

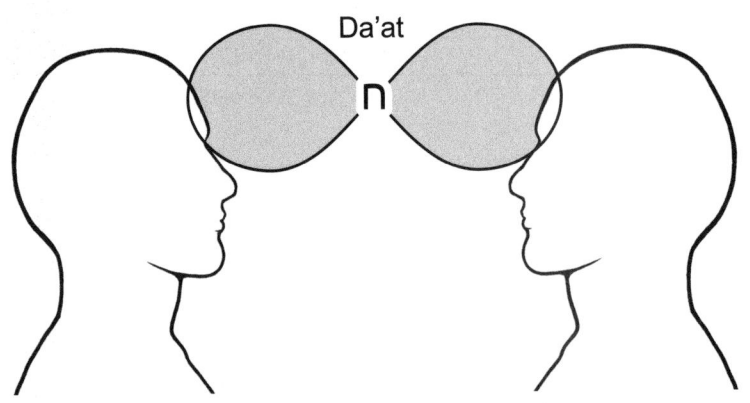

Image 110—Facing Partner with *Da'at*

Continue to trace horizontal infinity patterns between you, at the level of the third eye. Between you, at the center of your combined *Da'at* infinity pattern, lies your *chuppa*. You can imagine the chuppa resting between you there or mentally expand it to cover you. Perhaps imagine yourselves as the cherubs that are guarding the sacredness of your relationship. As you trace the horizontal infinity patterns to your partner and back, visualize the golden letters of YHVH/הוה -י flowing out from the center of your shared *chuppah*.

The letters weave around and through each other in the light of the infinity path that connects you. They expand to create an infinity sign of golden intertwined letters encircling your heads. If you wish to add a vocalization, exhale with the continual sound *eee*, as in the word "see."

This is the special vowel sound of *Da'at*.

Stop tracing but continue to see the golden letters flowing from the *chuppah* between you. Gently place your hands on each other's knees. Begin moving your heads and bodies together in <u>slow</u> horizontal infinity patterns, back and forth. Circle toward each other and away. Reverse direction whenever desired. Between your two foreheads lies the *chet* of your *chuppah*. Eyes can be open or closed. As you smoothly and slowly move together in the infinity shape, continue to visualize the golden letters encircling your heads.

Tiferet

Continue breathing and slowly moving your bodies in the infinity shape as the letter flow expands down to the area of the heart, activating the *sefira* of *Tiferet*, beauty. At *Tiferet*, the golden letters harmonize, balance, and connect your deepest hearts.

If you wish to add a vocalization, exhale with the continual sound of *ohhhh* (as in the word "slow"). This is the special vowel sound of *Tiferet*.

Send love to your partner from the depths of your heart. Open your heart to safely receive their love and the light of their inner beauty. Continue to breathe and move together. When the connection at *Tiferet* feels complete, move the focus to the area of *Yesod* in the low belly.

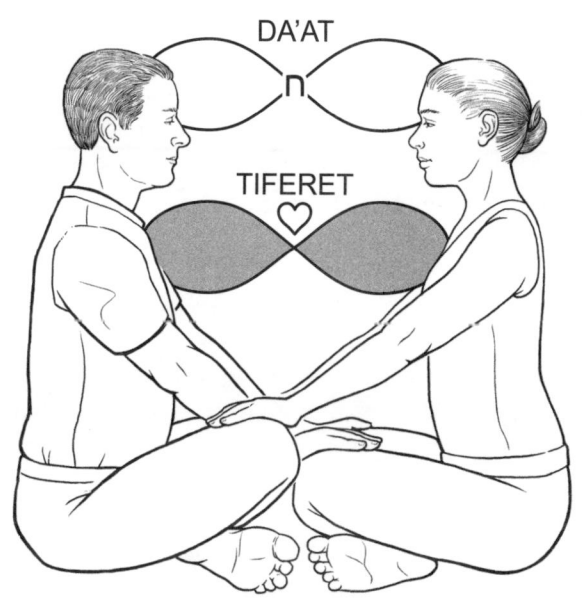

Image 111—*Sefira* of *Tiferet*

Yesod

Yesod is the center of sexuality and relationship. As your bodies continue to move rhythmically and slowly, back and forth in the infinity pattern, allow the letters to move down further, to the area of the low belly. Stay connected at *Da'at* and *Tiferet* as you visualize the lights of the golden letters of the Name activating *Yesod*. Feel the harmony and connection between your *Yesod* and that of your partner.

If you wish to add a vocalization, exhale with the continual sound *uuu*, as in the word "you." This is the special vowel sound of *Yesod*.

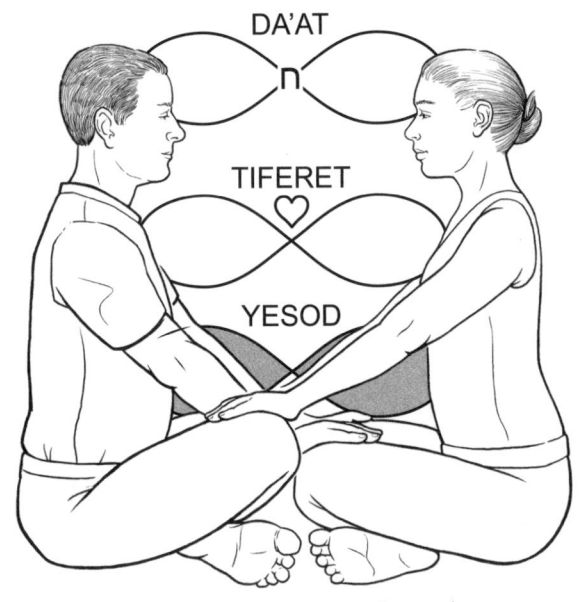

Image 112—*Yesod*

Malchut

Stop moving. You have connected at *Da'at, Tiferet, and Yesod*. The central column in your shared Tree is activated and glowing. When the connections between the upper *sefirot* have been made, the light finally reaches the level of *Malchut*—the stabilizing, grounding force of the Tree. *Malchut* is like an empty vessel waiting to be filled. She has no light of her own and like the moon, reflects back light she receives. *Malchut* receives the intense energy generated from the higher *sefirot,* and in a geyser of fireworks, sends the light back out. The letters of the Name weave around you, and the weaving strengthens the vessel of your relationship. Together, you are grounded and protected by your shared *Malchut*. You have created a vessel strong and flexible enough to hold and process whatever arises between you.

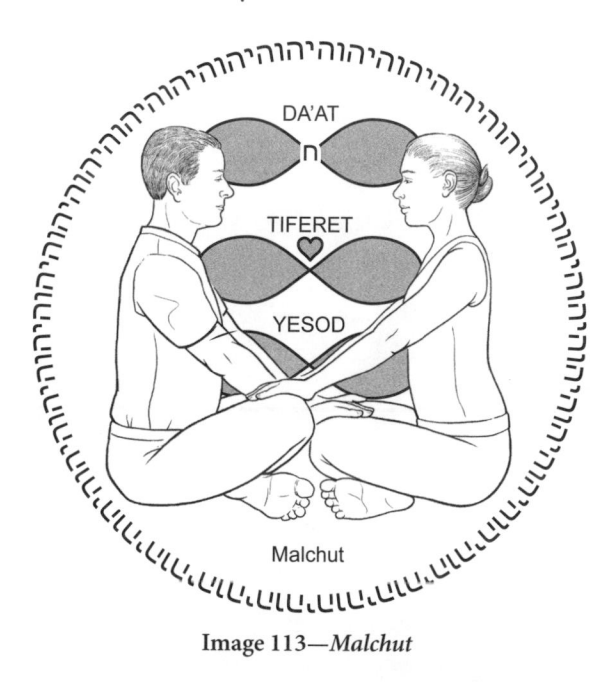

Image 113—*Malchut*

The space between you is charged, electric with anticipation. End as you began with your left hand over your own heart and your right hand over your partner's. Gaze softly at each other. Breathe together. Experience the joy of being surrounded by the letters of the Name. You are in harmony with the divine union which Shabbat ushers in.

PART 3

Healing

29

Kabbalistic Energy Healing

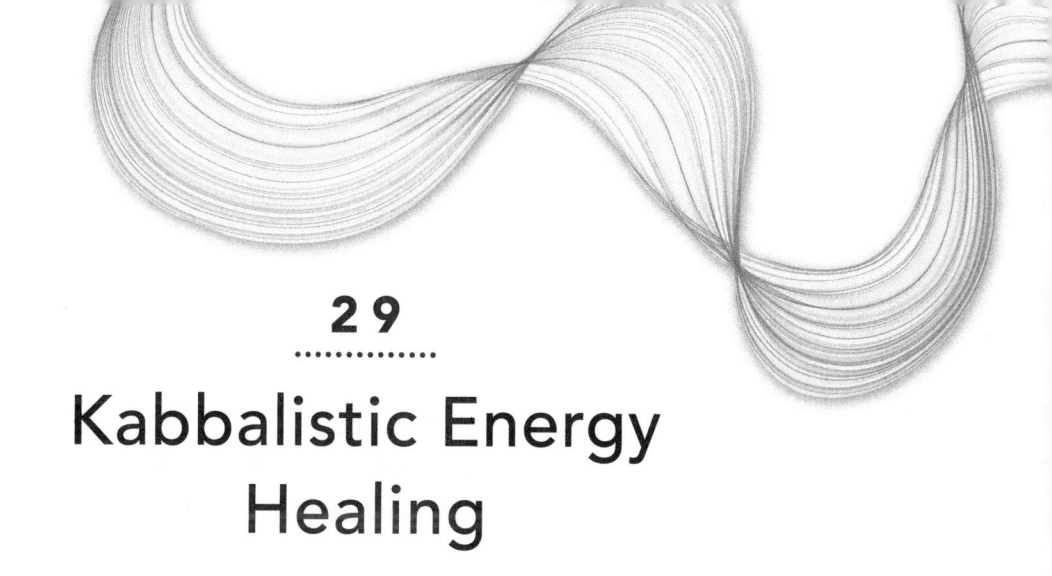

Love, the true flow of the universe and connection to God, is a great healer. In kabbalistic energy healing, a unification of masculine and feminine creates a field of divine love in the heart. The *gematria* of this unification is twenty-six. The twenty-six divides into 2 x 13/*ahava*/love. The wellspring of love in the heart then flows out the hands for healing. This technique is a modification of Quantum-Touch.[116]

Conscious breathing is the key to continually replenishing the healing energy. The word for breath, *neshima*, has the same root as the word for soul, *neshama*. The breath used in this healing is a breath of the soul. It cleaves to God, the Infinite Light. God's light is transformed to love, the source of healing.

As the healer, it is essential that you are comfortable with the breath. Two alternatives are given. I use them both and so have included both. First is the Breath of Love, also called *aleph* (א) breath, which was presented in chapter 15 and summarized below. Second is the YHVH breath, presented in detail. If you are familiar with a different form of healing touch than those presented here, try the addition of one of these breaths to your practice. They each connect to a different expression of God's Holy Name to create a field of healing love which then flows from the heart out the hands.

---

116 As taught by Richard Gordon, www.quantumtouch.com.

As extensions of the heart, the hands are the channels for healing energy. As divine love flows from the heart out the hands, the recipient resonates with this vibration at whatever level they are open to allowing, and healing occurs.

Remember that the word for hand is *yad*/יד and in Hebrew is spelled the same as the letter *yud*/יד.

The letter *yud* represents the light of the divine spark. In Kabbalah the name of something reflects its essence. Therefore, the essence of the hand/*yad* is also the divine spark. It can be helpful to visualize the love flowing from the hands as divine sparks.

- *Yad*/hand is the channel of healing
- *Yud*/י has the *gematria* of ten.
- There are ten fingers which connect to the power of the ten *sefirot* of the Tree of Life.

Therefore the breath has ten counts:

    4 count inhale
    1 count hold
    5 count exhale

1. The Breath of Love

    The Breath of Love is a visualization of the letter *aleph* with its three components (see Chapter 8).

        י   upper *yud*
     א ו   *vav*
        י   lower *yud*

    The upper *yud* refers to: heaven/the *K"BH*.
    The lower *yud* refers to: earth/the *Shechina*.
    The *vav*, meaning *and*—the connection—waits for them in the heart.
    There, the two *yuds* form a divine unification.
    Together with the *vav*, they create an *aleph*/א, יו/the Holy Name/YY,
    The *gematria* of the components of *aleph*: yud, vav, yud totals 26.
    The ten-count Breath of Love is divided into:

Inhale, 4 counts

Pause, 1 count

Exhale, 5 counts

Inhale, counts 1 through 4:

Imagine the breath rising up from the soles of the feet (earth/*Shechina*) and down from the crown of the head (heaven/*K"BH*) at the same time. Va*v*, centered in *Tiferet* at the heart attracts the upper *Yud* of heaven and the lower *Yud* of earth to each other.

The *Yud* of heaven and the *Yud* of earth together create the Holy Name name YY. YY joins with the *Vav* to create *Aleph*/א, (YVY)

Heaven

י

Inhale

אהבה　א　אהבה

Inhale

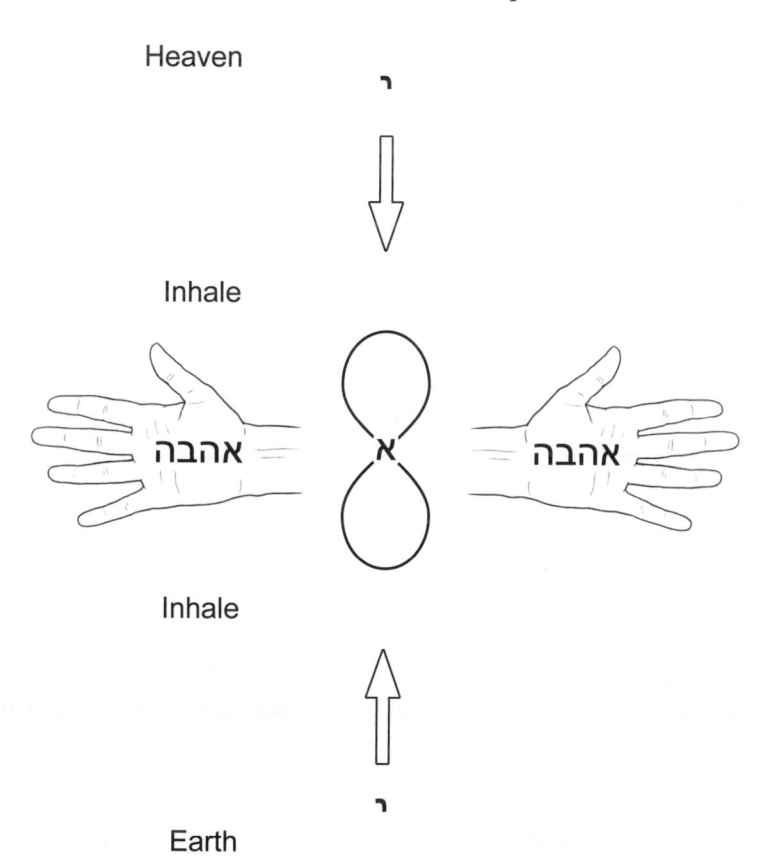

ו

Earth

Image 114—10 Counts Breath of Love

Pause, count 5:
In the heart, the coming together of YVY creates א, whose components add to *gematria* 26 . The 26 divides into 13 + 13/love + love.

As you pause on count 5, visualize the א **dividing into love-love**

Exhale, counts 6 through 10:
Feel love flowing from the heart into the **hands** activating them to **release divine sparks** of healing.

2. YHVH breath
The breath connects to YHVH and unites the four letters of the Name in the heart. Energy is gathered from earth beneath the feet and inhaled up the body out through *Keter* (the crown of the head). There it connects to the healing light of heaven. The energy is then exhaled back down to the heart. In the heart, YHVH, as *gematria* 26, is converted to 13 + 13/love + love and sent out the hands for healing. The Name YHVH is continuously visualized with the inhaled breath.

Image 115—YHVH Breath

Preparation for Connecting to YHVH through the Breath

Before working with a healee, practice the breath until it feels comfortable and natural. You will be visualizing the letters of the Name, so familiarize yourself with them, especially their shapes and names. The Name is also filled with symbolism, presented in Chapter 8. You may want to reread this chapter before you proceed, but once you have reviewed the material it is important to stay out of your head as much as possible. Do not dwell on the symbols, just appreciate that the Name has many layers of meaning, specifically the unification of divine masculine and feminine. It is beautiful when some associations arise naturally with the conscious breath, but as you visualize the letters, try to focus on the sensations in your hands and the breath moving through your body. Visualizing the letters can provide enough of a mental challenge.

As you inhale, project the letters of YHVH/יהוה in your mind, written vertically. Because the breath rises from earth to heaven, the Name is visualized backwards, from the final *hei*/ה to the *yud*/י at the beginning. The inhale is similar to the instructions for Earth Grounding in chapter 14.

Open your body to earth energy, the realm of the *Shechina*. Imagine the breath entering from beneath your feet.

Inhale the breath from earth up the body, from the end of the name to the beginning: H-V-H-Y—crown of the *yud*

י-ה-ו-ה

Repeat this visualization for every breath.

Inhale to a count of four visualizing ה/H- ו/V- ה/H- י/Y

As you inhale, imagine you are connecting deeply to each letter, breathing in the light and power of YHVH. Try to stay focused on the letters and the path of the breath. As the breath rises in the body, imagine the healing life force rising as well.

As you exhale, focus on sending divine love out the hands. If divine love is too abstract a concept, it may be helpful to imagine the deep love you have for a person or even a pet, filling and expanding the heart to overflowing. It may also help to visualize the healing love leaving the hands as divine sparks.

YHVH Breath

The Inhale

Count 1: the inhale travels from the "roots" of the final *hei*/ה up the legs

Count 2: the breath rises **up the spine** through the ו/*vav*

Count 3: the breath rises **up the chest and arms** through the ה/*hei*

Count 4: the breath rises up through the **neck, head, and crown** through the י/*yud*

Image 116—The Inhale

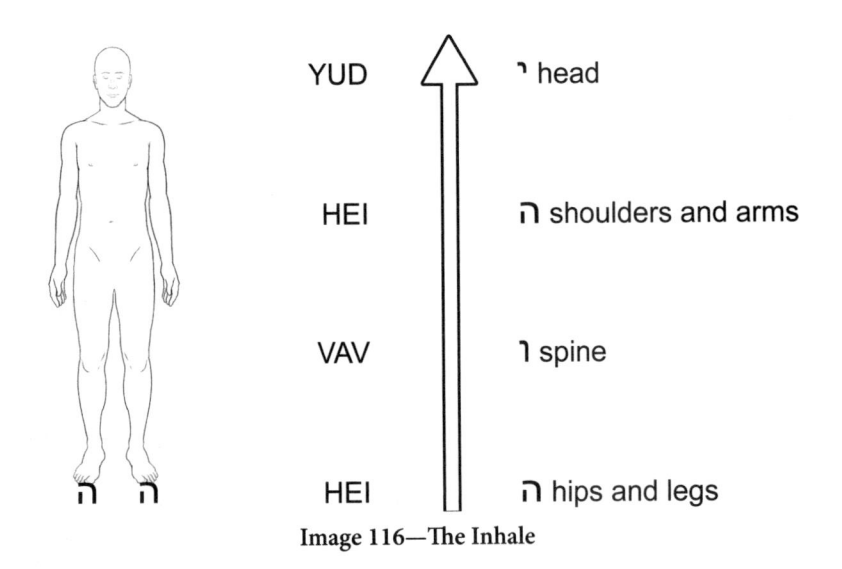

Count 5: **Pause**
Hold the breath briefly at *Keter*, at the tip of the *yud*. The tip of the *yud* symbolizes the closest connection to the influx of divine flow also called *shefa*/שפע. Open the top of the head with your imagination. Picture a large funnel or satellite dish there, and receive the abundant flow of *shefa*. This moment of pausing between the inhale and the exhale is the moment that all the letters of the Name, here representing Heaven/K"BH and Earth/*Shechina*, come together.

The Five-Count Exhale

Count 1: The heart fills with love
Use your imagination to direct the YHVH/י-הוה breath down from *Keter* into your heart.
In the heart, *Tiferet*, the *gematria* of YHVH/י-הוה 26, divides in 13/love+13/love.

Counts **2, 3, 4, 5**
Feel the **flow** of this powerful love/life force from the heart out **through** each of your **hands**.

Suggestion

"AH" is the natural sound of the exhaled breath. "AH" is also considered by many mystical traditions to be the sound of the heart chakra and is the vowel sound of *ahava/love*. It may help to experience the flow of love by ending the ten-count breath by slowly exhaling AH-HA-VA:

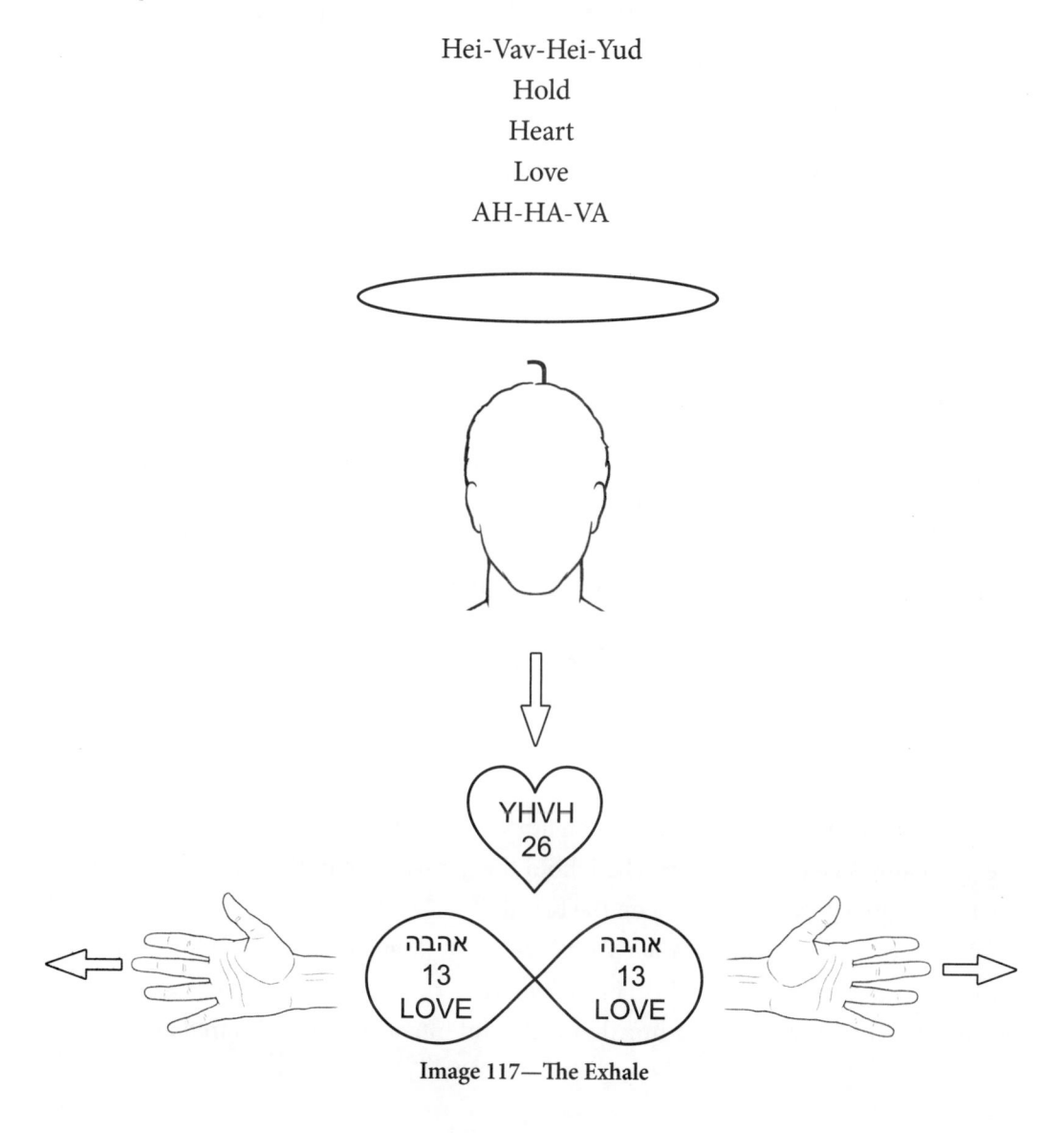

Hei-Vav-Hei-Yud
Hold
Heart
Love
AH-HA-VA

Image 117—The Exhale

General Preparation

1. Set an **intention** to be a channel of healing energy. Ask that the highest good of the recipient be realized through the healing. Trust in the process.

2. **Wash** the hands and bless them with the traditional blessing (chapter 16) or one of your own creation.

3. **Connect heaven and earth** to activate the hands (chapter 19).

4. **Set energy boundaries** (chapter 17). It is important to stay in your own field and not take on another's energy.

5. Optional: Fill yourself with light via the **Light Weave** (chapter 23).

The field of healing created by running the energy through the body and out the hands is non-willful. Non-willful means that your own agenda must not be a part of the process. Healing takes many forms. Set your intention that the healing be for the highest good and then trust in the power of divine love and a higher knowing. We cannot fathom the mystery nor see the bigger picture. You are the vessel for healing so relax and allow the energy to flow freely through you. You may want to begin with a personal prayer or an appropriate psalm, but then get yourself out of the way.

Connecting to the Healee

Always discuss the process with the person you will be touching before you begin. They need to feel comfortable and safe to receive your touch. Check in with them as often as needed.

Place the hands lightly and gently on any body part that needs special attention. If the part cannot be touched or reached, hold the hands close to the body without making direct contact. Keep focusing on the breath.

Wherever the energies of the two hands meet, *ahava* reconnects with *ahava* and creates the healing power of YHVH or *aleph*, restoring Oneness, wholeness. Send this beam of healing love with your breath, touch, and intention, to the injured area.

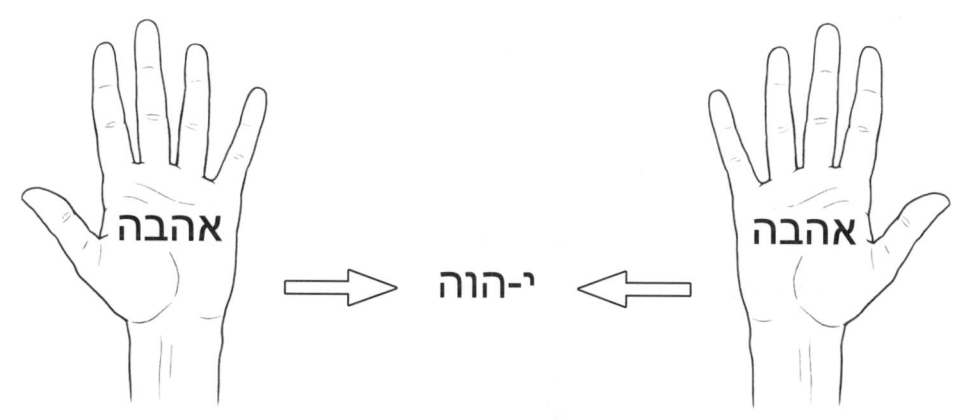

Image 118—Love Restores Wholeness

Be aware of sensation in the hands. This sensation varies from person to person, but some sensation should be present such as vibration, tingling, pulsing, or heat. Keep the hands relaxed and soft throughout the session so healing energy can flow easily and smoothly through them. If you sense that you are taking on energy from the person you are healing, stop and shake your hands off before you continue. It is important to keep your boundaries secure.

Repeat the breath sequence throughout, building your endurance to 20 to 30 minutes. As you end the session, slowly remove the hands and both you and the recipient offer thanks and say Amen.

Emotional Healing

In addition to physical issues, it is possible to use the Breath of Love or YHVH Breath to help with emotional situations. The handholds shown are energy techniques that help to balance emotions and reduce stress. They allow the recipient to feel safe which enables greater openness to the power of the healing. These hand positions are also an excellent way to either begin or end a session for they bring feelings of comfort, calmness, and safety to the person being healed. Continue to connect to the flow of love throughout the healing as you practice either the Breath of Love or the YHVH Breath. Check in with the recipient as often as needed to ensure they are comfortable and feel safe to receive your touch.

Place your hands *very lightly* on the person's head; there is no need to press. It may be uncomfortable for the person if anything more than the most gentle touch is used. The hands can also be positioned slightly off the body, although this may become tiring.

Remain in one position, shift if it feels right, or use your intuition to place your hands where they want to go on the head. Trust in the process. In the safe and non-willful field of love between your hands, the emotions can begin to heal themselves. Relax your hands as much as possible to facilitate the flow of healing love.

Following are two suggestions.

The hands create the position of the Priestly Benediction (see chapter 16). The fingers circle the ears. The thumbs rest gently on the main stress points of the body, halfway between the center of the eyebrow and the hairline.

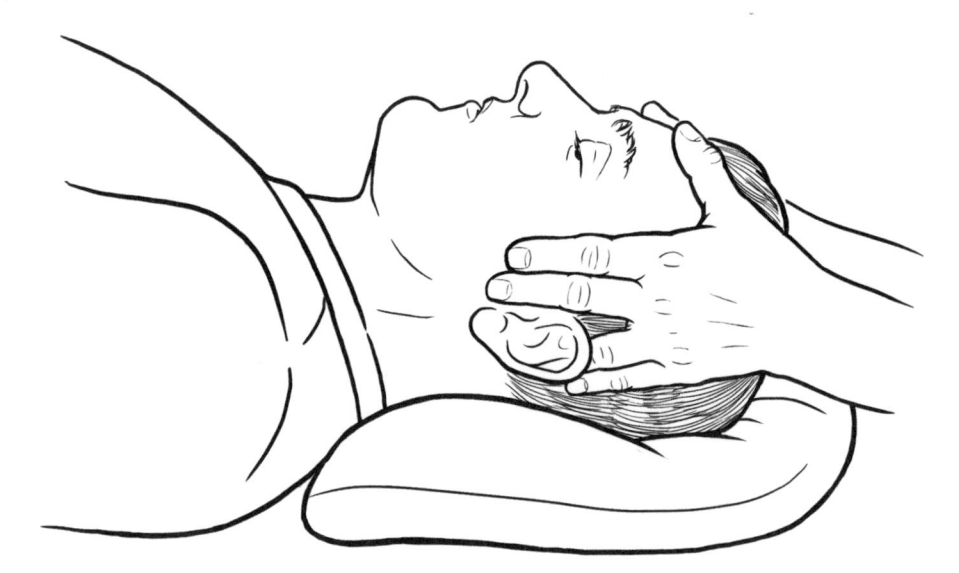

Image 119—Healing Touch diagram #1

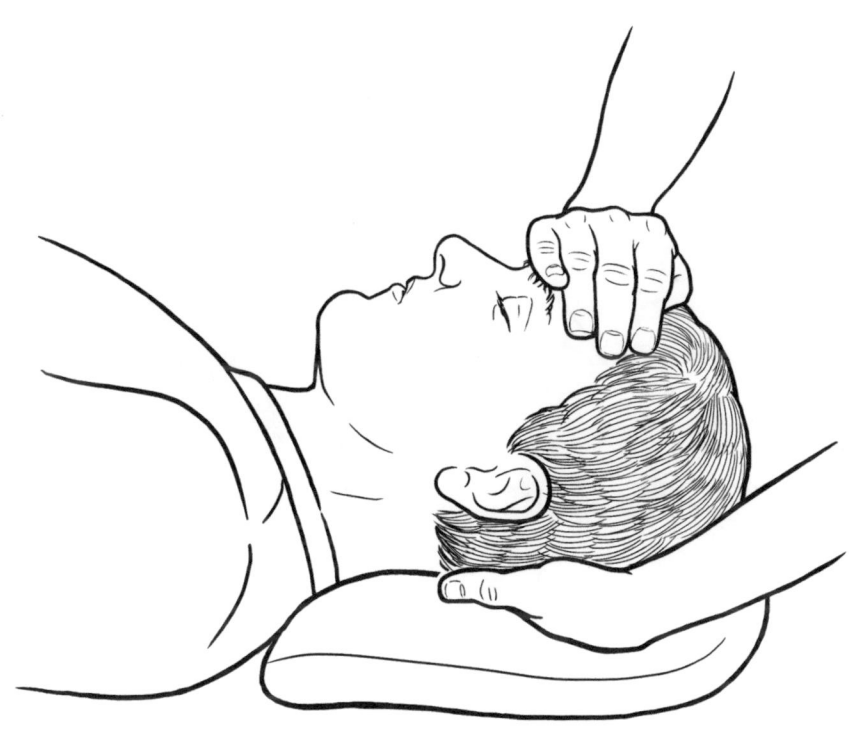

Image 120—Healing Touch diagram #2

Alternatively, one hand rests gently on the forehead, the other under the head. For the comfort of the giver, the person being healed can also turn the head to the side. It is important that you both are very comfortable.

Hold for five to ten minutes or until you and your subject sense you are done. This may be indicated by the feeling of steady pulsing in your hands. Advise the healee that you will be lifting your hands off their head, and slowly, gently, do so.

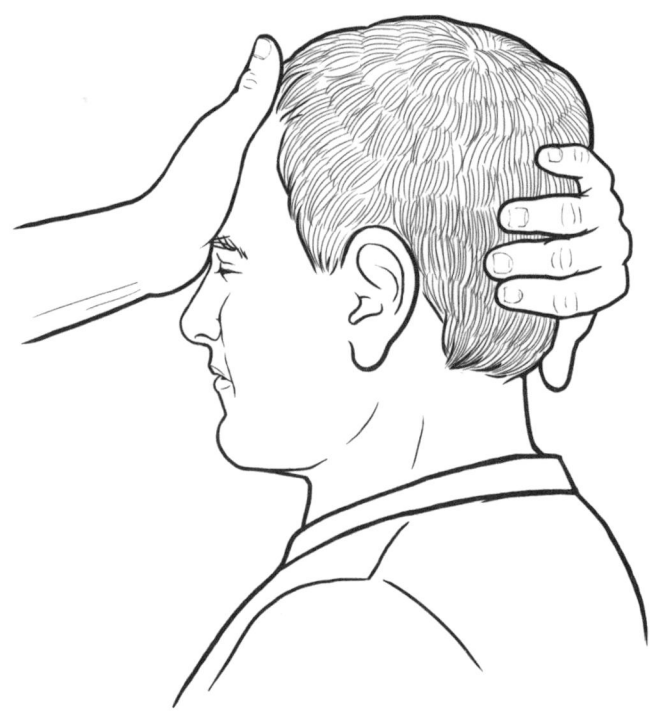

Image 121—Healing Touch diagram #3

Self-Healing

Using either the Breath of Love or the YHVH Breath, place your hands on any part of yourself requiring extra love and attention.

Distance Healing

Prepare as if the person were with you. Picture them in front of you and then shrink the image and place it between your hands. Breathe and let the energy run as if the person were there. Sitting or lying directly on the earth will facilitate this transmission.

~~~

Do not be afraid to attempt these healings. The worst mistake you can make is to imagine that you are doing something wrong. Remember, these healings are non-willful and your intention is for the highest good. Place your trust in the love, light, and goodness of YHVH and you will create *tikun*, the reunion of soul and body, heaven and earth.

PART 4
Summary

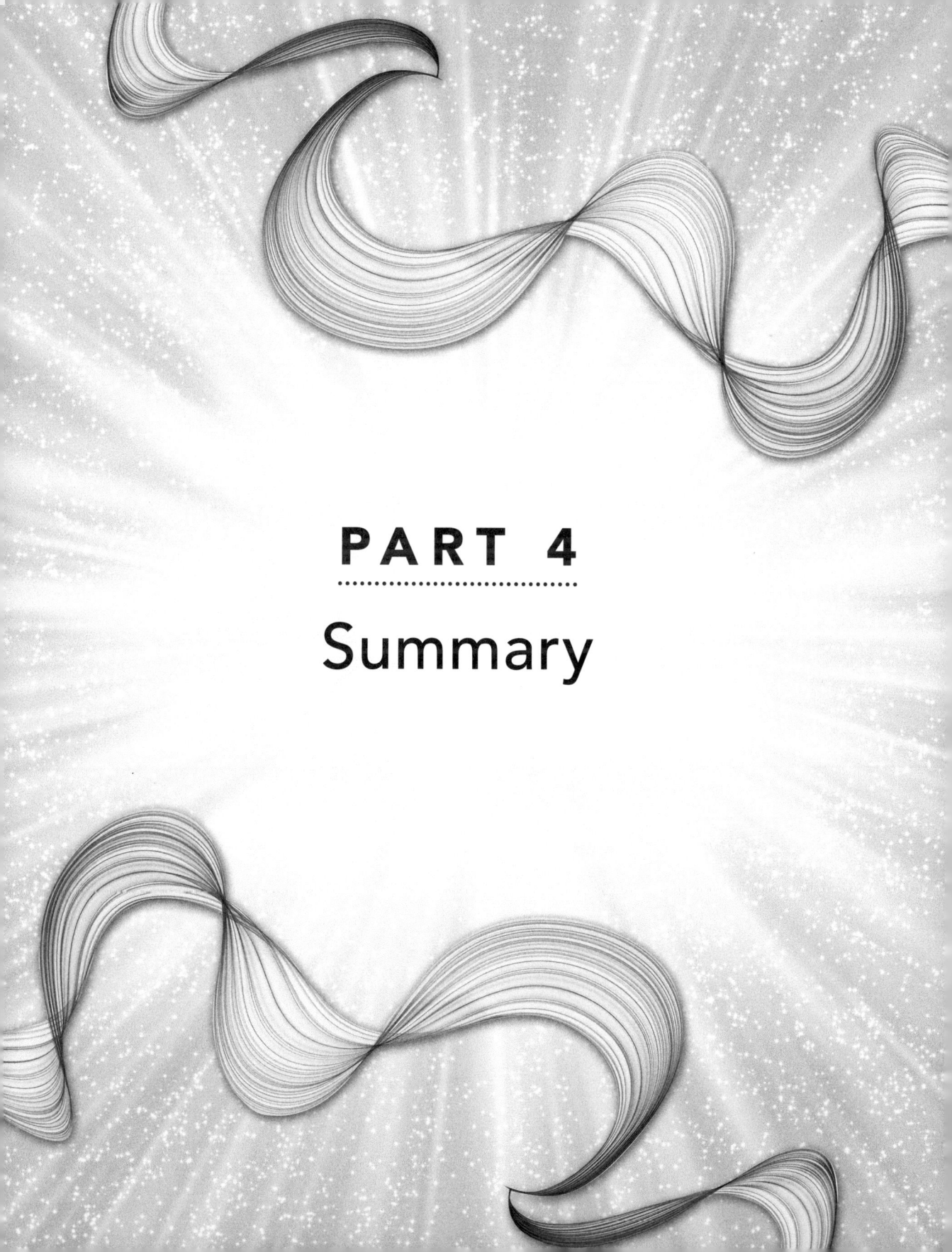

30

The Dragonfly

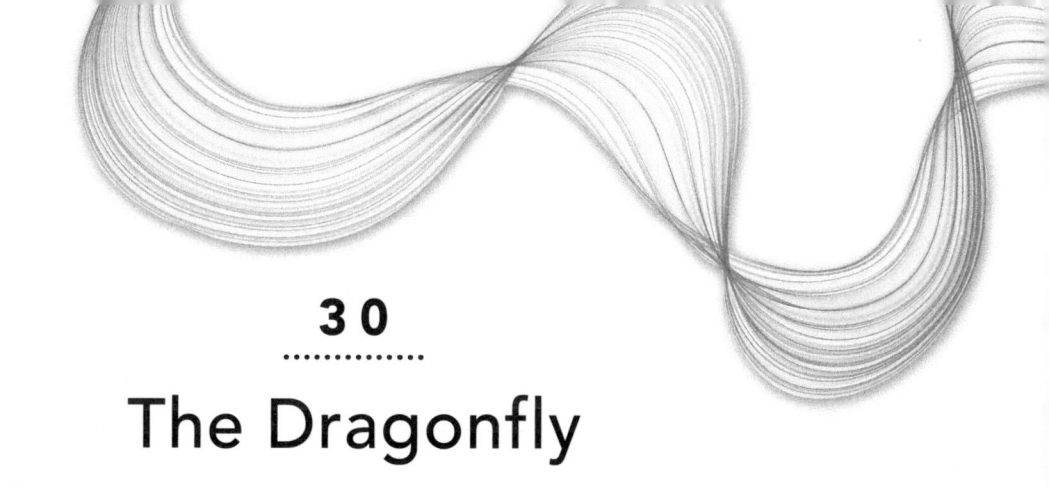

In many cultures, dragonflies are revered as instruments of enlightenment and transformation, but they did not start out that way for me. As a child I feared them. Because we called them darning needles I thought they could bite or pierce me. I would run from them in terror. I could not have imagined then how my studies of Kabbalah and energy medicine would combine to slowly reveal layers of dragonfly secrets.

The dragonfly ties together many of the ideas presented in this book. The four-letter Name י-הוה /YHVH, is a good place to begin. For this discussion, recall that the four letters of the Name symbolize the balance of masculine and feminine. Within YHVH all opposites become one. The letter א /aleph, as the number one, also symbolizes the balance of opposites through its letter components. In addition, the deconstructed *aleph* and the letters of YHVH both share *gematria* 26 and both are symbols of one and the infinite (see chapters 7 and 8).

How did these ideas lead to the dragonfly? Energy medicine provided the key, and the key was the infinity sign (see chapter 9). I learned the energetic significance of infinity patterns at about the same time I noticed references to them in kabbalistic texts I was studying. I began to use infinity signs for healing, clearing, connecting, in any situation I thought might benefit. It was a match made in heaven…and earth…for the infinity sign, like YHVH and aleph, symbolized the balance of opposites and the oneness of everything.

My background in science as well as dance led me to experiment with transforming the mental constructs of Kabbalah into physical movement. I even developed a yoga-like practice to embody the Hebrew letters (chapter 21 is an example). I was able to better understand some of the mental abstractions of Kabbalah by grounding them in the physical body. I often played with infinity patterns in this way.

The Dragonfly Is Revealed

One day, I was practicing alternate nostril breathing for balance and calming: inhaling through the right nostril, exhaling with the left, inhaling left, exhaling right…repeating this sequence many times. There were four parts to the breath, so I decided to try adding the four-letter Name. To help me stay focused on alternating right and left, I traced infinity signs over my face as I breathed. Two breaths in and out, two connected infinity signs, completed the Name. I saw that what I had been drawing was a dragonfly's wings, each lobe containing a letter of the Name. I found this image to be a helpful way to visualize the breath and so continued to trace the dragonfly wings when I practiced (see the image in chapter 15).

Several months later while I was practicing this breath in preparation for Yom Kippur (which would begin that evening), I suddenly became very curious about the Hebrew word for "dragonfly." I looked it up. It was "*sh'pirit*" שפירית. The similarity to the word *spirit* was only the beginning.

I added the *gematria* of the letters:

Shin	ש	200
Pei	פ	80
Yud	י	10
Resh	ר	300
Yud	י	10
Taf	ת	400
		1000 = א

To my amazement, the *gematria* of *sh'pi'rit* was 1000. One thousand in Hebrew is the word *eleph*, spelled in Hebrew exactly like *aleph*, and considered a giant version of *aleph*. This had to be more than a coincidence.

Guidance can come in mysterious ways. Just a week later, I was invited to lunch in the sukkah of Reb Rachmiel and his wife, Tamar. I was delighted to discover that Rabbi Ariel Bar Tzardok, whose kabbalistic writings I had been exploring, was at lunch as well. With Tamar's encouragement, I drew the dragonfly for him with the holy letters in the wings and explained what I discovered about the gematria.

Rabbi Bar Tzardok immediately led me to a text written by the famous sixteenth-century kabbalist Moshe Cordevero. He carefully opened to a page and showed me a drawing of a large *aleph* (facsimile below) with the letters ה/ו/ה/י written in its sections, just as I had visualized in the two infinity signs of the dragonfly wings.

Image 122—Aleph with the Letters YHVH

I was in awe. I had confirmation that the dragonfly, *sh'pirit*, 1000, giant *aleph*, could be regarded as a living spiritual symbol of the oneness of all creation.

Entrance to the Spiritual Plane

Through my Zohar studies with Sarah Yehudit Schneider, I discovered another interpretation of *eleph*/1000.

Single digit numbers: 1–9
correspond to the world of *Assiyah*, the physical plane.

Double digit numbers: 10–99
correspond to the world of *Yetzira*, the emotional plane.

Triple digit numbers: 100–999
correspond to the world of *Briya*, the mental plane.

Four digit numbers 1000–9999
correspond to the world of *Atzilut*, the spiritual plane.

As the first number in this series, one thousand represents the symbolic entrance to *Atzilut*. According to Schneider, the *Zohar* presents the idea of a thousand *maphtechot*, a thousand keys. When a person possesses a thousand keys on their metaphoric keychain, it allows them passage from the mental plane into the spiritual plane. The spiritual plane, *Atzilut,* is also called the world of *Kulo Elokut*, totally divine. Oneness consciousness permeates it completely. The thousand keys represent the gateway to *Atzilut* for at that point, the soul has passed all the tests and repairs that it needs for transit into the spiritual plane. The dragonfly, as *gematria* 1000, represents the doorway to the highest level of consciousness.

Love

And what of love? We began with the letters of YHVH in the dragonfly's two infinity-shaped wings, totaling *gematria* 26. Twenty-six divides into a wing of thirteen plus a wing of thirteen.

Recall that thirteen is the gematria of love/*ahava* (see chapter 10). The two lobes of each wing are opposites in balance. Throughout this book, six and seven, as masculine feminine, have represented all our opposites. In healthy relationships, opposites maintain individual expression and also enjoy a shared place of commonality and growth. Then six plus seven becomes thirteen—love.

If each lobe in the pair of wings is drawn with a six on one side and a seven on the other, then each set adds to thirteen, love. The two pairs of wings represent the relationship of one individual (6 + 7) to another (6 + 7). This is the Infinity sign of Love: 13 + 13 = 26 = 1. (See chapter 10.)

The dragonfly can be regarded as a symbol of all balanced and loving relationships, a miniature flower of life!

Fifty-Two

Thirteen is also the *gematria* of *echad*/one. if each lobe of the dragonfly's wings is regarded as *echad*/one, the four wings then become 4 x 13, which equals 52, the number of weeks in one cycle, a year. Fifty-two is also the *gematria* of BaN/בן, a special spelling of YHVH that corresponds to *Malchut* and the *Shechina*. This name represents more than just spelling or numbers. It represents the inner energetic force of the physical plane, that is, the energy in our world that connects to God.

A Final Lesson

I no longer shrink in fear when I see a dragonfly. Instead, the infinity shape of its wings connects me to YHVH, love, *aleph/eleph*, the balance of opposites, relationship, spirit. Although that is a lot of symbolism, there is one more lesson the dragonfly can teach us.

The dragonfly travels in its lifetime from water to earth to sky. At each stage it transforms until it reaches its full potential. Its four wings, the balance of its opposites in relationship, are what finally allow it to soar and display its iridescent magnificence. The path to manifesting our unique gifts leads us in many directions as well, and the challenges we encounter require us to transform in order to grow. Ultimately, it is the union of our opposites, our body and soul, our inner masculine and feminine as reflections of the divine One, that enable us to soar and shine.

May we support each other's journeys with open hearts. May the insights gained from this book help you recognize and shine your unique lights into the world. May the intensity of our combined light heal the world and bring us finally to the time of ultimate oneness.

Amen

Glossary

Abba: The *partzuf* of Father, partner of *Ema*/Mother; encompassing the *sefira* of *Chochma*/wisdom in the plane of *Briya*/mental.

Acupuncture: A form of alternative medicine used throughout Asia, especially in China, Japan, and Korea. Commonly used for pain relief and a wide range of other conditions, acupuncture involves stimulating specific points of energy using very fine needles. Acupressure uses the hands for this same stimulation without piercing the skin.

Adam Kadmon: The primordial man made of light upon whom the *sefirot* can be projected in order to relate them to the anatomy of a physical body. *Adam Kadmon* existed in the spiritual plane, *Atzilut*.

Aramaic: An ancient language written in Hebrew letters, found in many Jewish prayers and writings such as the Zohar.

(The) *Ari*: The term of affection and respect given to the brilliant sixteenth-century kabbalist Rabbi Isaac Luria (1534–1572), leader of the Safed kabbalists during his brief lifetime. *Ari* means "lion." The Ari is also referred to as the *Arizal*, meaning the Ari of blessed memory.

Assiya: The physical plane in Kabbalah, the lowest of the four planes of existence (physical, emotional, mental, and spiritual).

Atzilut: The spiritual universe, literal meaning: nearness; highest of the four planes of existence—physical, emotional, mental, and spiritual.

Ba'al Shem Tov: Also known as the Besht, Rabbi Yisrael ben Eliezer was the eighteenth-century founder of the Chassidic movement in Eastern Europe.

Bible: The twenty-four books that comprise Hebrew scripture: Torah (5), Prophets (8), Writings (11).

Bina: The third *sefira* when counting from *Keter*. Called "understanding," it is the analytic componant of the mind, and can refer to the left brain. It lies with Chochma in the mental plane, *Briya*. *Bina* is also the *partzuf Ema*/Mother.

Briya: The mental plane of existence.

Chabad: From the first letters of *Chochma, Bina,* and *Da'at*, a worldwide Orthodox Jewish movement involved in education and outreach.

Chakras: From the Sanskrit word meaning "wheel," chakras are powerful vortex-shaped energy patterns. There are seven major chakras running up the center of the body.

Chashmal: The final barrier Eziekiel encountered in his vision of the *merkava* (chariot). Translated as "electrum," it is the combination of two opposites, *mal*/speech and *chash*/silence.

Chesed: The fourth *sefira* when counting from *Keter*. *Chesed* represents the divine attribute of loving kindness. It lies in the emotional plane, *Yetzira*.

Chochma: The second *sefira* when counting from *Keter,* translated as "wisdom," is the place of insight. It lies with *Bina*/understanding, in the mental plane, *Briya*. *Chochma* is also the *partzuf Abba*/Father.

Da'at: "Knowing." Lower *Da'at*, located in the area of the throat, connects the mind to the heart. Upper *Da'at*, located in the area of the midbrain called corpus callosum, integrates the right and left hemispheres of the brain. It can be accessed symbolically at the third eye, located between the eyebrows. When dealing with the conscious mind, *Da'at* is counted instead of *Keter* as one of the ten *sefirot*.

Devekut: A mystic experience of intimate and direct connection between an individual and divinity; literally, "cleaving to God."

Ema: Mother; the *partzuf* created by *Binah*. *Ema* is the partner of *Abba*, Father.

Gematria: Every Hebrew letter possesses a number value called *gematria*. Words or phrases with the same *gematria* have a special relationship that is the basis of many kabbalistic teachings.

Grounding: The process of connecting to life-sustaining earth energies.

Gvurah: The fifth *sefira* when counting down the Tree from *Keter*. Translated as "might" or "justice," it is the boundary making force in creation. It lies in the emotional plane, *Yetzira*.

Hod: The eighth *sefira* when counting down the Tree from *Keter*, translated as "splendor," *Hod* is the power of surrender and gratitude. It is one of the six *sefirot* in the emotional plane, *Yetzira*.

Immanent: The divine presence manifested in the physical world.

Kabbalah: The Jewish mystical tradition.

Keter: The highest *sefira*, the crown, the root of the soul. It lies in the spiritual universe of *Azilut*, "nearness."

Kohen: Temple priest. Descended from Moses' brother Aaron, the priests were responsible for performing religious rituals on behalf of the people and maintaining the purity of the Temple.

Lecha Dodi: A mystical hymn composed in the sixteenth century by the Safed kabbalist Shlomo Halevi Alkabetz. Lecha Dodi is sung as a part of the Kabbalat Shabbat (welcoming the Sabbath) service on Friday evenings. As the last stanza is sung, the congregation rises and faces west to the setting sun to welcome the Sabbath queen. The song is also an acrostic—the first letter of each stanza spells the author's name.

Ma'aseh Merkava: Literally, "workings of the chariot," a phrase that refers to the practice of mystical ascension for the purpose of receiving divine influx. It is based on the prophet Ezekiel's vision of the heavenly throne.

Malchut: The lowest of the ten *sefirot*, translated as "majesty." It corresponds to the physical plane, *Assiya*, and the realm of the divine feminine, and the *partzuf* of the daughter, *Nukva*.

Meridians: Energetic pathways that run along channels in the body. They are the basis of oriental medicine, including acupuncture.

Merkava: The chariot, throne of God, in Ezekiel's vision.

Mingmen: An acupuncture point called the Gate of Life, located behind the navel on the back. The mingmen is said to be where the original life essence of the individual is based.

Mishkan: The portable sanctuary containing the Ten Commandments; carried throughout the forty-year journey in the desert following the the Israelites' exodus from Egypt. Home of both the *Shechina* and the cherubs who guarded the Ark of the Covenant.

Motzi: A term referring to the Hebrew blessing for bread, also recited at the beginning of a meal that includes bread as a grace over all the food that will be eaten.

Nadi(s): An ancient Sanskrit term for channels through which the energies of the body flow.

Netzach: The seventh *sefira* when counting down the Tree from *Keter*. Its meaning can be thought of as victory, eternity, or endurance. It one of the six *sefirot* in *Z"A*, corresponding to the emotional plane, *Yetzira*.

Nukva or *NOK*: The partzuf of the daughter, the archetype of Woman. Corresponds to the *sefira* of *Malchut*/majesty and the physical plane, *Assiya*. The root of the word *Nukva* literally means concave, implying a receptacle. The word for feminine in Hebrew, *N'kayva,* is from the same root.

Olam Haba: Literally, the world to come, envisioned as a time of Oneness and mutual cooperation.

Partzuf, pl. *partzufim*: The kabbalistic human-like archetypes in the Tree of Life that create a family system of grandfather/father/mother/son/daughter. They can also function as sub-personalities in an individual.

Radiant circuits: Subtle energy flows that support and assist all other energy systems, especially the meridians. Highly responsive to thoughts and emotions, they fuel joy and other positive feelings.

Rakia: Hebrew for "firmament." According to the creation story in the book of Genesis, the firmament was created on the second day as a boundary between heaven and earth.

Sefer Yetzira: *The Book of Formation*; the oldest known kabbalistic text.

Sefira/pl. *sefirot*: The ten channels of divine flow that link the transcendent light of the Creator with the creation.

Shabbat: Sabbath, the seventh day of the week, lasting from sunset on Friday evenings to dusk on Saturday. Work is forbidden for observant Jews. It is a time of spiritual reflection rather than creation.

Shakti: A Hindu goddess, considered the concept or personification of divine feminine creative power, sometimes referred to as the Great divine Mother. Hindus believe Shakti is both responsible for creation and is the agent of all change.

Shechina: In Kabbalah, the indwelling divine presence, the feminine expression of God associated with the *partzuf Nukva*, the daughter, the archetype of woman.

Shefa: Divine flow or influence.

Shiva: A supreme Hindu male deity, regarded as limitless, transcendent, unchanging, and formless.

Soul: Spiritual essence, life force, consciousness. The aspect of living creatures more closely connected to the light of Source.

Talmud: The teachings and opinions of thousands of rabbis on a variety of subjects, including the Torah, law, ethics, philosophy, customs, history, and many other topics, codified in the fifth century.

Transcendent: Existing apart from and not subject to the limitations of the physical word.

Tiferet: The sixth *sefira* down the tree when counting from *Keter*, translated as beauty and harmony, and corresponding to the heart. It lies on the the central column, in the center of six *sefirot* in the *partzuf* of *Ze'er Anpin (Z"A)*, the son, the archetype of Man.

Tikun olam: "Repair of the world," including social reforms leading to a time of peace, prosperity, health, and justice for all.

Torah: The five books of Moses: Genesis, Exodus, Leviticus, Numbers, Deuteronomy.

Tzimtzum: The withdrawing of God's light to form a space for creation, the *chalal*.

Yesod: The ninth *sefira* when counting from *Keter*, translated as foundation, it lies in the central channel. One of the six *sefirot* of *Yetzira*, the emotional plane.

Yetzira: The emotional plane; literally, "universe of formation."

Yichudim: Hebrew for unifications; kabbalistic practices meant to unite the practitioner with the divine Oneness.

Yin and *Yang*: In Chinese philosophy, a description of how opposite forces are actually complementary, interconnected, and create a whole greater than the assembled parts. Yin is associated with dark, cold, feminine; Yang with light, heat, masculine.

Ze'er Anpin (Z"A): The *partzuf* of the son/man. It is composed of the six *sefirot* of the word of *Yetzira*, the emotional plane. Sometimes referred to as the *KB"H, Kadosh Baruch Hu*, the Holy One Blessed be He.

Zohar: From the Hebrew זֹהַר, literally "splendor" or "radiance." It is the foundational work in Kabbalah. It is a group of books including commentary on the mystical aspects of the Torah and scriptural interpretations as well as material on mysticism. The Zohar contains discussions of the nature of God, the origin and structure of the universe, the nature of souls, redemption, the relationship of ego to darkness and "true self" to the "Light of God," and the relationship between the "universal energy" and man. The Zohar was first published in Spain in the thirteenth century by Moses de Leon. De Leon ascribed the work to Shimon bar Yochai (*Rashbi*), a rabbi of the second century during the Roman persecution who, according to Jewish legend, hid in a cave for thirteen years studying the Torah and was inspired by the prophet Elijah to write the Zohar.

Appendix 1: The Hebrew Letters

gematria (numeric values) and pronunciation

There are twenty-two letters in the Hebrew alphabet. Five of them are written in special forms when appearing at the end of a word. Although pronounced the same, the final forms have different numeric values than the regular forms and are listed in order at the bottom of this list. The letter values range from 1 to 1000.

א	1	aleph	silent letter pronounced as the accompanying vowel
ב	2	bet	B/V
ג	3	gimel	G
ד	4	dalet	D
ה	5	hei	H
ו	6	vav	V
ז	7	zayin	Z
ח	8	chet	CH—a gutteral sound from the throat
ט	9	tet	T
י	10	yud	Y
כ	20	kaf	K/CH
ל	30	lamed	L
מ	40	mem	M
נ	50	nun	N
ס	60	samech	S

ע	70	ayin	silent letter pronounced as the accompanying vowel
פ	80	peh	P/F
צ	90	tzadi	Tz
ק	100	kuf	K
ר	200	resh	R
ש	300	shin	Sh/S
ת	400	tav	T
ך	500	final kaf	כ
ם	600	final mem	מ
ן	700	final nun	נ
ף	800	final peh	פ
ץ	900	final tzadi	צ
א	1000	eleph/the giant aleph (the word *eleph* means "a thousand")	

Appendix 2: *Gematria* and Translation of Words Cited

Hebrew/transliteration	Meaning	*Gematria*
א/*aleph*	one	1
ו/*vav*	masculine	6
ז/*zayin*	feminine	7
ח/*chet*	chuppa	8
אחד/*echad*	one	13
אהבה/*ahava*	love	13
י-הוה/YHVH	unpronounceable Name	26
א/components of *aleph*	one, first letter	26
לב/*lev*	heart	32
יחד/*Yachid*	Singularity/Divine Name	32
י-הוה//YHVH..............		26
א -דני/*Adonai*		+65 =
אמן/Amen		91
אין סוף/*Ein Sof*	Infinity/Divine Name	207
אור/*aur*	light	207
רז/*raz*	mystery	207
נר/*ner*	candle	250
שפירית/*sh'pirit*	dragonfly	1000

Bibliography

Rabbi Ariel bar Tzadok. *Walking in the Fire.* Tellico Plains, TN: Tarzana, Kosher Torah Publishing, 1993.

_____. www.koshertorah.com/PDF/tefilin.pdf.

Chabad. www.chabad.org

Rabbi David Cooper. *Ecstatic Kabbalah.* Boulder, CO: Sounds True, 2005.

Pamela Dussault. "The Benefits of Being in a Higher Vibration," http://m.huffpost.com/us/entry/positive-energy_b_1715767.html

Donna Eden. *Energy Medicine.* New York: Tarcher Penguin, 1998.

Eden Energy Medicine, www.innersource.net

Riane Eisler. *The Chalice and the Blade.* New York: HarperOne, 1988.

Masaru Emoto. *The Hidden Messages in Water*, trans. David A. Thane. Tokyo: Beyond Words Publishing, 2004.

Lawrence Fine. *Physician of the Soul, Healer of the Cosmos: Isaac Luria and his Kabbalistic Fellowship.* Stanford, CT: Stanford Studies of Jewish History and Culture, 2003.

Rabbi Yitzchak Ginsburgh. www.galeinai.org (5764#29).

Richard Gordon. *Quantum-Touch.* Berkeley, CA: North Atlantic Books, 2002.

David R. Hawkins, MD, PhD. *Power vs. Force.* Carlsbad, CA: Hay House, 2002.

Dr. Gayle Hubatch, OMD. *Fabric of the Soul: 8 Extraordinary Vessels.* Denver, CO: Outskirts Press, 2012.

Rabbi Aryeh Kaplan translator. *Sefer Yetzirah.* York Beach, ME: Weiser Books, 1997.

———. *Innerspace.* New York: Moznaim Publishing Corporation, 1990.

———. *Meditation and Kabbalah.* York Beach, ME: Feldheim Publishers 1977.

Eliahu Klein. *Kabbalah of Creation: The Mysticism of Isaac Luria, Founder of Modern Kabbalah.* Lanham, MD: Jason Aronson, 2000.

Leonora Leet. *Sacred Doctrine of Kabbalah.* Rochester, VT: Inner Traditions, 1999.

Dr. Bruce Lipton. *The Biology of Belief: Unlocking the Power of Consciousness, Matter & Miracles.* Carlsbad, CA: Mountain of Love, 2005.

Rabbi Moshe Chaim Luzzato. *Derech Hashem, The Way of God.* Trans. Rabbi Aryeh Kaplan. Jerusalem, Israel: Feldheim Publishers, 1977.

Lynn McTaggart. *The Field: The Quest for the Secret Force of the Universe.* Rockport, ME: Element Books, 2003.

Ellen Meredith. www.listening-in.com.

Caroline Myss. *Anatomy of the Spirit.* New York, Three Rivers, 1996.

Stephen A. Rapp and Tamar Frankiel. *Aleph-Bet Yoga: Embodying the Hebrew Letters for Physical and Spiritual Well-Being.* Woodstock, NY: Jewish Lights Publishing, 2002.

Sarah Yehudit Schneider. *Kabbalistic Writings on the Nature of Masculine and Feminine.* Jerusalem, Israel: A Still Small Voice, Jason Aronson, 2001.

Steven Schram. "Tefillin: An Ancient Acupuncture Point Prescription for Mental Clarity." *Journal of Chinese Medicine* number 70 (October 2002).

Leonard Shlain. *The Alphabet and the Goddess.* New York: Viking Adult, 1998.

Llewellyn Vaughan-Lee. *Signs of God*. Inverness, CA: The Golden Sufi Center, 2001.

Chaim Vital. *Shaarei Kedusha: The Gates of Holiness*. Translated by Yaron Ever Hadani. Otterburne, Canada: Providence University, 2006.

Art Credit List

Image 1—Tree of Life created by Llewellyn art department   35

Image 2—Partzufim in the Tree created by Llewellyn art department   39

Image 3—Star of David with Shabbat created by Llewellyn art department   47

Image 4—Upward-Pointing Triangle created by Llewellyn art department   47

Image 5—Downward-Pointing Triangle created by Llewellyn art department   47

Image 6—Chet with Bridge created by Llewellyn art department   48

Image 7—Infinite 8 supplied by David Friedman   51

Image 8—The Combined Name created by Llewellyn art department   61

Image 9—Yin/Yang symbol created by Llewellyn art department   63

Image 10—Infinity Sign created by Llewellyn art department   65

Image 11—Influx of Light created by Llewellyn art department   67

Image 12—Infinity Sign 6 + 7 = 13 created by Llewellyn art department   73

Image 13—Infinity Sign of Love created by Llewellyn art department   74

Image 14—The Flower of Life created by Llewellyn art department   77

Image 15—The Tree of Life Superimposed on the Flower of Life created by Llewellyn art department   77

Image 16—Double Infinity Symbols with Yuds created by Llewellyn art department   79

Image 17—The Infinity Sign of Love with the Infinity Sign of א created by Llewellyn art department   79

Image 18—The Chakras created by Mary Ann Zapalac and Llewellyn art department   87

Image 19—The Two Channels created by Mary Ann Zapalac and Llewellyn art department   88

Image 20—The Meridians created by Mary Ann Zapalac and Llewellyn art department   89

Image 21—Soldier Wearing Tefillin created by Mickie Mueller   92

Image 22—The Chakras Revisited created by Mary Ann Zapalac and Llewellyn art department   95

Image 23—Tree of Life created by Llewellyn art department   96

Image 24—Seated Man showing Chakra/Nadi Connections created by Mary Ann Zapalac and Llewellyn art department   99

Image 25—Elements and the Tree of Life created by Llewellyn art department   101

Image 26—Kidney 1 created by Mary Ann Zapalac and Llewellyn art department   113

Image 27—Kabbalistic Grounding created by Mary Ann Zapalac and Llewellyn art department   115

Image 28—Connecting to Heaven created by Mary Ann Zapalac and Llewellyn art department   116

Image 29—Heaven and Earth created by Llewellyn art department   120

Image 30—Heaven Divine Masculine K"BH created by Llewellyn art department   121

Image 31—Earth Divine Feminine Shechina created by Llewellyn art department   121

Image 32—The Breath of Love created by Mary Ann Zapalac and Llewellyn art department   122

Image 33—Nose with Letters created by Llewellyn art department   123

Image 34—How diagram #1 created by Mary Ann Zapalac   124

Image 35—How diagram #2 created by Mary Ann Zapalac   124

Image 36—Dragonfly with Letters created by Llewellyn art department   125

Image 37—The Hands created by Llewellyn art department   127

Image 38—Divine Spark Hands created by Mary Ann Zapalac and Llewellyn art department   129

Image 39—Infinity Sign created by Llewellyn art department   130

Image 40—Atzilut created by Llewellyn art department   132

Image 41—Hands with Heart Center created by Mary Ann Zapalac and Llewellyn art department   136

Image 42—Body with Hands in Front created by Mary Ann Zapalac and Llewellyn art department   137

Image 43—Body with Hands at Mouth created by Mary Ann Zapalac and Llewellyn art department   138

Image 44—Aura Protector created by Mary Ann Zapalac and Llewellyn art department   139

Image 45—Bring Your Energy diagram #1 created by Mary Ann Zapalac   141

Image 46—Bring your Energy diagram #2 created by Mary Ann Zapalac   142

Image 47—Bring your Energy diagram #3 created by Mary Ann Zapalac   142

Image 48—Infinity Sign of Love created by Llewellyn art department   143

Image 49—Infinity Sign of Divine Sparks created by Llewellyn art department   143

Image 50—Body with Hands with Infinity created by Mary Ann Zapalac and Llewellyn art department   144

Image 51—Central Meridian created by Mary Ann Zapalac and Llewellyn art department   149

Image 52—Governing Meridian created by Mary Ann Zapalac and Llewellyn art department   150

Image 53—Microcosmic Orbit created by Llewellyn art department   151

Image 54—The Belt Flow created by Llewellyn art department   152

Image 55—Rakia Flow created by Llewellyn art department   154

Image 56—Rakia Flow diagram #1 created by Mary Ann Zapalac   155

Image 57—Rakia Flow diagram #2 created by Mary Ann Zapalac   155

Image 58—Rakia Flow diagram #3 created by Mary Ann Zapalac   156

Image 59—Rakia Flow diagram #4 created by Mary Ann Zapalac   156

Image 60—Rakia Flow diagram #5 created by Mary Ann Zapalac   156

Image 61—Palms at Heart Center created by Mary Ann Zapalac   160

Image 62—Stretch Arms with Palms Flat created by Mary Ann Zapalac   161

Image 63—Right Arm Upward created by Mary Ann Zapalac   162

Image 64—*Sh'ma* created by Llewellyn art department   169

Image 65—Energy Exercise created by Mary Ann Zapalac   171

Image 66—*Sh'ma* Hook-In created by Llewellyn art department   172

Image 67—Father Inhale created by Mary Ann Zapalac and Llewellyn art department   176

Image 68—Mother Exhale hhhhh, Son Inhale, Daughter Exhale hhhh created by Mary Ann Zapalac and Llewellyn art department   177

Image 69—Infinity Eyes created by Llewellyn art department   179

Image 70—Creating the Chet created by Llewellyn art department   181

Image 71—Golden Chuppa created by Llewellyn art department   185

Image 72—Palms on Temples created by Mary Ann Zapalac   187

Image 73—Smooth Behind the Ears created by Mary Ann Zapalac   187

Image 74—Hei of *Ema* created by Llewellyn art department   188

Image 75—*Hei* & *Yud* to *Chet* created by Llewellyn art department   188

Image 76—Fingers at Third Eye and Heart created by Mary Ann Zapalac   188

Image 77—Hands on Thighs created by Mary Ann Zapalac   198

Image 78—Hands in Front of Heart created by Mary Ann Zapalac   199

Image 79—Hands Cupped at Ears created by Mary Ann Zapalac   200

Image 80—Elbows In and Arms Out diagram #1 created by Mary Ann Zapalac   201

Image 81—Elbows In and Arms Out diagram #2 created by Mary Ann Zapalac   201

Image 82—Cross Arms, Arms to Side diagram #1 created by Mary Ann Zapalac   202

Image 83—Cross Arms, Arms to Side diagram #2 created by Mary Ann Zapalac   202

Image 84—Cross Hands at Ankles created by Mary Ann Zapalac   203

Image 85—Palms Up at Feet created by Mary Ann Zapalac   204

Image 86—Stretch Arms over Head created by Mary Ann Zapalac   205

Image 87—Braided Candle created by Llewellyn art department   210

Image 88—Lulav and Etrog created by Llewellyn art department   213

Image 89—8x Circles created by Llewellyn art department   214

Image 90—Palm Facing Away from Body Right created by Mary Ann Zapalac   216

Image 91—Palm Facing Away from Body Left created by Mary Ann Zapalac   217

Image 92—Spirals in Front created by Mary Ann Zapalac   218

Image 93—Spirals Behind created by Mary Ann Zapalac   219

Image 94—Above the Head created by Mary Ann Zapalac   220

Image 95—Spirals Down created by Mary Ann Zapalac   221

Image 96—Palms Toward You created by Mary Ann Zapalac   222

Image 97—Cupped Hands Over Head diagram #1 created by Mary Ann Zapalac   223

Image 98—Cupped Hands Over Head diagram #2 created by Mary Ann Zapalac   224

Image 99—Fingers Together created by Mary Ann Zapalac   228

Image 100—Counterclockwise Circles created by Mary Ann Zapalac   229

Image 101—Clockwise Circles created by Mary Ann Zapalac   229

Image 102—From Bread to Heaven created by Mary Ann Zapalac and Llewellyn art department   230

Image 103—Connect the Food to You with 8's created by Mary Ann Zapalac and Llewellyn art department   230

Image 104—*Mayim* Man created by Mary Ann Zapalac and Llewellyn art department   241

Image 105—Tree of Life with Mother Letters created by Llewellyn art department   244

Image 106—Triangle Over Lower Belly created by Mary Ann Zapalac   246

Image 107—Hands on Forehead created by Mary Ann Zapalac   247

Image 108—Heart Fire created by Mary Ann Zapalac and Llewellyn art department   249

Image 109—Infinity Sign with Yuds created by Llewellyn art department   253

Image 110—Facing Partner with *Da'at* created by Mary Ann Zapalac and Llewellyn art department   258

Image 111—*Sefira* of *Tiferet* created by Mary Ann Zapalac and Llewellyn art department   259

Image 112—*Yesod* created by Mary Ann Zapalac and Llewellyn art department   260

Image 113—*Malchut* created by Mary Ann Zapalac and Llewellyn art department   261

Image 114—10 Counts Breath of Love created by Mary Ann Zapalac and Llewellyn art department   267

Image 115—YIIVH Breath created by Mary Ann Zapalac and Llewellyn art department   268

Image 116—The Inhale created by Mary Ann Zapalac and Llewellyn art department   270

Image 117—The Exhale created by Mary Ann Zapalac and Llewellyn art department   271

Image 118—Love Returns to God created by Mary Ann Zapalac and Llewellyn art department   273

Image 119—Healing Touch diagram #1 created by Mary Ann Zapalac   274

Image 120—Healing Touch diagram #2 created by Mary Ann Zapalac   275

Image 121—Healing Touch diagram #3 created by Mary Ann Zapalac   276

Image 122—Aleph with the Letters YHVH created by Llewellyn art department   283

Index

A

Abraham, 17, 19, 21

Abulafia, Abraham, 21

Adam breath, 119

Adam Kadmon, 37–40, 49, 57, 98, 180, 255, 287

Adonai, 12, 52, 60–62, 129, 133, 167, 168, 173, 195–198, 205, 226, 229, 235, 236, 253, 297

Aleph, 45, 51–53, 62, 63, 67, 68, 71, 78–81, 100, 102, 110, 119, 120, 129, 147, 154, 157, 159, 163, 164, 168, 169, 171, 172, 186, 197–200, 208, 227, 243, 265–267, 272, 281, 283, 285, 295–297

Allen, Dr. Sara, 136

Alternate nostril breathing, 123, 125, 282

Aura, 67, 85, 86, 138–141, 143, 144, 170, 191, 196

Aur chadash, 72

B

Baruch Shem Prayer, 172, 173, 223, 224

Bar Tzadok, Rabbi Ariel, 193, 194

Belt flow, 147, 148, 152–154, 157

Bet, 46, 295

Bina, 34, 38, 40, 59, 98, 100, 180, 243, 288

Breath of Light, 119, 196, 238

Breath of Love, 120, 122, 123, 136, 159, 176, 265–267, 273, 276

Bridge flow, 173, 224, 257

C

Celtic weave, 193, 195

Central channel, 86, 97, 99, 136, 148, 292

Central column, 34, 66, 67, 72, 97, 99, 136, 182, 256, 257, 261, 292

Chakras, 2, 44, 84–87, 91, 93–95, 97–100, 112, 136, 170, 212, 288

Chanuka, 1, 9

Chashmal, 66, 288

Cherubs, 180, 181, 183–185, 189, 191, 258, 290

Chesed, 34, 38, 59, 72, 74, 102, 211, 213, 214, 243, 255, 288

Chet, 48, 49, 181, 185, 188, 255, 259, 295, 297

Chinese medicine, 21, 65, 68, 84, 91–93, 100, 102, 233, 243

Chochma, 34, 38, 39, 59, 98, 102, 180, 243, 287, 288

Chuppa, 49, 181–185, 189–191, 209, 253, 257, 258, 297

D

Da'at, 34, 36, 98, 124, 172, 181–186, 188–190, 256–258, 260, 261, 288

Dalet, 18, 46, 56, 129, 164, 295

Devekut, 24, 175, 182, 183, 193, 289

Divine Feminine/Divine Presence, 9–14, 24, 25, 34, 36, 37, 40, 41, 60–62, 80, 97, 107, 121, 135, 147, 148 168, 175, 181, 209, 234, 236, 238, 289, 290, 291

De Leon, Moses, 19, 293

Dragonfly, 5, 125, 133, 281–285, 297

Drizin, Reb Rachmiel, 173

E

Eden, Donna, 3, 67, 68, 84, 85, 103, 159, 183, 195, 227, 228

Eden Energy Medicine, 3, 4, 67, 68, 84, 85, 91, 135

Ein Sof/Aur Ein Sof, 52, 68, 80, 94, 297

Eisler, Riane, 11, 15

Elements, 92, 101, 102, 233, 243, 245

Elohim, 12, 30, 44, 45, 52, 119, 147, 168, 195–197, 199, 205, 207

Ezekiel's vision, 20, 65, 290

F

Feinstein, Dr. David, 84

Forty-two letter Name, 207, 209

Four Worlds:

> *Atzilut,* 40, 58, 59, 132, 194, 196, 205, 284, 287, 288
>
> *Briya,* 40, 58, 59, 196, 200, 206, 284, 287, 288
>
> *Yetzira,* 17, 19, 33, 36, 40, 43–45, 58, 59, 65, 66, 98, 128, 195, 199, 206, 212, 245, 284, 288–293
>
> *Assiya,* 40, 58, 59, 61, 112, 195, 196, 198, 206, 287, 290

Flower of Life, 76, 77, 191, 285

G

Gartel, 20

Gematria, 43–45, 48, 53, 60, 63, 68, 71, 73–75, 78–80, 122, 136, 143, 157, 164, 168, 169, 189, 191, 195, 206, 208, 209, 226, 227, 234, 258, 265, 266, 268, 270, 281–285, 289, 295, 297

Gimel, 46, 295

Governing meridian, 148, 150

Grounding, 18, 36, 37, 97, 111–116, 160, 186, 195, 254, 261, 269, 282, 289

Gvurah, 34, 38, 72, 74, 102, 213, 214, 243, 289

H

Hawkins, Dr. David, 71

Havdala, 38

Healing:

> emotional, 273
>
> with the hands, 130
>
> kabbalistic energy healing, 5, 265

Heart, 5, 14, 36, 40, 44, 72, 74, 84, 86, 93, 98, 103, 110, 119–123, 127, 129, 131–133, 136, 137, 141, 159–165, 167, 169, 170, 172, 173, 176, 182, 184–186, 188–190, 195, 196, 199, 213, 214, 222, 237, 246, 248, 249, 253, 254, 257, 259, 262, 265–271, 288, 292, 297

Hei, 46, 57–59, 63, 115, 124, 178, 180, 181, 184, 185, 188, 208, 254, 255, 269, 295

Hod, 34, 38, 59, 102, 213, 214, 234, 243, 289

I

Infinity, 49, 51, 52, 65–69, 71, 73, 74, 78–81, 103, 110, 119, 120, 125, 130, 135–138, 140, 143, 144, 163, 169, 171–173, 179, 182–184, 189, 191, 195, 196, 200, 206, 211, 212, 224, 230, 236–238, 243, 246, 248, 253, 256–260, 281–285, 297

Infinity sign:

of love, 74, 79, 110, 137, 143, 169, 171, 172, 284

J

Jacob, 23, 65

Jewish star, 47, 213

K

Kabbalah, 1–5, 10, 11, 15, 17–23, 25, 28, 29, 31, 36–38, 40, 43–45, 49, 55, 60, 65, 67, 74, 79, 83, 84, 90–94, 97, 100, 102, 107, 111–113, 116, 128, 130, 131, 135, 147, 153, 163, 168, 180, 184, 186, 195, 196, 207, 208, 211, 225, 234, 239, 252, 254–256, 266, 281, 282, 287, 289, 291, 293

Kadosh Baruch Hu (KB"H), 12, 13, 40, 59–61, 164, 172, 208, 226, 293

Keter, 34, 36, 38–40, 57–59, 94, 97, 98, 116, 182, 186, 196, 206, 268, 270, 288–290, 292

Klein, Rabbi Eliahu, 28, 49

Klipa (klipot), 29, 30, 75

L

Leet, Leonora, 93, 168

Lecha Dodi, 60, 209, 251, 289

Light *(Aur),* 1, 4, 6, 10–12, 14, 15, 17, 18, 20, 21, 23–25, 27–34, 36–41, 45, 52, 55, 58, 63, 65–69, 72–74, 76, 80, 85, 86, 90, 91, 93, 94, 97, 102, 103, 108, 109, 111–113, 116, 119, 120, 128, 131–133, 138, 145, 148, 163–165, 169, 170, 172, 173, 175, 179, 181–184, 189–191, 193–196, 198, 203, 206, 207, 209, 224, 225, 227, 233, 236–238, 240, 248, 251–254, 256, 258, 259, 261, 265, 266, 268, 269, 272, 277, 285, 287, 291–293, 297

Love *(Ahava),* 1, 4, 6, 12, 15, 24, 25, 40, 44, 48, 52, 71–76, 78–81, 98, 108–110, 119–123, 129, 133, 135–137, 140, 143–145, 153, 154, 157, 159, 163, 169, 171, 172, 176, 178, 180, 184, 186, 189, 191, 207, 209, 210, 223, 225, 235, 237, 238, 240, 246, 248, 253, 255, 257–259, 265–274, 276, 277, 284, 285, 297

Lulav and etrog, 213

M

Malchut, 12, 34, 36–38, 40, 47, 48, 59, 97, 100, 112, 113, 172, 173, 186, 211, 213, 214, 223, 255, 256, 261, 285, 290

Matt, Daniel, 24

Mayan calendar, 9, 15

Meridians, 84–86, 89, 100, 102, 152, 169, 170, 290, 291

Midot, 74

Mishkan, 22, 29, 180, 181, 183, 185, 258, 290

Mem, 102, 227, 234, 237–240, 243, 245, 246, 248, 295, 296

Meredith, Ellen, 114, 131, 138, 211

Moses, 19, 24, 52, 74, 194, 208, 234, 289, 292, 293

Myss, Carolyn, 2

Mystery (raz), 3, 19, 80, 81, 168, 252, 272, 297

N

Nadis, 99, 100

Netzach, 34, 38, 59, 102, 213, 214, 234, 243, 290

Nimoy, Leonard, 128

Neshima, Neshama yiteira, 119, 254, 256, 265

O

Olam Ha Ba (the world to come), 11, 14, 22, 24, 30, 41, 291

P

Pardes, 18, 111, 112

Priestly benediction, 128, 133, 274

Prinzivalli, Dr. Shems, 94

R

Akiva, Rabbi, 19, 111, 112

Radiant circuits, 68, 85, 86, 90, 102, 103, 109, 131, 136, 148, 169, 170, 291

Rakia, 103, 147, 148, 153–157, 291

Ruach Hakodesh, 17, 18, 20, 21, 24, 98, 182, 190

S

Schneider, Sarah Yehudit, 14, 29, 41, 66, 194, 255, 256, 283

Sefira, sefirot, 12, 27, 28, 31, 33, 34, 36–41, 44, 46, 47, 48, 58, 59, 66, 72–74, 93, 94, 97–100, 112, 116, 128, 136, 172, 180, 181, 182, 196, 208, 211–213, 215, 234, 243, 255, 256, 257, 259, 261, 266, 287–293

Sefer Yetzira, 17, 19, 33, 36, 43–45, 65, 66, 98, 128, 212, 245, 291

Seven spirals exercise, 215, 253

Shabbat, 12, 47, 164, 209–211, 213, 251–256, 262, 289, 291

Sh'ma, 103, 133, 167–173, 224, 254

Shechina, 9, 12–14, 22, 24, 25, 30, 31, 36, 38, 40, 41, 59–62, 71, 76, 78, 79, 97, 100, 112, 120, 121, 128, 133, 148, 153, 163, 164, 168, 170, 172, 175, 181, 184, 186, 207–211, 213, 214, 226, 228, 234, 251–255, 266, 267, 269, 270, 285, 290, 291

Shefa, 117, 270, 291

Shiviti, 190, 253

Shlain, Dr. Leonard, 10

Shin, 102, 127, 128, 133, 243, 245–248, 282, 296

Shivirat Ha Kaylim (shattering of the vessels), 27–29

Soul:

    levels of, 60

    extra soul, 254

Szent-Gyorgyi, Albert, 83

T

Tefillin, 92, 93

Ten Commandments, 22, 24, 29, 52, 55, 180, 290

Tree of Life *(Etz haChayim)*, 27, 28, 33, 35, 36, 44, 57, 65, 72, 77, 85, 93, 96, 100–103, 116, 136, 180, 208, 212, 243, 244, 266, 291

Tiferet, 34, 38, 40, 59, 72, 74, 98, 213, 214, 256, 259–261, 267, 270, 292

Tikun olam, 25, 28–31, 164, 182, 255, 292

Torah, 11, 18, 20–23, 43, 45, 46, 55, 60, 93, 111, 147, 167, 178, 179, 181, 182, 194, 209, 257, 288, 292, 293

Tzfat (Safed), 5, 20, 51, 251, 287, 289

Tzimtzum, 27, 40, 76, 292

V

Vaughn-Lee, Llewellyn, 14, 15

Vav, 45–49, 53, 57–60, 62, 63, 67, 73, 78–80, 115, 119–121, 124, 129, 147, 148, 154, 157, 163, 164, 168, 177, 184, 207, 266, 267, 269, 295, 297

Vessel, 12, 13, 24, 25, 27, 29, 36, 37, 40, 94, 97, 111–113, 148, 170, 175, 236, 254, 256, 261, 272

Vital, Chaim, 20, 21, 24, 58, 175, 190, 225

W

Water *(Mayim)*, 9, 12, 47, 92, 102, 133, 147, 225, 233–241, 243, 245–248, 285

Y

Yachid, 44, 297

Yad, 49, 120, 128, 131, 132, 164, 266

Yang, 46, 47, 63, 65, 100, 116, 131, 148, 152, 153, 159, 170, 245, 292

Yesod, 34, 38, 59, 97, 213, 214, 255, 256, 259–261, 292

Yichud (Yichudim), 24, 168, 175, 178, 184, 193, 196, 208, 228, 292

Yin, 47, 63, 65, 100, 116, 131, 135, 136, 148, 152, 153, 159, 170, 233, 245, 292

YHVH, 12, 46, 49, 55–63, 75, 78, 80, 81, 102, 110, 116, 123, 129, 132, 136, 143, 147, 164, 168, 170, 173, 175, 178, 180–185, 189–191, 193–196, 205, 209, 226, 235, 236, 253, 258, 265, 268–270, 272, 273, 276, 277, 281, 283–285, 297

YHVH breath, 265, 268–270, 273, 276

Yud, 49, 53, 57–60, 62, 63, 78, 79, 100, 110, 115–117, 119, 120, 124, 128, 129, 131, 132, 147, 148, 154, 163, 164, 168, 177, 180, 181, 185, 188, 208, 239, 253–255, 266, 267, 269, 270, 282, 295

Z

Zayin, 12, 46–49, 73, 79, 80, 207, 295, 297

Zip-Up, 135, 136, 140

Zohar, 12, 14, 15, 19, 20, 22, 24, 27, 29, 30, 32, 43, 45, 47, 49, 62, 65–67, 73, 74, 78, 102, 119, 128, 135, 147, 168, 182, 194, 251, 255, 256, 283, 284, 287, 293

Zygote, 148, 151, 152, 170

GET MORE AT LLEWELLYN.COM

Visit us online to browse hundreds of our books and decks, plus sign up to receive our e-newsletters and exclusive online offers.

- Free tarot readings • Spell-a-Day • Moon phases
- Recipes, spells, and tips • Blogs • Encyclopedia
- Author interviews, articles, and upcoming events

GET SOCIAL WITH LLEWELLYN

Find us on **f**
www.Facebook.com/LlewellynBooks

@LlewellynBooks

GET BOOKS AT LLEWELLYN

LLEWELLYN ORDERING INFORMATION

Order online: Visit our website at www.llewellyn.com to select your books and place an order on our secure server.

Order by phone:
- Call toll free within the US at 1-877-NEW-WRLD (1-877-639-9753)
- We accept VISA, MasterCard, American Express, and Discover.
- Canadian customers must use credit cards.

Order by mail:
Send the full price of your order (MN residents add 6.875% sales tax) in US funds plus postage and handling to: Llewellyn Worldwide, 2143 Woodale Drive, Woodbury, MN 55125-2989

POSTAGE AND HANDLING

STANDARD (US):
(Please allow 12 business days)
$30.00 and under, add $6.00.
$30.01 and over, FREE SHIPPING.

INTERNATIONAL ORDERS, INCLUDING CANADA:
$16.00 for one book, plus $3.00 for each additional book.

Visit us online for more shipping options. Prices subject to change.

FREE CATALOG!

To order, call 1-877-NEW-WRLD ext. 8236 or visit our website